The Gospel of the Kingdom

Studies in the Sermon on the Mount

Edwin Crozier

The Gospel of the Kingdom: Studies in the Sermon on the Mount
© 2017 by DeWard Publishing Company, Ltd.
P.O. Box 6259, Chillicothe, Ohio 45601
800.300.9778
www.deward.com

All rights reserved. No portion of this book may be reproduced in any form without written permission from the publisher.

Cover design by Evangela Creative.

The preponderance of Bible quotations are taken from the The Holy Bible, English Standard Version®, copyright © 2001 by Crossway Bibles, a publishing ministry of Good News Publishers. Used by permission. All rights reserved. Any emphasis in Bible quotations is added.

Reasonable care has been taken to trace original sources for any excerpts and quotations appearing in this book and to document such information. For material not in the public domain, fair use standards and practices were followed. Should any attribution be found to be incorrect or incomplete, the publisher welcomes written documentation supporting correction for subsequent printing.

Printed in the United States of America.

ISBN: 978-1-936341-96-2

GRATITUDE

Special thanks to Marita, my wife, and Tessa, Ethan and Ryan, my children. You support me in my work, put up with me on my bad days, remind me of what I preach and write when I am not walking the walk and sacrifice so I can get these books finished. Thank you.

Special thanks to the Franklin Church of Christ in Franklin, Tenn. You have given me the opportunity to teach and write, hearing most of what I say in its initial raw form. Thank you.

Special thanks to Max Dawson. You have helped me spiritually more than just about anybody I know. I hope I am finally half the preacher you are. Thank you.

Therefore everyone who hears these words of Mine and acts on them, may be compared to a wise man who built his house on the rock.

And the rain fell, and the floods came, and the winds blew and slammed against the house; and yet it did not fall, for it had been founded on the rock.

Matthew 7.24-25

The Gospel of the Kingdom
A Month in the Sermon on the Mount

Table of Contents

Preface	7
Week One: Introduction and Matthew 5.3-4	13
The Jesus Who Preached the Sermon	15
How to Read the Sermon: Matthew 7.21-27	27
The Sermon's Purpose: Matthew 5.13-20	35
Blessed are the Beggars: Matthew 5.3	45
Happy are the Sad: Matthew 5.4	55
Group Discussion	64
Week Two: Matthew 5.5-5.9	67
The Kingdom's Ladder: Matthew 5.5	69
From Starvation to Satisfaction: Matthew 5.6	81
God Helps Those Who Help Others: Matthew 5.7	91
Undivided Devotion: Matthew 5.8	99
Lovely Feet: Matthew 5.9	109
Group Discussion	119
Week Three: Matthew 5.10-5.42	121
The World Strikes Back: Matthew 5.10-12	123
Anger Management: Matthew 5.21-26	133
Morality and Marriage: Matthew 5.27-32	143
Integrity Matters: Matthew 5.33-37	153
My Personal Space: Matthew 5.38-42	163
Group Discussion	174
Week Four: Matthew 5.43-6.34	177
Love's Response: Matthew 5.43-48	179
Secret Service: Matthew 6.1-18	187
Pray This Way: Matthew 6.7-15	195
Membership Has Its Privileges: Matthew 6.19-24	205
Money Talk: Matthew 6.25-34	215
Group Discussion	223
Week Five: Matthew 7.1-23	225
Righteous Judgment: Matthew 7.1-6	227
Our Loving Father: Matthew 7.7-11	237
The Golden Rule: Matthew 7.12	247
Choices: Matthew 7.13-23	257
The Sermon in the Real World	267
Group Discussion	277

Preface

"Blessed are the poor in Spirit, for theirs is the kingdom of heaven."
"The meek shall inherit the earth."
"Treat others the way you want to be treated."
"Walking the strait and narrow."
"Turn the other cheek."

Each of these phrases has its origin in one of the greatest discourses of all time—The Sermon on the Mount. Who, among Christians, has not spent time within the Sermon recorded in Matthew 5-7?

Who has not rejoiced in the promise to "ask, and it will be given to you; seek, and you will find; knock, and it will be opened to you"? Who has not quaked at the warning that "many will say to Me on that day, 'Lord, Lord,'...and then I will declare to them, 'I never knew you; depart from Me, you who practice lawlessness'"? Who has not struggled with the instruction to "not resist an evil person; but whoever slaps you on your right cheek, turn the other to him also"?

Who has not been refreshed, challenged and rebuked by Jesus within this Sermon? Yet, we keep coming back to it. We are drawn to it, knowing it contains the concentrated essence of what Jesus wants us to be, even when we don't always like what it says or how we look in comparison.

In Matthew 4.23, just five verses before the Sermon begins, Matthew wrote, "Jesus was going throughout all Galilee, teaching in their synagogues and proclaiming *the gospel of the kingdom*..." (emphasis mine- ELC). This Sermon is the gospel of *the kingdom*. When we read it, we cannot help but see why Jesus said before Pilate, "My kingdom is not of this world..." (John 18.36).

In his book, *Letters from a Skeptic*, Gregory Boyd published an ongoing correspondence between his skeptical father and himself. One of the skeptical father's complaints against Christianity was how impractical and even impossible the requirements were. The father, Edward Boyd, wrote:

> But it's not only the rigidity of the Bible's sexual ethics which bothers me. I remember hearing a priest preach on Jesus' command to "love your enemies," and I thought to myself that this command would be the ruin of any nation that actually tried to live it![1]

The son's response was:

> Concerning the political applicability of Jesus' ethics, you're right that a nation would come to disaster if it tried to survive with a "turn the other cheek" mentality.[2]

Dr. Boyd proceeded to tell his father the point of the Sermon was not to provide a standard for Christians, but to demonstrate the standard of holiness is impossible, causing us to fall at the feet of Jesus, begging for mercy. While these two expressed the thoughts of many, I think both men missed the point.

This Sermon is the gospel of *Christ's* kingdom. It is not a constitution for physical nations. It is a declaration of citizenship in the kingdom that is not of this world. God is not interested in ruling nations. He is interested in ruling hearts. As Jesus said in Luke 17.21, the kingdom is in our midst or "within you" (KJV). In Matthew 6.10, Jesus taught His disciples to pray, "Your kingdom come, Your will be done on earth as it is in heaven." We cannot pray this if we are not willing to allow the King dominion within *our* hearts or the King's will to be done in *our* lives.

What does this mean? While I certainly agree with Dr. Boyd, that the gospel's standards of righteousness are too high for you and me, that does not make the Sermon any less our standard. We must not shrug our shoulders or throw up our hands, saying, "Well, that's why Jesus died." Certainly, we must seek God's aid, as Jesus also taught in Matthew 6.13, teaching us to pray, "And do not lead us into temptation but deliver us from evil." Yet, *we* must strive for God's will to be done in our lives. We must "work out [our] salvation with fear and trembling" (Philippians 2.12). We can do this confidently knowing God is at work within us (Philippians 2.13). Nevertheless, we must work. This Sermon is God's will for our lives. This Sermon outlines the work we must do to be saved.

---

1. *Letters from a Skeptic*, Gregory and Edward Boyd, Life Journey, Colorado Springs, 2004, p. 167.
2. *Ibid.* p. 170.

This Sermon is the *gospel* of the kingdom. That is, it is the good news of the kingdom. Will we view it that way? No doubt, we view Matthew 7.7-11 as good news. We love hearing that God will respond to our requests. But what about Matthew 6.14-15, which says we must forgive others if we want to be forgiven? What about Matthew 5.44, which says we must love our enemies and pray for those who persecute us? What about Matthew 5.39-42, which says we should let someone hit us a second time, go the extra mile or give to whoever asks of us? Are all of these teachings good news to us?

Christ's good news doesn't look all that good to those who are anchored in this world. If we approach the Sermon judging it based on societal standards or cultural norms, we will constantly fall short of it. Many will think we are insane or abnormal. They will laugh at us. We have come to expect it (1 Peter 4.4). They will persecute us. But, when they do, we are blessed (Matthew 5.10-12).

The Sermon is only three chapters long. It can be read in 10 to 15 minutes. Yet, it can be studied for a lifetime. It is the good news of the kingdom. But it is the good news of the kingdom in concentrate. Like a powdered drink to which we can add water and refresh numerous people, if we add study and time, the Sermon grows. It will lead us to nearly every major aspect of Christ's doctrine for Christian living. It will refresh our spirits but it will also challenge us to the core. Whichever the case, if we study it deeply, we cannot leave unchanged.

This month in the Sermon on the Mount will refresh us at times, instruct us at times, challenge us at times and rebuke us at times. Most of all, it will change us. That is what Bible study should do. If we complete this study and our lives have not changed, we should either rejoice that we had already attained perfection before studying the Sermon or we should repent. We should approach this study as Paul approached life in Christ in general:

> Not that I have already obtained it or have already become perfect, but I press on so that I may lay hold of that for which also I was laid hold of by Christ Jesus. Brethren, I do not regard myself as having laid hold of it yet; but one thing I do: forgetting what lies behind and reaching forward to what lies ahead, I press on toward the goal for the prize of the upward call of God in Christ Jesus.
>
> *Philippians 3.12-14*

Before we enter wholesale into the study of the Sermon, I want to share something interesting. This Sermon is about being a part of Christ's kingdom, Christ's nation. It is about being a "chosen race, a royal priesthood, a holy nation, a people for God's own possession, so that you may proclaim the excellencies of Him who has called you out of darkness into His marvelous light" (1 Peter 2.9). We have not always been in this kingdom. We are not in this kingdom because we are Americans or Englishmen or whatever nationality. We must rid ourselves of the idea of the "Christian Nation." Jesus did not die to establish Christian nations. He died to establish His kingdom (Matthew 16.18-19). We have to be transferred by God from the domain of darkness into the kingdom of His beloved Son (Colossians 1.13). We are foreigners immigrating into the kingdom of God.

With that in mind, we ought to consider what this kind of immigration means. If a foreigner immigrates to the United States and seeks to become a citizen, one of his final steps is to take the Naturalization Oath of Allegiance:

> I hereby declare, on oath, that I absolutely and entirely renounce and abjure all allegiance and fidelity to any foreign prince, potentate, state or sovereignty, of whom or which I have heretofore been a subject or citizen; that I will support and defend the Constitution and laws of the United States of America against all enemies, foreign and domestic; that I will bear true faith and allegiance to the same; that I will bear arms on behalf of the United States when required by the law; that I will perform noncombatant service in the armed forces of the United States when required by the law; that I will perform work of national importance under civilian direction when required by the law; and that I take this obligation freely without any mental reservation or purpose of evasion; so help me God.[3]

Citizenship in earthly kingdoms is not a light matter. How much more important is it in the heavenly kingdom? Let me share with you some profound words by David Bercot in his book, *The Kingdom That Turned the World Upside Down*.

> I want to make one final comment before we take a look at some of the ground-breaking laws and "upside-down" values of the Kingdom. Most of us have heard these teachings of Jesus so many times, that we have virtually become numb to what they actually say. The revolutionary teachings of Jesus have been reduced to clichés, trite sayings, and nice "thoughts for the day." We talk about the "Beatitudes," the "Golden Rule" and "going the extra mile." Something nice to think about, but nothing to take too seriously or too literally.

---

3. http://uscis.gov/graphics/aboutus/history/teacher/oath.htm

In my Bible, the first seven verses of the Sermon on the Mount (i.e. the "Beatitudes") are printed in poetic format—as though these were simply beautiful words, not meant to be taken too seriously. Poetry? Jesus wasn't reciting poetry to the crowd that came to hear Him that day. He didn't want them to go home and talk about the beautiful words He had shared. No, He wanted to challenge them to the core of their very souls. He wanted to give them a new set of values and a new set of laws—together with a new life.[4]

I hope this study is enjoyable for you. I hope you recommend it to others. But most of all, I hope the Sermon changes your life to be more like Jesus. Please, don't take the Sermon lightly. Please, do not pass over its challenges with a wave of the "it's figurative" wand. Let the Sermon mold you and renew your mind, making you different from the world.

May God richly bless you as you draw closer to Him. But more importantly, may you richly bless God.

---

4. *The Kingdom That Turned The World Upside Down*, David Bercot, Scroll Publishing, Tyler, TX, p. 25.

The Gospel of the Kingdom

Week One

You are the salt of the earth; but if the salt has become tasteless, how can it be made salty again? It is no longer good for anything, except to be thrown out and trampled under foot by men. You are the light of the world. A city set on a hill cannot be hidden; nor does anyone light a lamp and put it under a basket but on the lampstand, and it gives light to all who are in the house. Let your light shine before men in such a way that they may see your good works, and glorify your Father who is in heaven.

Matthew 5.13-16

The Jesus Who Preached The Sermon

More than a Great Teacher

Think back to your school days. Who were your best teachers? What made them so great? Was it the relationship you had with them? Was it their ability to make the complex seem simple? Was it their ability to impart information in an entertaining and enjoyable way? Did everyone else view that teacher as the best? Probably not.

Viewing someone as a great teacher is a very subjective judgment. What I find to be great, you may not, and vice versa. If I conducted a poll, most who claim to be Christian would likely claim Jesus Christ as the greatest teacher to ever live. However, at times I fear this response may be like the little child's response in Bible class. The teacher posed the question, "I am thinking of something that is gray, furry, has a fluffy tail, climbs trees and eats nuts. Of what am I thinking Johnny?" Johnny thought, "Well, that sounds like a squirrel to me, but this is Bible class. The answer must be...," "Jesus," he said out loud.

I am afraid when many of us think of great teachers, we don't really think of Jesus except for the fact that we are Christians and we know that is the right answer. He wasn't that entertaining. He certainly didn't make the complex simple, in fact at times it seems He made the simple, complex. He didn't stick with one particular style. He incessantly made use of figures of speech that slow down our study. He made enemies through His teaching nearly everywhere He went. His teaching was known to run off thousands of people at a time. By the end of His earthly teaching ministry, the rulers wanted Him dead, the masses were willing to let Him die and His closest associates abandoned Him. Even after His resurrection, the people He spent the most time teaching were slow to accept the evidence. After 40 more days of teaching, Jesus only had about 120 disciples (Acts 1.15). By most of our subjective standards, we would probably say that was pretty lousy.

All that being said, we have to admit Jesus is the greatest teacher to have ever lived. We do not admit that because of any particular subjective standard. We admit that because of what Jesus taught. Jesus taught the truth from God. He did it without partiality, without compromise and without pretense. He simply taught the truth of God and allowed it to work on his listeners' hearts, leaving a legacy for us as we teach nearly 2000 years later.

Matthew, more than the other three gospel accounts, presents Jesus as the *teaching* Messiah. In fact, one natural outline of the book will demonstrate the introduction of Jesus' supernatural birth and the conclusion of His death and supernatural resurrection. In between, the book is divided into five sections of teaching. Each one ends with a phrase similar to "When Jesus had finished these words..." (Matthew 7.28; 11.1; 13.53; 19.1; 26.1). For all Jesus was (and is), He was a teacher. That was His main work, teaching the truth from God. Jesus said, "The word which you hear is not Mine, but the Father's who sent Me" (John 14.24). Jesus was the greatest teacher simply because He only taught God's truth.

When Jesus prayed with His disciples before going to the garden where He was betrayed, He said:

> I have manifested Your name to the men whom You gave Me out of the world; they were Yours and You gave them to me, and they have kept Your word. Now they have come to know that everything You have given Me is from You; for the words which You gave me I have given to them; and they received them and truly understood that I came forth from you, and they believed that You sent Me...I have given them Your word; and the world has hated them, because they are not of the world...I do not ask on behalf of these alone, but for those also who believe in Me through their word.
>
> *John 17.6-8, 14, 20*

Jesus was a teacher and He expected His followers to be teachers. He was a teacher of God's word and He expected His followers to be teachers of God's word.

Having said all of that, we must recognize, however, that Jesus was more than just a great teacher. He was more than a man who should be listed in the annals of history with the likes of Socrates, Plato and Aristotle as so many of His modern opponents would like to do. According to eye-witness testimony, Jesus made claims that bar us from merely viewing Him as a great teacher. He made claims to be a divine Savior. Belief on Him, He claimed, would provide forgiveness of sins. He is either far more than just the greatest teacher among great teachers or He is a nutcase that should be dismissed or He is a sinister liar offering hope where there is none.

Matthew recognized Jesus for who He was and is. Before entering into Jesus' teaching, Matthew established exactly why Jesus' teaching was so important to the Jews who were looking for the Messiah's kingdom and for us who are in or are entering the Messiah's kingdom.

The King

Any writer will tell you the very first part of a book needs to be attention grabbing. It has to pick the reader up, shake him around a bit and cause him to say, "I can't put this down." Whether it is the intro to the book, the first section of a chapter, the first paragraph of a section, the author has to cause people to say, "I want more."

I try to accomplish this, but I am not very good. However, I must be light years ahead of Matthew. He started his book with a genealogy. Talk about mind-numbingly boring. Of course, if Matthew had been writing for folks like me, he would have begun differently. Instead, he was writing for first century Jews who were looking for the "righteous Branch of David" (Jeremiah 33.15; see also Isaiah11:1 and Jeremiah 23.5) through the tribe of Judah (Genesis 49.10) who was the seed of Abraham (Genesis 22.16). Considering what the Jews were searching for, you can imagine they were ecstatic about genealogies. Matthew 1.1 would grab their attention. They would have immediately wanted to know more about this man who was the son of both Abraham and David. Could He be the promised Messiah?

What was the point of this lineage? According to Jeremiah 23.5, this righteous Branch of David would be the king who saved Israel. Of the 40 names in the lineage, 15 were kings of Judah. Jesus is the heir to Judah's throne, the rightful King.

But Matthew didn't stop with the genealogy. He proceeded to tell the story of the wise men from the east traveling to see Jesus as a child (Matthew 2.1-12). Their question of Herod was, "Where is He who has been born King of the Jews? For we saw His star in the east and have come to worship Him" (Matthew 2.2). The wise men were told to look in Bethlehem, because that would fulfill Micah 5.2, 4:

> But as for you, Bethlehem Ephrathah, too little to be among the clans of Judah, From you One will go forth for Me to be ruler in Israel…And He will arise and shepherd His flock in the strength of the Lord, in the majesty of the name of the Lord His God.

As we read the Sermon, the Gospel of the Kingdom, we must understand we are not just reading the words of a great teacher. We are reading the dictates of the King. Ecclesiastes 8.4-5 says, "Since the word of the king is authoritative, who will say to him, 'What are you doing?' he who keeps a royal command experiences no trouble." Jesus is authoritative, as is His Sermon. If we want to avoid trouble, we had better submit to His royal commands.

The Son of God

At the same time, Jesus is more than a teacher and more than the King. He is not a reincarnation of David and his role. After the genealogy, Matthew told the story of Jesus' birth.

"Now the birth of Jesus Christ was as follows: when his mother Mary had been betrothed to Joseph, before they came together she was found to be with child by the Holy Spirit" (Matthew 1.18). You can imagine what a shock that was for Joseph. Yet, the angel of the Lord appeared to him and said, "Joseph, son of David, do not be afraid to take Mary as your wife; for the Child who has been conceived in her is of the Holy Spirit" (Matthew 1.20).

Matthew further related the prophecy of Isaiah 7.14 to Jesus. Jesus was "'Immanuel,' which translated means, 'God with us'" (Matthew 1.23). Then while demonstrating Jesus' troublesome beginning to be consistent with God's previous work, Matthew related God's statement from Hosea 11.1 about the nation of Israel to Jesus saying, "Out of Egypt I called My Son."

Finally, Matthew recorded the events of Jesus' baptism. Coming to John in the wilderness, Jesus asked to be baptized to fulfill all righteousness. As Jesus arose from His immersion in the water, the Spirit of God descended as a dove, lighting upon Jesus "and behold, a voice out of the heavens said, 'This is My beloved Son, in whom I am well-pleased'" (Matthew 3.17).

Jesus was more than a teacher and the King. He was and is the Son of the living God. He was incarnate deity as Paul taught in Colossians 2.9, "For in Him all the fullness of Deity dwells in bodily form."

Matthew drove home exactly what this means for us in Matthew 16.15-19.

> He said to them, "But who do you say that I am?"

Simon Peter answered, "You are the Christ, the Son of the living God."

And Jesus said to him, "Blessed are you, Simon Barjona, because flesh and blood did not reveal this to you, but My Father who is in heaven. I also say to you that you are Peter, and upon this rock I will build My church; and the gates of Hades will not overpower it. I will give you the keys of the kingdom of heaven; and whatever you bind on earth shall have been bound in heaven, and whatever you loose on earth shall have been loosed in heaven."

Jesus is the Christ, the Son of the living God. As such, He is the head of the kingdom. Read what the Spirit spoke through the psalmist prophet in Psalm 2.6-12:

"But as for Me, I have installed My king Upon Zion, My holy mountain."

"I will surely tell of the decree of the Lord: He said to Me, 'You are My Son, today I have begotten You. Ask of Me, and I will surely give the nations as Your inheritance, and the very ends of the earth as Your possession. You shall break them with a rod of iron, you shall shatter them like earthenware.'"

Now therefore, O kings, show discernment; take warning, O judges of the earth. Worship the Lord with reverence and rejoice with trembling. Do homage to the Son, that He not become angry and you perish in the way, for His wrath may soon be kindled. How blessed are all who take refuge in Him.

All things are subject to Him as proclaimed in Matthew 28.18. His right to the throne is not merely because He was the descendant of David (how many others might have made that claim) but because He is the Son of God. He is deity Himself.

He is the creator and sustainer of the world. He, therefore, has the absolute right to tell us exactly what to do and how to live. As we read the Sermon, the good news of His kingdom, we must realize we are not just reading the suggestions of a good teacher. We are reading the very word of God. This is no less binding on our lives than were the 10 commandments on the Israelite nation.

A Teacher with Authority

Understanding that the Jesus who preached this sermon was more than a teacher, more than a king, He was God in the flesh can help us understand the people's reaction.

In Matthew 7.28-29, Matthew wrote, "When Jesus had finished these words, the crowds were amazed at his teaching; for He was teaching them as one having authority and not as their scribes."

Jesus taught with authority. Why? Because He is *the* authority. Jesus did not have to appeal to other authorities. Jesus did not have to hem and haw His way around saying, "I think, perhaps, maybe, possibly this is the way it is." He was able to say unequivocally, "This is the truth. This is the standard. If you base your life on My words, you will do well. If not, you will fail" (Matthew 7.24-27).

As Jesus taught the Sermon, He did not appeal to any other authority. He did not say, "You have heard it said, but Moses says…" He did not say, "You have heard it said, but Elijah says…" He said "I say." Jesus appealed to His own knowledge and authority saying "I say to you" 14 times.

Matthew closed his entire book with the statement of Jesus' authority. "All authority has been given to Me in heaven and on earth" (Matthew 28.18). Paul drove Jesus' authority home in Ephesians 1.19-23.

> These are in accordance with the working of the strength of [the Father's] might which He brought about in Christ, when He raised Him from the dead and seated Him at His right hand in the heavenly places, far above all rule and authority and power and dominion, and every name that is named, not only in this age but also in the one to come. And He put all things in subjection under His feet, and gave Him as head over all things to the church, which is His body, the fullness of Him who fills all in all.

Tying all this together is Colossians 1.13-18.

> For He rescued us from the domain of darkness, and transferred us to the kingdom of His beloved Son, in whom we have redemption, the forgiveness of sins. He is the image of the invisible God, the firstborn of all creation. For by Him all things were created, both in the heavens and on earth, visible and invisible, whether thrones or dominions or rulers or authorities—all things have been created through Him and for Him. He is before all things, and in Him all things hold together. He is also head of the body, the church; and He is the beginning, the firstborn from the dead, so that He Himself will come to have first place in everything.

As we read the Sermon on the Mount, we are not reading a great self-help discourse from one who is passing on his personal experience and study. We are reading the words of the One who has absolute authority. With that in mind, we should read the Sermon with the exact same intent as directed in Ecclesiastes 12.13-14, "The conclusion, when all has been heard, is: fear God and keep His commandments, because this applies to every person. For God will bring every act to judgment, everything which is hidden, whether it is good or evil."

The Serving Example

I remember my Dad telling me something I never quite believed. When he told me to do something and I complained about it, he often said, "Listen, Son, I have never asked you to do something I have not had to do or wouldn't do myself." That may have been true, but it was awfully hard to believe back then. I spent most of my childhood thinking the reason my dad started having kids was because the remote control for the TV hadn't been invented yet.

Looking back, I think my Dad may have been telling the truth. But as a child, I often thought he was just trying to flex his fatherly muscles, proving he was the authority and was just allowed to tell me what to do. Granted, he was a fallible human, and I could probably pinpoint a time or two where that was true.

However, as we read the discourse of our King, the Son of God, who has authority over us, we must realize what kind of king we have. In Matthew 20.25-28, our King described what His view of leadership is:

> But Jesus called them to Himself and said, "You know that the rulers of the Gentiles lord it over them, and their great men exercise authority over them. It is not this way among you, but whoever wishes to become great among you shall be your servant, and whoever wishes to be first among you shall be your slave; just as the Son of Man did not come to be served, but to serve, and to give His life a ransom for many."

In John 13, Jesus demonstrated His great capacity as a servant leader. While the disciples gazed on in astonishment, He girded Himself with a towel and washed their dirty feet. The Master performed the slaves' duty for His disciples.

Jesus is the King. However, He exercises His kingly authority by serving His subjects. He even served us to the point of dying for us. The Sermon is not Jesus flexing His kingly muscles. The Sermon is Jesus' serving us. He is graciously letting us know what is for our own eternal good.

The first nine statements in the Sermon begin "Blessed are…" The term translated here means happy or fortunate. Jesus isn't telling us to be poor in spirit, mourners, gentle, etc. because He is simply exercising His kingly right to issue edicts. He is telling us what is for our good. He is telling us what will make us happy. Even when we can't see how it is for our good, we need to trust that our heavenly Father, through His Son, does give us good gifts (Matthew 7.11).

Further, Jesus did not ask anything of us in this Sermon that He was not willing to do Himself, even in most literal ways. Jesus, in His own earthly life, exemplified some of the hardest and most difficult parts of the Sermon.

Consider the Beatitudes. Who has been poorer in spirit than Jesus? Yet He is God. He has every reason to be proud and flaunt Himself before us. He doesn't. He did not have any personal sins to mourn about, but He did mourn over the sins of the world. He was most gentle. His dealings with children, lepers, mourners and sinners demonstrated this. He hungered and thirsted for righteousness. He was certainly merciful and pure in heart. He died on a cross to bring peace between man and God. And He was persecuted to the point of death on that cross.

Prayer? He was so much of an example in prayer His disciples asked Him to teach them how. Forgiveness and loving your enemies? "Father, forgive them; they do not know what they are doing." Do I need to say anything else about that?

What about not worrying about food, clothing and shelter? Do we remember Jesus' words that the Son of Man did not have any place to even lay His head in Matthew 8.20? Of course, there was the statement in the wilderness that He would not live by bread alone but by the word of God (Matthew 4.4).

When I think about some of the more difficult and "tricky" parts of the Sermon, I see Jesus lived by them in very literal ways. For instance, the series of statements about not resisting evil people from Matthew 5.39-42. Jesus did not resist the evil Pharisees or Romans. When He was slapped and beaten, He could have called 12 legions of angels to stop it, but He didn't. He was scourged and mocked and then crucified. He allowed it all. He turned the other cheek most literally. The soldiers took every stitch of clothing and Jesus did nothing. He was forced to travel the road to the cross and He did, though His beaten human body could not bear up under the cross. What about giving to Him who asks of you? Did we ask for forgiveness? He gave it to us through the cross to which we nailed Him.

Jesus was not only *willing* to do what He taught, He *did* do what He taught. Many times we gasp at the statements made in this Sermon, "Surely Jesus wouldn't expect me to endure that!" Yet, Jesus endured it all Himself. Remember, a disciple is not above his Teacher. Rather, it is enough for the disciple to become like his Teacher (Matthew 10.24-25).

We haven't even started studying the Sermon yet. However, just knowing the Jesus who preached it should impress us with how important it is. The Sermon is not to be taken lightly. It is not to be read quickly with little thought. It is not to be glossed over as though we know it all already (no matter how many times we have studied it).

This Sermon is God's word. It is the edict of *the* King, the word of *the* Son of God, the command of *the* Authority. But it is for our good from the One who was willing to live it. We must approach it with care, handle it with caution and be prepared for it to change us.

Responding to the Sermon

What, in your mind, made Jesus such a great teacher?

What are some of your favorite examples of Jesus' teaching?

What do you believe are some of the hardest parts of Jesus' teaching?

Look at the above list again, what makes those hard teachings good news?

Meditating on the Sermon

Philippians 4;8 says, "Finally, brethren, whatever is true, whatever is honorable, whatever is right, whatever is pure, whatever is lovely, whatever is of good repute, if there is any excellence and if anything worthy of praise, dwell on these things." No doubt, Jesus, His life and His teaching fall within these categories. We ought to meditate daily upon Jesus, just taking time to think about Him and what we have read from His word. In the space below list what you believe are some of the most amazing aspects of Jesus' life, teaching and sacrifice for you. Then, take some quiet time today and meditate on those things, thinking about what they mean for your life.

_____

_____

_____

_____

_____

Praying the Sermon

Almighty God

Thank You for sending Your Son. Thank You for revealing His life and teaching by Your Spirit through the Word. I am in awe of Your mercy bestowed through Him. You, Your Son and Your Spirit are worthy of praise, adoration and glory. I humble myself in Your presence.

Thank You for Your sacrifice. Thank You for Jesus' sacrifice. Help me remember today, and every day, Your Son's teaching and example. Strengthen me to study this Sermon with an open heart and an open mind, loving You by obeying Your will.

Father, Yours is the kingdom and the power and the glory and I love You. Through Your Son, my King, I pray.

Amen.

How to Read The Sermon:

Matthew 7.21-27

"Not everyone who says to me, 'Lord, Lord,' will enter the kingdom of heaven, but he who does the will of My Father who is in heaven will enter. Many will say to me on that day, 'Lord, Lord,' did we not prophesy in Your name, and in Your name cast out demons, and in Your name perform many miracles?' and then I will declare to them, 'I never knew you; depart from Me, you who practice lawlessness.'

"Therefore everyone who hears these words of mine and acts on them, may be compared to a wise man who built his house on the rock. And the rain fell, and the floods came, and the winds blew and slammed against that house; and yet it did not fall, for it had been founded on the rock. Everyone who hears these words of Mine and does not act on them, will be like a foolish man who built his house on the sand. The rain fell, and the floods came, and the winds blew and slammed against that house; and it fell—and great was its fall."

Begin with the End in Mind

In *How to Read a Book*, Mortimer Adler and Charles Van Doren suggest we read the last pages of a book first, especially of a non-fiction book. Usually, authors will wrap up and summarize all they have said in that last chapter, giving the reader a bird's eye view of the book's message.[5]

---

5. Adler and Van Doren; *How to Read a Book*, Simon and Schuster, New York, 1972, p 35.

We are going to follow their advice in the Sermon. However, we are doing so for a different reason. Jesus did not end His Sermon with a summation of what He taught. Rather, the whole lesson seems to be a summation of His entire ministry's message. We are going to examine the last verses of the Sermon because that is where Jesus explained the importance of it.

As we work through the rest of the Sermon, we need to keep these last verses in mind. It is no light read. It is an anchor, a foundation, for our lives. We must read it to learn from it and let it mold our lives.

Read what God said to Ezekiel in Ezekiel 33.30-32:

> But as for you, son of man, your fellow citizens who talk about you by the walls and in the doorways of the houses, speak to one another, each to his brother, saying "Come now and hear what the message is which comes from the Lord."
>
> They come to you as people come, and sit before you as My people and hear your words, but they do not do them for they do the lustful desires expressed by their mouth, and their heart goes after their gain. Behold, you are to them like a sensual song by one who has a beautiful voice and plays well on an instrument; for they hear your words but they do not practice them.

We must not come to Jesus or His Sermon in this fashion. Sadly, we can very easily do so. How easy it is to come to the Sermon, pick out the parts we like, mollify the parts we don't, make minor changes and act as though we have heeded the word of the Lord when all we have done is followed our own desire. In 2 Timothy 4.1-4, Paul warned Timothy not to twist his teaching to please the ears of his hearers. Jesus most certainly withheld no punches. He laid it on the line. However, it is very easy for us to deceive ourselves into believing the Sermon is beautiful but asks very little. It is easy to sit at the feet of the Master Teacher and walk away affirming we are already compliant with His will. If we are complying, that is great. However, we must make sure we are honest with ourselves. We must not twist Jesus' words to fit our lives. Rather, we must twist our lives to fit Jesus' words.

A Test of Lordship

In Mark 10.17-22, a rich young ruler faced a test of lordship. He came to Jesus calling Him, "Good Teacher." There was the rich young ruler's fundamental problem. He did not see Jesus as Lord and Master; he saw Jesus as merely a good teacher. The ruler wanted to know what he could do to inherit eternal life. He was conscientiously religious. He had kept the laws of God. Or had he? There was one law he really had not kept. He was deceiving himself.

Exodus 20.3 said, "You shall have no other gods before Me." The rich young ruler did in fact have a god above Jehovah—the rich young ruler's god was stuff. Jesus told the ruler to sell all he had and give it the poor—he refused. The rich young ruler faced a test of lordship and failed. The Bible said, "But at these words he was saddened, and he went away grieving, for he was one who owned much property" (Mark 10.22).

At least the ruler had the wherewithal to be grieved, admitting he wasn't doing what he was told. I don't believe Jesus' specific command to this young man is His absolute law for all Christians, but I can imagine how some of us might respond if Jesus did say it directly to us. Many would not sell their possessions, but would not walk away grieving. They would say, "I can't believe God would really expect me to sell off all my possessions. He was using hyperbole. I'll sell off some of my possessions." Or they might say, "Jesus simply meant I needed to be willing to sell my possessions if necessary. I could do that. All He has to do is tell me and I will." These people would walk away rejoicing, not grieving, convincing themselves they were doing exactly what Jesus commanded when they were actually doing exactly opposite.

This Sermon is a lordship test for us just as that scenario was for the rich young ruler. We have come to Jesus asking, "What must I do to enter the kingdom of heaven?" He has responded with this Sermon. Matthew 7.21 says, "Not everyone who says to Me, 'Lord, Lord,' will enter the kingdom of heaven, but he who does the will of My Father who is in heaven will enter." It is not enough to merely declare Jesus as our Lord. We must actually let Him be our Lord, by obeying His will. Then and only then will we enter the kingdom of heaven.

Proverbs 3.5 says, "Trust in the Lord with all your heart and do not lean on your own understanding." We have already learned the Jesus who is preaching this Sermon is our King and our God. He is the one in authority. He is our Lord. Will we let Him be our Lord by doing what He said? By following His example? Or will we talk our way out of it?

No doubt, there are some tricky passages in this Sermon. I certainly believe Jesus does use figurative language. I do not believe every statement within the Sermon is to be followed to its absolute literal extreme. However, we must understand this very simple fact, if our only argument for not doing exactly what is said is simply, "I just can't believe God would expect this of us," then we are trusting ourselves and not the Lord.

In Isaiah 55.8-9, God said:

> "For My thoughts are not your thoughts,
> Nor are your ways My ways," declares the Lord.
>
> "For as the heavens are higher than the earth,
> So are My ways higher than your ways
> And My thoughts than your thoughts."

Trusting in the Lord means doing what He says, even when His ways are different from our ways, even when His ways are different from the world's ways. There may be times when we say, "I can't believe God expects this of me." However, letting Jesus be Lord in our life means trusting what He says is right and good for us in the big picture, even when we can't understand how.

With each passage we study in the Sermon, we need to ask ourselves whether we will trust Jesus as Lord or lean on our own understanding. Will we do what He says? Will we follow His example? Or will we talk our way out of it?

A Foundation

I am saddened we adults so often look down on children's songs as simply children's songs. Because we typically make the children's songs simple and straightforward, they are often basic and yet most profound. Songs like "This Little Light of Mine," "Jesus Loves Me" and "Oh, Be Careful Little Eyes" are among the most profoundly helpful and edifying songs we will ever sing.

Another reason many children's songs are so great is because we often just repeat what the Bible says without feeling the need to make it more grown up. For me, "The Wise Man Built His House upon the Rock" tops this list. It comes directly from Matthew 7.24-27.

The wise man builds his house upon the rock. The foolish man builds his house upon the sand. The rains fall and the floods come. The winds blow and slam against the house. The foolish man's house on a bad foundation slides off and crumbles. The wise man's house on a solid foundation withstands the storms. The wise man is the one who hears and heeds Jesus' words. The foolish man doesn't.

Psalm 127.1 says, "Unless the Lord builds the house, they labor in vain who build it." Is the Lord building our spiritual house? This Sermon is a good gauge. Does our life look like Jesus' Sermon? If not, then all the work we are doing is in vain. When the storms come, our house will fall—and great will it be.

Did you see the subtle message in this parable? Jesus does not tell us if we heed His Sermon our lives will be tranquil and easy. He did not say when we obey Him we avoid the storms of life. Rather, He said when we obey Him, we are building our house on a foundation that will hold when we face the storms, which will inevitably come. Our loved ones will still die. We will still lose our jobs. People will still persecute us. Satan will still tempt us. But we are building our spiritual house on Jesus Christ. We can withstand the storms by the strength Jesus gives when we heed His word. As Paul said, "I can do all things through Him who strengthens me" (Philippians 4.13).

Here is the key. We must read this Sermon as a guide for building our house on the proper foundation. As I write this book, some of my best friends in Beaumont, TX are preparing to build a new house. The first thing they had to do in the process was get a set of blueprints drafted. We would not even remotely think about building a house without developing plans. Then we follow the plans every step of the way. Do we view life and our spiritual house differently? The Sermon is a blueprint for our spiritual house. We must read it that way.

As Jesus said in Matthew 7.21-23, it is not enough to hear Jesus words. It is not enough to believe Jesus' words. It is not enough to say Jesus is our Lord. It is not enough to rest on religious experiences. We actually have to do what He says. We actually have to align our lives to Jesus' Sermon.

Hard Work

I remember some of my dad's more creative disciplinary measures. We had a pile of bricks I used to have to move from one point in the yard to another. We had a bunch of wood in our garage from which I would spend hours pulling nails. One of the worst was digging holes. There was a time when I had to just dig a hole only to fill it back up. I think he may have done it in conjunction with a project he was working on. But I was the one digging the ditch because I was in trouble. Digging a hole is hard work.

How did the wise man of Matthew 7.24 build his house on the rock? He had to dig down to it. He had to remove the sand shovelful by shovelful until he struck bedrock. The wise man builds his house by the sweat of his brow and the work of his back.

Reading this Sermon is like that. It is hard work. This Sermon is not easy. Jesus did not intend to spoon feed us. Much of what He says is difficult to grasp. Much of what He says is difficult to put into action.

This Sermon takes work. It takes work to figure out what Jesus meant when He said, "The eye is the lamp of the body; so then if your eye is clear, your whole body will be full of light…" (Matthew 6.22). It takes work to implement Jesus' teaching, "For if you forgive others for their transgressions, your heavenly Father will also forgive you. But if you do not forgive others, then your Father will not forgive your transgressions" (Matthew 6.14-15).

As Jesus concluded His Sermon, He explained that listening to Him was like building on a strong foundation. Just like building a house on a foundation takes lots of work and lots of digging, so does building our spiritual house on the Lord's foundation. This study is not going to be simple. It is going to take commitment and work. Some of it will be hard and challenging.

However, it will be worth it. Isn't it interesting that we all love the secular version of this story, "The Three Little Pigs"? We have all learned about being industrious in the face of the big bad wolf. We love to teach our kids the importance of working hard in this life. We even love Jesus' story as a kid's story or song. But actually applying it to our spiritual lives as grown up Christians and letting it make its demands on us becomes tough. We must remember the hard work is worth it. Like the pig who worked hard and built with bricks safely endured the wolf's attack, like the wise man who worked hard and safely endured the storms, when we work hard at the Sermon we will safely endure the storming attacks of Satan. We will stand in the ranks of Abraham, Moses, Rahab, Deborah, David, Daniel, Esther and all the faithful who leaned on God.

Do not skim the Sermon. Read it fully. Read it repeatedly. Do not read it lightly. Read it as an absolute guide. Dig deep and rest your spiritual house on God's foundation, letting Jesus be Lord of your life.

Responding to the Sermon

What is your initial response to Matthew 7.21-27 and the chapter you have just read?

What do you expect to get out of this study of the Sermon on the Mount?

What parts of the Sermon do you already find to be difficult to understand or implement?

Meditating on the Sermon

In the space provided on the next page, list some of the "storms" biblical characters faced and how relying on God's word helped them endure. List some of the storms you have faced in your life and how relying on the Lord has already helped you. Meditate on this list today.

_____

_____

_____

_____

Praying the Sermon

Father in heaven,

Great are You Lord and worthy of praise and honor. Thank You for Your word, which explains how I might live to please You. Thank You for Your word, which strengthens me to face the storms of life.

Father, give me the discipline to study Your word. Give me the wisdom to understand Your word. Give me the honesty to measure my life by Your word. Give me the strength to obey Your word.

Father, help me make Your Son the Lord of my life. Let me live as Paul, crucified with Christ, allowing Him to live through me.

Thank You for the forgiveness in Your Son, which allows me to serve You. Thank You for the revelation of Your Spirit, which allows me to serve You.

Please forgive me, for I have too often followed my own course and built my house upon the sand of my desires and cultural norms. Please cleanse me. Help me be different from the world, building my life on Your foundation.

I love You, Father. Thank you for loving me.

Through Your Son I pray,

Amen.

The Sermon's Purpose:

Matthew 5.13-20

"You are the salt of the earth; but if the salt has become tasteless, how can it be made salty again? It is no longer good for anything, except to be thrown out and trampled under foot by men.

"You are the light of the world. A city set on a hill cannot be hidden; nor does anyone light a lamp and put it under a basket, but on the lampstand, and it gives light to all who are in the house. Let your light shine before men in such a way that they may see your good works, and glorify your Father who is in heaven.

"Do not think that I came to abolish the Law or the Prophets; I did not come to abolish but to fulfill. For truly I say to you, until heaven and earth pass away, not the smallest letter or stroke shall pass from the Law until all is accomplished. Whoever then annuls one of the least of these commandments, and teaches others to do the same, shall be called least in the kingdom of heaven; but whoever keeps and teaches them, he shall be called great in the kingdom of heaven.

"For I say to you that unless your righteousness surpasses that of the scribes and Pharisees, you will not enter the kingdom of heaven."

Read, not Heard

I know my first statement here is going to sound odd. However, I firmly believe the Sermon on the Mount, as presented in Matthew, is primarily meant to be read and not heard. The reality is if we were simply to hear the 10 to 15 minute presentation of these three chapters, our heads would be spinning. Jesus addressed everything from the basic attitudes of the Christian heart to prayer to marriage and divorce to anger management to…I think you get the picture.

The Gospel accounts are not moment by moment biographies of Jesus' life and words. Therefore, I do not think we have to believe the Sermon as recorded in Matthew 5-7 was actually preached as an outlined sermon like the ones we commonly hear on Sundays. I tend toward the same understanding as John Stott, who in turn piggy-backed off A.B. Bruce. Jesus likely traveled up on the mountain to have some extended time with His disciples, getting away from the crowds (Matthew 5.1). This is likely the "Cliff's notes" version of a much longer discourse or a summation of several days' worth of instruction on the mount.[6]

As such, this condensed version really is meant to be read and studied deeply. It is meant to give the highlights of Jesus' teaching, which will in turn force us to study throughout the rest of the Bible to gain the full meaning of what Jesus taught.

I am sharing this with you simply to explain why I am taking some of the passages out of order. We have already examined Jesus' conclusion to the Sermon, but before we get into the beatitudes and the further teaching, we need to see the overall purpose of the Sermon. That purpose is demonstrated in Matthew 5.13-20.

If we were simply listening to this presentation of Jesus' teaching as it is recorded, we would hear several shocking statements causing us to tune in and listen up (the Beatitudes). Then we would hear this brief, but thorough explanation of Jesus' mission for this instruction. Then we would hear the deeper commentary on those first eight statements. Jesus demonstrated that the purpose of His Sermon was to make His disciples different from the world so the Father might be glorified (vss. 13-16), to fulfill the Law and the Prophets (vss. 17-19) and to teach His disciples to surpass the Pharisees' righteousness (vs. 20). As we study the rest of the Sermon, we need to hang each part on the understanding of Jesus' purpose.

---

6. Stott, John R.W.; *The Message of the Sermon on the Mount*, Inter-Varsity Press, Downers Grove, Illinois, 1978, pp 23-24.

Different from the World

"You are the salt of the earth."

"You are the light of the world."

In the South, you often hear people talk about others, saying, "He's good people" or "She's good people." Grammar notwithstanding, when southerners say that, they have paid a high compliment. "Good people" is a cut above the rest. No doubt there are bad people, there are average people. But this person is "Good people." As much of a compliment as that is, I think many have altered the meaning of "You are the salt of the earth" to mean nothing more than "You are good people."

When Jesus talked about salt and light, He was not primarily referring to the goodness of the disciples. He was referring to the difference in the disciples. What is it that gives salt and light their power? Their difference. Because the food is bland, the salt adds flavor. Because the room is dark, the light brightens. If the salt tasted just like the bland food, it would be useless. If the light was no brighter than the room, it would be useless.

Three times in the sermon, Jesus specifically mentions the Gentiles. They greet and love their brethren (Matthew 5.47). They pray with vain repetitions (Matthew 6.7). They seek material things first (Matthew 6.32). We are to be different. Jesus wants us to be salt in a bland world, light in a dark world. He wants us to stand out like a city set on a hill. He wants us to live lives that simply cannot be hidden.

Jesus wants us to be different. To do that, however, our minds have to be renewed. In Romans 12.2, Paul wrote, "And do not be conformed to this world, but be transformed by the renewing of your mind, so that you may prove what the will of God is, that which is good and acceptable and perfect." He wrote in Ephesians 4.22-24, "...in reference to your former manner of life, you lay aside the old self, which is being corrupted in accordance with the lusts of deceit, and that you be renewed in the spirit of your mind, and put on the new self..."

Do you see what those passages mean? Being different from the world means being different from what we have been. Even if brought up by Christians, we have been brought up in this world. It is impossible that the world has had no impact and naively shallow to act as if it has had none. In fact, Paul, a man brought up in a godly Jewish home spoke of himself along with all Christians, saying, "Among them *we* too *all* formerly lived in the lusts of our flesh, indulging the desires of the flesh and of the mind and were by nature children of wrath, even as the rest" (Ephesians 2.3; emphasis mine).

As tempted as we are to believe we have been different from the world our entire lives, it is simply not so. Each of us has been influenced by this sinful world and each of us has pursued our own fleshly and worldly desires (*cf.* Romans 3.23). We can, no doubt, find those who are "worse sinners," but our souls have been just as defiled by our sins, as their souls by theirs. We are in the same boat. If we will enter the kingdom of heaven, we have to change. We have to be different from the world. We have to be different from ourselves.

We referred to Ephesians 4.22-24 above. As Paul continued his discussion there of being renewed, he wrote, "and put on the new self, which in the likeness of God has been created in righteousness and holiness and truth." Peter, when talking about the holiness we are to have, wrote, "As obedient children, do not be conformed to the former lusts which were yours in you ignorance, but like the Holy One who called you, be holy yourselves in all your behavior" (1 Peter 1.14-15). God is our standard. We are not different from the world when we are different in one or two areas. We are not different from the world when we are only slightly better than the world. We are different from the world when we are like God.

This concept is demonstrated by Jesus mere statement that we are the light of the world. After all, didn't Jesus say, "I am the light of the world" (John 8.12; 9.5; 12.46). Jesus is the true light of the world. We are the light only to the extent that people can see Jesus living in us (*cf.* Galatians 2.20). In like manner, Psalm 119.105 speaks of God's word saying, "Your word is a lamp to my feet and a light to my path." We are the light of the world only to the extent that we display God's word in our lives.

Do you see how serious this is? Jesus is the light. His word is the light. However, many people in the world will only ever see the light of Jesus and His word if they see it in us. How bright is our light? How flavored is our salt?

This sermon is about making us different. It is about making us stand out so we cannot be hidden. Many will think we are strange (*cf.* 1 Peter 4.3-4). Lets face it, being different from the world means the advice we hear around the water fountain at the office just won't be good enough. The advice that our locker room buddies or our worldly girlfriends suggest just won't get the job done. We are to think differently, act differently, *be* differently. Therefore, they will mock us. They will ridicule us. They will persecute us. But they cannot stop us and our influence. We are to be too obviously different.

Understand what this means for us on a practical level as we study the Sermon. We are going to read instruction that doesn't sit well. At times, we may be tempted to say, "Well, Jesus can't mean *that* because nobody on earth would do that." At times, when we follow the Sermon, our worldly friends will say, "That is just ridiculous, nobody thinks like that. I can't believe your Jesus expects that of you." At times, we might be tempted to think, "This is just not natural. Nobody would do this." That is exactly the point. Jesus has called us to do exactly what nobody else would do. After all, didn't Jesus do what no one else would do? Remember, God doesn't think like us (Isaiah 55.8-9).

Many of us hit a wall here. Nobody really likes to stand out, which causes one of the two problems demonstrated by Jesus' metaphors. There is the tasteless salt. It is no longer the seasoning it once was, having become corrupted by the leaching of its distinctiveness. Here is a picture of the Christian who is no longer living God's way. He started on the path of righteousness, but for whatever reason he veered away and become a friend of the world (cf. James 4.4; 1 John 2.15-16). He is no longer effective in the world, because he has become like the world, enjoying the same things as the world, entertained by the same things as the world, acting the same way as the world. There is also the covered light. Under the basket, the light is still as bright as it ever was. Here is a picture of the Christian with personal righteousness. She has not gone headlong into sin and is still different from the world. However, she keeps her differences hidden. She will not venture out into the world to be an influence, but sits quietly in her corner seeking to avoid notice. In either case, the great benefit of salt and light is lost on the world. Jesus wants His kingdom citizens to be seasoned salt and exposed light. He wants us to stand out. He wants us to be a city set on a hill, which cannot be hidden.

Finally, Jesus also said, "Let your light shine before men in such a way that they may see your good works, and glorify your Father who is in heaven" (Matthew 5.16). We do all of this to glorify God. We do nothing to be noticed for our own sake. We do nothing to stand out for ourselves. According to John 15.8, this is what proves we are disciples. "My Father is glorified by this, that you bear much fruit and so prove to be my disciples."

Why are we poor in spirit, gentle, merciful, forgiving? Why do we turn the other cheek, seek first God's kingdom and righteousness, pursue honesty and integrity? We do all of this to turn the world's attention to God. Our prayer is that through our difference, the world will see God. Even though they slander and mock us, we hope they will come to glorify God and be redeemed in the day of His visitation (1 Peter 2.12).

Fulfilling the Law

One of the most difficult aspects of this Sermon is how it relates to Moses' Law. Some suggest Jesus refers to the Law and then says, "But I say to you…" (*cf.* 5.31-32, 38-42). That is, Jesus was establishing a completely new law for the New Covenant. Others suggest Jesus is highlighting distortions of the Law and calling Jews back to the real standard of Moses' Law to prepare them for the coming New Covenant (*cf.* 5.21-26, 27-30). I believe there is a little of both involved in the Sermon.

Jesus recognized the struggle Jews were going to have. Therefore, He explained His relationship to the Law in Matthew 5.17-19. He was not abolishing the Law of Moses; He was fulfilling it. Galatians 3.24 explains the Law was a tutor to lead us to Christ. Romans 10.4 says Jesus is the end or goal of the Law. Jesus and His teaching, while being sometimes different from specific commands in the Old Law, are the fulfillment, the logical conclusion, the goal to which the Law was pointing.

No doubt, some aspects of the Old Law would be directly carried into the New. On these points, we do not need to hear a completely new law, we simply need to be called back to the ultimate meaning of the Old. On the other hand, some aspects of the Old Law would be superseded by aspects of the New. The fact that the New supersedes the Old in no way means the New abolishes the Old. The Old Law was never intended to remain authoritative forever. It was intended to point us to our need for the Christ and what He would teach us.

Therefore, those who truly believed and followed Moses' law would most naturally come into Jesus' kingdom and most naturally follow this Gospel of the Kingdom. Coming into Christ's kingdom did not equal abandoning Moses' law. It meant believing it and following it through to its logical conclusion. Paul explained this in Romans 3.31. Submitting to the Gospel of the Kingdom does not mean we have nullified the Law. It means we have accepted it. It means, in a sense, we are following it.

When Marita and I go out on a date, we rarely carry the kids with us. Instead, we let some friends babysit. As we pull into our friends' driveway, we always have "the talk." You know the one, "While I am gone, you obey Mr. and Mrs._____. If I come back and find out you have disobeyed, you are going to get it." Then we list all the infractions we know they have weaseled in during other babysitting stints and warn them of the consequences if they try it again this time. When my children obey the babysitter, are they abandoning me? Are they nullifying my authority? Absolutely not. They are submitting to it. Not because I gave the specific direction they are following, but because I told them to obey the babysitter. In like manner, since the Law leads us to Christ, preparing us to follow Him, when we actually follow Jesus, we are, in a sense, submitting to the Law. We have not abandoned it or nullified it. We have accepted it and obeyed it.

Jesus knew folks would have difficulty seeing He was not abolishing Moses' law. So He explained what He was doing. At times, people may accuse us of abolishing the Old Law. After all, we no longer submit to its specific rules. We, however, have not abolished the Law. Rather, we are fulfilling it by following after the One who fulfilled it.

Surpassing Righteousness

There was, perhaps, nothing in this Sermon more shocking to Jesus' original audience than, "For I say to you that unless your righteousness surpasses that of the scribes and Pharisees, you will not enter the kingdom of heaven."

The scribes were the students of the Law, who studied it and copied it. The Pharisees were a sect of Jews devoted to absolute standards of righteousness. They were so concerned with following God's law to the jot and tittle that they had established many of their own rules just to be on the safe side. They washed before they ate to make sure none of the defilement of sinners that they might have accidentally contacted would enter their bodies. They offered elaborate prayers. They had developed extensive sets of rules about everything. How could these disciples have more righteousness than the Pharisees?

There are probably many things we could say about how the Pharisees fell short. However, there are two main points highlighted in the Sermon. First, the Pharisees were concerned about looking righteous on the outside, but not so concerned about being righteous on the inside. Consider Jesus' statements in Matthew 23.25-28 about how the Pharisees cleaned the outside of the cup but not the inside. Then compare that to Jesus' teaching about murder and adultery in the Sermon. The Pharisees didn't seem to mind what went on in the mind as long as on the outside one didn't actually murder or commit sexual immorality. Second, the Pharisees were performing their acts of righteousness to be seen of men. See Jesus statements on alms-giving and praying in Matthew 6.

Our righteousness surpasses the Pharisees when it starts in the heart and when it is about glorifying God and not ourselves. Keep in mind what this means on a practical level. Much of what the Sermon teaches is going to be about our heart—our attitudes, motivations and thoughts. The Sermon should govern our worldview. When we let the Sermon dictate how we think and feel about what happens to us, then it will dictate how we react to what happens to us. Further, we adjust our thoughts and actions without thought to temporal, earthly rewards. We may be holy and spiritual and never even be noticed by anyone. We may never get a certificate or trophy. We may never get the honorable mention among men. We may be godly and righteous and only ever receive persecution and abuse. However, we have glorified God. That is the goal. When we do, we will receive our reward from Him in the end.

There is a further conclusion we need to draw. The Pharisees were the cream of religion in Jesus' day. Yet, they were one of the biggest thorns in His side (and vice versa). The Sermon means we are to be different from the world. It also means we will be different from a great deal of religion. Amazingly, a lot of the religious world is no different from the ungodly world. The big difference is they "go to church" on Sundays (sometimes). Whether conservative or liberal, most religious people just are not following the Gospel of the Kingdom. We are to be different from the world and our righteousness is to surpass the righteousness of the merely religious. Therefore, we must not be surprised when the instruction and demands of the Sermon are different even from what our good religious friends do.

Perhaps we can already begin to see why the last beatitude is, "Blessed are the persecuted." When we stand out, the unrighteousness of others is highlighted and they won't like it. Don't be surprised when the Sermon makes shocking challenges that will cause others, even religious people, to think you are an oddball. We are salt. We are light. We are different. Following this Sermon will make us so.

Responding to the Sermon

What is your initial response to the Sermon's purpose as presented in this chapter?

What are some issues in the Sermon you already know will make you different from the world? How will they make you different?

What fears or reservations do you have about standing out and being different? What are some steps you can follow to overcome those?

Meditating on the Sermon

In the space provided on the next page, list how Jesus was different from the world and different from what the religious world expected and wanted.

Take some time today to meditate upon and think about how we can follow His example and why being different is important for the salvation of the worldly.

_____

_____

_____

_____

_____

Praying the Sermon

Almighty Father in heaven,

Thank You for Your mercy. I have been like the world. I have followed the lusts of the flesh and become by nature a child of wrath like the rest. Yet Your Son died to cleanse me of sin. Thank You.

Father, it is not going to be easy to be different from the world. I have been like them for too long. Please, be my strength and my shield. Deliver me from the tempter and from the traps he will set for me.

I am weak Father, but You are strong. Strengthen me to accomplish all the things You have revealed in this Sermon. Strengthen me to be the salt of the earth and the light of the world. Strengthen me to demonstrate Your pure Son to this corrupt world. Strengthen me to be different from the world and surpass the righteousness of the merely religious.

Forgive me of my iniquities. Purify my heart. Cleanse my hands. Give me a single mind to follow after Your will.

I love You, Father. Thank You for loving me.

Through Your sacrificed Son I pray,

Amen.

Blessed are the Beggars:

Matthew 5.3

"Blessed are the poor in spirit, for theirs is the kingdom of heaven."

Blessed

Three and a half centuries before Jesus taught, Aristotle proclaimed every action we perform is for a purpose. However, achieving that purpose was simply a stepping stone to achieving a greater purpose and achieving that purpose a stepping stone to a greater purpose and so on. For instance, we go to school to learn. We learn so we can get a job. We get a job so we can make money. We make money so we can buy things, etc.

Aristotle wondered if there was any final purpose to man's activities. Is there anything for which man strives just to have and not reach an even higher goal? He decided there is. The ultimate goal of all our activities, said Aristotle, is happiness.

A little more than 2000 years later, Thomas Jefferson wrote in *The Declaration of Independence* that we all have certain inalienable rights granted by our Creator "that among these are Life, Liberty, and the Pursuit of Happiness."

What a noble pursuit. Happiness. And yet, how many have marred that pursuit by thinking they can achieve a truly happy, content, satisfied and blessed state by pursuing their every whim and fleshly desire? How many times have we heard someone justify sin and selfishness by saying, "God wants me to be happy"?

God does want us to be happy, content and satisfied. He wants us to be blessed and He wants to bless us. However, He wants to accomplish this His way. Further, since He is our Creator, He likely knows the best way. With the opening statements of the Sermon on the Mount, Jesus shows us how to be Blessed.

Though many prefer the translation "happy," I prefer "blessed." "Happiness" connotes an internal feeling welling up inside us, "blessedness" a contentment resulting from external gift. We may be happy because of a proclivity for happiness. We are only blessed, however, when given a blessing.

The blessing-giver in this case is Jesus. Be warned, however. The blessing-receivers are a bit shocking. The kind of person described by Jesus seems on the surface to be wretched and abandoned, not blessed. Jesus turns our ideas on their heads and calls us back from our selfish and self-serving pursuit of momentary pleasure and pushes us along the slow and arduous path to true happiness, true contentment, true satisfaction—true blessedness. As we read this list, we will begin to see why Jesus' path is indeed the small and narrow way and why so few find it (Matthew 7.13-14).

Blessed are the Beggars

"Blessed are the poor in spirit for theirs is the kingdom of heaven." We have heard this so often its sharp edge has been blunted. Not to mention the English translation, while odd, is not nearly as extreme as the Greek. Therefore, we might easily miss the lightning bolt with which Jesus opened this instruction.

When you look these words up in your Strong's Enhanced Lexicon, you find there are three words used in the Greek New Testament for "poor." *Penes* and *penichros* are similar words describing those who have to toil for their daily existence. The word used in Matthew 5.3, however, is the most common word used in the New Testament. It is *ptochos*. The root word from which it derives means "to crouch." Thus, it referred to one who was forced to crouch in poverty; that is, those who were crouching as they begged for assistance.

Blessed are those reduced to begging? How does that work? Those who have to beg aren't blessed, they are abandoned. So it would seem to us when we look at life from the world's perspective. We have a natural revulsion for begging. Like the unjust steward of Luke 16.3, we are ashamed of it. Jesus, however, is looking for destitute beggars to bless.

Poverty in Spirit

Though some look at the parallel statement in Luke 6.20 and believe Jesus' more fundamental point was about financial poverty, Matthew's rendering provides Jesus' main thrust. This statement is not about the guy on the corner with the "Can't work, need food" sign. It is about the person who comes into God's presence saying, "Can't work, need forgiveness."

We might too easily say poverty of spirit is humility. However, I am not sure that takes us quite far enough. Look again at those words translated "poor" in the New Testament. *Penes* and *Penichros* are the kind of poverty we naturally picture in our mind, the one that just scrapes by a meager existence. Being poor in spirit, being humble, in our minds is often a mindset that says, "I can scrape by, but I sure would like help sometimes."

Ptochos, the word used here, is a different mindset altogether. It says, "If I don't get help, I'm going to starve." This is the spiritual equivalent of Lazarus in Luke 16.19-21. Or perhaps more closely akin to the Syrophoenician woman of Matthew 15.21-28 who entreated the Lord to heal her daughter. The poor in spirit are the broken who realize they have nothing to lay on the table. The poor in spirit are the destitute who realize they can do nothing more than cry out for mercy and hope for crumbs to fall their way.

Poverty of spirit is perhaps best seen in two stories from Luke. The first is the story of the Pharisee and the tax collector in Luke 18.9-14. The Pharisee declared his own greatness. "Look at me. I do this, I do that. I am not like him." The tax collector, unable to lift his eyes to heaven, beat his breast and begged, "Be merciful to me the sinner." Here was one who was crouching in the presence of God. He understood his position—destitute, broken, beggar. He needed forgiveness and there was nothing he could do to achieve it except beg for mercy.

Why was he broken? His problem was not that he wasn't as spiritually awesome as the Pharisee. His problem was that he was a sinner and had fallen short of God's glory, as have we all according to Romans 3.23. He deserved death as explained to Ezekiel in Ezekiel 18.20. Paul described just how destitute we have all become in Ephesians 2.1-3:

And you were dead in your trespasses and sins, in which you formerly walked according to the course of this world, according to the prince of the power of the air, of the spirit that is now working in the sons of disobedience. Among them we too all formerly lived in the lusts of our flesh, indulging the desires of the flesh and of the mind and were by nature children of wrath, even as the rest.

Further, notice for what the tax collector asked—Mercy. Mercy is undeserved benevolence and relief. Mercy is seeking what we are not owed. This is where the poor in spirit are so different from so many of the materially poor in our society. In our society, the materially poor often believe they are owed something by the materially rich. We deserve to be on equal financial footing; therefore, the rich should give us some of their stuff. When we are poor in spirit, we understand we are asking for mercy. We are sinners. We deserve nothing. God owes us nothing. He has every right to tell us, "No." We do not come into His presence swaggering like old buddies expecting to get everything we want. We come humbly, begging for mercy, crouching in our spiritual poverty.

However we can be thankful that unlike the roadside beggar who never knows if someone will fill his needs, God has promised that when we come into His presence with poverty of spirit, He will bless us. Are we willing to beg for mercy, knowing all the while we don't deserve it?

The story of Simon and the sinful woman in Luke 7.36-50 is the second enlightening story. Poverty of spirit is demonstrated to be an issue of perception, not reality. Think about it. Was Simon any better spiritually than the sinful woman? Did she really have more need for forgiveness than he? The problem was he didn't realize how poor he was. Like the Laodiceans of Revelation 3.14-22, he thought he was rich, wealthy and had need of nothing. He did not realize he was wretched, miserable, poor, blind and naked. The sinful woman did.

Simon came to Jesus viewing himself as an equal, reclining at the same table. The woman came to him on hands and knees washing His feet with her tears and wiping them with her hair. That is not mere humility. That is abject poverty of spirit.

Are we willing to crawl to the feet of Jesus, keeping our eyes on His feet knowing we have no right to look Him in the face, washing and anointing His feet, hoping against hope He might toss the crumbs of mercy we so desperately need our way? Or are we looking to sit across the table from Him communing on an almost equal level?

Jesus' Plan of Salvation

In Matthew 5.3-6 we are seeing Jesus' "plan of salvation." This is the beginning of the journey to righteousness, which we will receive if we follow the path outlined in these verses. Where does it begin? It begins with brokenness.

Have you ever been to or heard anyone talk about military bootcamp? The initial goal of bootcamp is to absolutely break the individual. It is to rid him of all his conceptions. Once the individual is broken, then he can be built up to be the soldier the military wants him to be. Entering the kingdom of the Lord is quite similar. Before we can do the Lord any good, we must first be broken. We must lose all sense of self-accomplishment. We must be shed of any idea that somehow God is lucky to have us in His army. Like the prodigal who returned to his father begging to merely be a servant in the household (Luke 15.18-19), we must be beggars in spirit. Once we are broken, then the Lord can build us up to be the soldier He wants us to be. Consider the great men of the Bible—Abraham, Jacob, Moses, Peter and Paul. How many of them were not first broken? This is the first step to salvation, it is the first step to usefulness in the kingdom. Remember what Matthew 21.44 says. Jesus is the stone the builders rejected. Our choices are this. We either fall on the stone and allow it to break us or the stone will fall on us and it will grind us into dust. Neither is a pleasant experience. But the first is beneficial, because the kingdom belongs to the broken.

Do you understand why so few people find Jesus' narrow way? How many people want to be broken? How many people want to be beggars? We don't want to be broken down, we want to be pumped up. We get upset when preachers blast away at our sinfulness. We want to hear about how great we are and what we are doing right. However, before the positive messages can do us any good, we have to know and understand how utterly broken we are. Even once we enter Jesus, we must be reminded lest we puff ourselves up with our obedience and lose sight of our own weakness.

A Christian's Example

If you desire to see this poverty of spirit in action in the Christian's life, look to the apostle Paul. In Romans 7.14-25, Paul outlined what trying to win spiritual battles on his own was like. Despite his desire, despite his knowledge, despite his personal commitment and personal strength, he failed again and again and again. He was left only to wail in abject destitution, "Who will set me free from the body of this death?" His reply, "Thanks be to God through Jesus Christ our Lord!"

Consider also his statements in 2 Corinthians 12.7-10. When Paul was denied the removal of his thorn in the flesh, he learned this great lesson. He was only strong when he was weak. That is, the thorn reminded him of his destitute nature before God. The thorn reminded him he was nothing special on his own merit. Everything he accomplished spiritually was because of the grace of God. The thorn reminded him of his weakness. He couldn't even get rid of a simple thorn in the flesh. But in that poverty stricken spiritual state, he could rely on the strength of God. Then God, through Paul, would accomplish more than he could possibly imagine (*cf.* Ephesians 3.20-21).

Because of his poverty of spirit, Paul was unwilling to hold on to his old life. In Philippians 3.7-8, Paul said everything which had once been so important to him as an increasingly elite Jewish Pharisee was now rubbish. He was willing to throw it all out with the trash to come to Jesus. In Galatians 2.20, he had given up control of his life. Instead of pursuing his own desires and will, Jesus was his master. He crucified himself with Jesus and let Jesus live through Him. That is poverty of spirit.

A Foundation

Being poor in spirit is the foundation for the rest of the Sermon. It is the recognition of our weakness that makes us the good soil allowing God to work in us and make us strong. Before we can be the salt of the earth and the light of the world, before we can have the strength to love our enemies, before we can learn to truly judge with righteous judgment, we have to have poverty of spirit.

We must not approach the rest of this Sermon with the mindset of, "I am going to give this my best shot. I am sure I can do better than others I have seen." Rather, we must come with the mindset of, "I can't live this Sermon. I need God's mercy. I can do all things through Him who strengthens me."

It is a paradox. The very people who realize they cannot keep the standards of this Sermon and stop trying to on their own strength are the ones God will strengthen to obey the Sermon. Consider the promises of God.

According to Psalm 34.18, "The Lord is near to the brokenhearted and saves those who are crushed in spirit." In Isaiah 57.15, God said, "I dwell on a high and holy place, and also with the contrite and lowly of spirit in order to revive the spirit of the lowly and to revive the heart of the contrite." In Isaiah 66.2, God promised, "But to this one I will look, to him who is humble and contrite of spirit, and who trembles at My word." Of course, there is the great promise about which we often sing recorded in Isaiah 40.28-31:

> Do you not know? Have you not heard?
>
> The Everlasting God, the Lord, the Creator of the ends of the earth.
>
> Does not become weary or tired.
>
> His understanding is inscrutable.
>
> He gives strength to the weary,
>
> And to him who lacks might He increases power.
>
> Though youths grow weary and tired,
>
> And vigorous young men stumble badly,

Yet those who wait for the Lord

Will gain new strength;

They will mount up with wings like eagles,

They will run and not get tired.

They will walk and not become weary.

Theirs is the Kingdom of Heaven

"Help Wanted!" the sign reads. "Establishing a kingdom in Jerusalem that will spread out and conquer all kings and all nations. Looking for men and women to fight battles, pull down fortresses, release captives. Apply within."

What are the list of qualifications for that position? Strength, intelligence, leadership potential, money, successful experience? Oddly enough, that is not who Jesus was looking for. He was looking for broken, destitute, weak beggars.

Keep in mind how much this statement would grab His Jewish audience. Since the writing of Psalm 2, they had been awaiting God's kingdom of heaven. They had awaited the Son who would provide victory over the kings who counseled together and the nations that devised vain things. Since the days of Isaiah and his prophecy in Isaiah 2, they had waited for the day when Jerusalem would be established as the chief of mountains, the day the law would go forth from Zion and people stream to that hill. From the time Daniel detailed Nebuchadnezzar's dream in Daniel 2, they had waited for the rock that was to be cut out without hands to grow and crush the kingdoms of bronze, silver and gold.

Yet, they had missed the real point. They were awaiting a Messiah who would bring in a kingdom of this world, like the ones it would destroy, only stronger. They did not realize this kingdom would win because it was completely different. They were looking for a kingdom that would have the strongest warriors, wisest generals and wealthiest treasury (not to mention wealthiest citizens). They were looking for and wanted to be a part of that kingdom.

But let's be realistic. Who among the poor rabble of the Galilean countryside would really be worthy to be part of that great kingdom? Jesus was speaking to people who wanted that kingdom, but had little hope of being anyone important in it.

He turned that notion on its head. The great kingdom of God that would overturn Rome and all kingdoms to come, is not of this world (John 18.36). It is not made up of the world's worthies. Rather, it is made up only of the world's realized unworthies.

In John 3.3, 5, Jesus said, "Truly, truly, I say to you, unless one is born again (born of water and the Spirit) he cannot see the kingdom of God." Rebirth is only possible for those who are poor in spirit. The kingdom of heaven is theirs and theirs alone.

Having said the above, please remember poverty of spirit, like all aspects of Christian spirituality, is a matter of growth. As I study this and write this chapter, I look back and wonder, "Was I poor in spirit enough for my submission to count when I was baptized?" Naturally, the more we Christians learn about God, His will and our shortcomings, the more poor in spirit we will become. That doesn't mean we did not become Christians earlier. We are just doing what the poor in spirit do. We are growing. That, according to 2 Peter 1.5-8, is what being in Christ's kingdom is all about. In fact, if we never look back and wonder if what we have done is enough, we probably are not as poor in spirit as we might think. That is the point of being commanded to work out our salvation in fear and trembling (Philippians 2.12).

When we realize our destitute station and are absolutely certain we are unworthy of God's grace, then be comforted. The poor in spirit are blessed. Theirs is the kingdom of heaven.

Responding to the Sermon

What is your initial response to poverty of spirit as presented in this chapter?

What makes poverty of spirit difficult for people today?

What advice would you give to someone who wanted to know how to be poor in spirit?

Meditating on the Sermon

What kind of people would you have expected someone who was establishing a kingdom that was going to take over the world to look for? Why is it surprising that Jesus is looking for the exact opposite? Then again, knowing Jesus, why is it perfectly natural that Jesus wants people so different from the world?

Answer these questions in the space below and meditate upon these things throughout your day.

_____

_____

_____

Praying the Sermon

Almighty Father in heaven, Please be merciful to me a sinner.

Thank You for Your mercy. Thank You for Your grace. Thank You for Your Son who paved the way to forgiveness for me. Strengthen me to lean upon Him.

Father, I am weak. I turned to sin too often and in so doing became by nature a child of wrath even as the rest. Too often, even after turning to You and becoming one of Your children, I have relied on my own strength in hopes to make You proud of me. But I realize I cannot win the battle. Please, be my strength, my rock, my shield, my deliverer. My life is Yours. Do with it what You want.

I am, at times, frightened by the standard Your Son revealed in this Sermon. I tremble at Your word. Please, be my strength and comfort, helping me live the standard You have established. Guide me through Your word and let me live the life You want me to have.

You are worthy of praise, glory and honor. You are the great God over all the earth. You are the Creator, the Redeemer and the Judge. I praise Your name.

I Love You, Father. Thank You for loving me.

Through Your Son I pray,

Amen.

Happy are the Sad:

Matthew 5.4

"Blessed are those who mourn,

For they shall be comforted."

An Apology
I'm sorry. I tried and tried and tried to think of a better title for this chapter. I know you have seen it in every book you have ever read about the Sermon on the Mount. Preachers everywhere have used it as their sermon title about this beatitude. I know you were hoping for something more original, new and shocking. The problem is this is the exact paradox Jesus was establishing. It is old hat to us. But when Jesus said it, it was stunning.

That is the problem with the Sermon among modern Christians. We have gotten so used to its message it doesn't seem quite as revolutionary anymore. We can yawn through the beatitudes with the best of them because we have read there, heard that. "Can't you come up with something new?" we plead.

Think what it must have been like for the disciples to hear this for the first time in history. No doubt, "Blessed are the poor in spirit" was a shock, but "blessed are those who mourn?" Happy are the sad? What is up with that?

This is not a blanket statement. Jesus was not teaching any and all mourning is equally beneficial or warrants divine comforting. Jesus is decidedly not making a social statement, as some teachers twist it. He was not saying blessed are those who bewail the sad condition of famine in third world countries, who campaign with tears to remove land mines or who cry over the increasing spread of communicable diseases. Nor was He making a psychological statement. He was not saying blessed are the depressed, despondent and despairing. He was not speaking of mourning the passing of loved ones, the sickness of friends or the loss of jobs. He was not speaking of bemoaning one's lot in life. There may be a place for any and all of these things, but Jesus was not talking about those mournings here. Jesus said this within a context. He was providing the next step of His plan for salvation.

Blessed are the poor in spirit for theirs is the kingdom of heaven, but not quite. That is, if all that is present is a recognition of personal worthlessness due to sin, we will not be part of Jesus' kingdom. We must also mourn our spiritual poverty.

Notice, Jesus did not say, "Blessed are those who confess." He said, "Blessed are those who mourn." It is not enough to acknowledge our sins. Too many are willing to admit they are sinners, but then act like sin is the normal course of things. After all, everyone does it. It must not make us feel better that others are as guilty as we are. In fact, that should cause us to mourn all the more.

How many Christians have we heard talking about their days in the world? Some sound like they long for those days of freedom when they could do what they wanted, messing up their lives with reckless abandon. Have you ever heard the sin competitions? "Oh, before I became a Christian I did such and such." And the sister responds, "Oh that's nothing, here is what I was like." They laugh and reminisce about the good ol' sins. Where is the mourning?

How many have we heard talk about their sins as if they were merely a sickness contracted through no fault of their own? They dismiss sin because of addiction and expect others to do the same. Addiction is serious and takes drastic measures, but it is no justification for sin. We cannot take our sins lightly because we are addicted. Where is the mourning?

How many treat their sins lightly with a seemingly spiritual tone of, "Well, that's why Jesus died"? Grace is good and worthy to be noted. But it does not come to those who expect it cheaply. There is most certainly a place to take comfort in Jesus' grace. However, that place is not before we have been broken in spirit and mourned our utter sinfulness.

Do we beat our breasts over our sinfulness as did the tax collector of Luke 18.13? Could we produce enough tears over our sins to dampen Jesus' little toe, let alone wash His feet, as did the sinful woman of Luke 7.38? Have we bewailed our own stupidity for running away from the Father who loved and cared for us as did the prodigal of Luke 15.17?

Sin is serious. Do you recall the occasion in which tribes of Israel, moving to the east of the Jordan, built an altar to signify their relationship with the rest of the nation in Joshua 22. When the western tribes learned what had been done and misunderstood, thinking it a matter of idolatry, they said, "What is this unfaithful act which you have committed against the God of Israel…Is not the iniquity of Peor enough for us, from which we have not cleansed ourselves to this day" (Joshua 22.16-17). The idolatry at Peor had been punished and forgiven, yet it still played on the minds of the children of those who had done it. They mourned over their sins, took them seriously and viewed their previous sins as reason not to sin more. Sadly, too many today view the forgiveness of their previous sins as the reason not to be too concerned if we slip and fall today.

If we simply dismiss our sins, even when we believe it is the spiritually mature matter of relying on God's grace, we are not blessed. Only those who mourn are blessed.

The House of Mourning

In Ecclesiastes 7.2-4, the Preacher said the wise are in the house of mourning, which is better than the fool being in the house of feasting. "Sorrow is better than laughter," he wrote, "for when a face is sad a heart may be happy." He was speaking of coming to grips with death. It is better to go to a funeral and remember it is where we are headed than to go to the nursery and reminisce about where we came from. It is folly to fill our time with partying and pleasure as though we will never give account. Are we allowed to enjoy life? Certainly. The preacher made that clear in Ecclesiastes 11.9-10. However, he reminded us we will be judged based on how we lived. As Hebrews 9.27 says, "It is appointed for men to die once and after this comes judgment."

I find it intriguing that when I study the word translated "mourn" in Matthew 5.4, Zodhiates[7], Vine[8], Robertson[9], Rienecker and Rogers[10] all say this term was used to describe one's mourning over someone's death. That is exactly what Jesus wants us to mourn—someone's death. Ours.

Romans 3.23 says all have sinned and fallen short of God's glory. Romans 6.23 says the wages of sin is death. In Romans 7.9, as Paul discussed his own past, he said when sin became alive, he died. In the beginning,

---

7. *The Complete Word Study Dictionary: New Testament*, AMG Publishers, Chattanooga, 1992, p. 1138.

8. *Expository Dictionary of New Testament Words*, Macdonald Publishing, McLean, VA, p. 769.

9. *Word Pictures in the New Testament*, Baker Book House, Grand Rapids, 1930, v. I, pp. 40-41.

10. *Linguistic Key to the Greek New Testament*, Zondervan Corporation, Grand Rapids, 1980, p. 12.

God told Adam and Eve if they ate from the tree of knowledge of good and evil, they would surely die (Genesis 2.17). They ate and they died—spiritually. When we ate of our forbidden fruit, we also died. We are not merely spiritually destitute beggars; we are spiritually dead sinners (Ephesians 2.1). We must mourn that death.

Our mourning is not merely for us. We also mourn the sinfulness of our brethren and the world around us. In 1 Corinthians 5.2, Paul rebuked the Corinthians because they did not mourn over the sin of their brother. Most Christians I know are great mourners when brethren die physically. We write cards, make phone calls, send food, sing at the funeral and more. Do we, however, mourn when brethren die spiritually? Sadly, today, many Christians only mourn when the church takes disciplinary action against a sinful brother. That mourning is often not for the sinning brother but against the congregation. This is tantamount to being upset with the mortuary for burying the physically dead. It seems many think this pretense of spiritual life is love for their family member or friend. Yet, love does not rejoice in unrighteousness but in truth (1 Corinthians 13.6). Love does not participate in, gloss over or blow off a sister's sin. Love mourns it.

In Ezekiel 9.4-7, when God proclaimed the judgment coming on Jerusalem, he showed Ezekiel a vision of angels marking those who would not be touched by God's judgment. Guess who received the mark—"the men who sigh and groan over all the abominations which are being committed in its midst." If God were going to judge our hometown and sent an angel to mark those who mourned over the abominations committed among them, would we get the mark? 2 Peter 2.7-8 speaks of righteous Lot whose soul was tormented by the sins of his society. What about us? Are we tormented by our society's sins or do we pay money to be entertained by them on TV, in the movies and on the radio?

As we mourn, we must make sure we are true mourners, not just going through the motions to look good. According to Fred Wight, the eastern lands of Bible times had a very interesting custom surrounding death. The bereaved called upon professional mourners (cf. Amos 5.16) to help lament the loss of a loved one.[11] But were those professional wailers mourning as was the mother of the dead child? In Joel 2.12-13, God told Judah, "Return to Me with all your heart, and with fasting, weeping and mourning; and rend your heart and not your garments." Don't just go through the motions of mourning, mourn. Weep and fast. Have we ever cried over our sins? Have we ever fasted because we were so devastated by our sinfulness? Even then, we might go through those

---

11. *Manners and Customs of Bible Lands*, Moody Press, Chicago, 1953, p. 143.

activities and still not mourn in the heart. God doesn't want rote action. He wants mourning.

Sadly, churches today fear becoming a house of mourning. They want to be a house of feasting and partying. Sadly, Christians today want to go to the houses of feasting more than the houses of mourning. Too many do not want to be reminded of their poverty and mourn. They want to be stroked and told everything is ok. They want to be told they are not that bad. But we do need to be told how bad we are. We do need to be told of our sins and we need to mourn.

Certainly, we should rejoice in the Lord always (Philippians 3.1; 4.4). But again, we must keep the proper perspective. The reality is, before we can truly rejoice in the Lord, we have to mourn in ourselves. We have to remember that mourning even as Christians. We must be like those Israelites in Joshua 22 who were not so overjoyed for forgiveness that they forgot their own sinfulness, caving in to more sin. We have to be people who mourn the sins of our brethren and even our world. We must not pass lightly over them.

Becoming a Mourner

If you want to be a mourner who is blessed by God, start confessing your sins. I don't mean just admit you are a sinner. I mean confess your sins. When you look up "confess," as used in 1 John 1.9, in any lexicon or Bible dictionary, you will learn it translates the Greek word, "homologeo," which literally means to say the same thing as. Confessing is more than admitting we sinned. It is more than even admitting specific sins. Confessing means saying the same thing God says about sin. If we want to mourn, then with brutally honest self-examination we should confess our sins.

We need to express to God and ourselves exactly how wretched, defiled, dirty, abominable, putrid and vile we have become through our own actions. We need to express what we have done to our relationship with God and His family because of our transgressions. We need to express how we have hurt God, His children and His world because of our iniquity. We must not sugarcoat it. We must not whitewash it. We must not justify it with excuses. We must lay bare the barrenness of our heart. When we do, true mourning will be the natural result.

Consider the great example of mourning in Daniel 10.2. Daniel said he had been mourning for three weeks. I do not believe it is a coincidence that this mourning is described in the chapter following his prayer of confession in Daniel 9. Read that chapter and see how confession will lead to proper mourning.

No doubt, there must be a step before this one. We can only say the same thing as God when we know what God says. The first step to becoming a mourner is to immerse ourselves in God's word. As 2 Timothy 3.16-17 says, Scripture is profitable for reproof and correction. We need to get into God's word and allow it to reprove us, showing us where we are wrong and where we have fallen short. Then we can confess and correct our sins, setting aright what has toppled over in our lives.

The God Who Mourns

Mourners are blessed because they have become like God. Obviously, God has no sins of His own to mourn. James 1.13 says He cannot be tempted by evil, let alone commit it. Yet He mourns over sin.

We often think of God as angry over sin, but the Bible presents another side. In Jeremiah 8.18, 21, we read God's words to Judah, "My sorrow is beyond healing, My heart is faint within Me!...For the brokenness of the daughter of My people I am broken; I mourn, dismay has taken hold of Me." Again in Isaiah 22.4, "Therefore I say, 'Turn your eyes away from Me, let Me weep bitterly, do not try to comfort Me concerning the destruction of the daughter of My people."

God mourns the sins of His people. He mourns the judgment that must be brought upon them for their sins. Jeremiah 9.1 goes on to say, "Oh that my head were waters and my eyes a fountain of tears, that I might weep day and night for the slain of the daughter of my people."

Jesus, God in the flesh, was called a man of sorrows and acquainted with grief in Isaiah 53.3. His grief and sorrow were so strong men would hide their faces from Him, despising Him. After all, someone with such sorrow must have problems.

When we mourn, we become like Jesus. We become like God. He is truly a God who mourns.

The God Who Comforts

Jesus promises the mourners they shall be comforted. Everyone has reason to mourn. Our iniquities have killed us all. We have all earned eternal damnation, a place in the fires of hell, through our sins. We should all mourn our lamentable state. Yet, only those who actually mourn will really be comforted.

Matthew 5.4 should not really have been as shocking as it likely was. Isaiah 61.1-3 had promised that the Lord's anointed would come...

> To bring good news to the afflicted...to bind up the brokenhearted, to proclaim liberty to captives and freedom to prisoners...to

comfort all who mourn, to grant those who mourn in Zion, giving them a garland instead of ashes, the oil of gladness instead of mourning, the mantle of praise instead of a spirit of fainting.

God's Anointed was coming to bless those who mourn. This should have been expected.

The true mourners are blessed, because they will not stop with their mourning. 2 Corinthians 7.8-10 explains that a godly sorrow, a sorrow caused not by getting caught or by facing the consequences, but by true poverty of spirit, produces repentance.

Why was the tax collector justified in Luke 18? …the sinful woman forgiven in Luke 7? …the prodigal returned to his status of son in Luke 15? Not simply because they mourned, but because their mourning produced a change. They repented. They reconsidered their actions and changed their lives.

Our mourning is so important God will even discipline us to bring us to mourning in order to comfort us. Hebrews 12.10-11 says our Father disciplines us for our good that we might share in His holiness. The text goes on to say the discipline is not joyful in the moment, but is sorrowful. While it produces mourning, "afterwards it yields the peaceful fruit of righteousness."

Psalm 119.67, 71 demonstrate God's affliction to produce mourning and repentance. The psalmist wrote, "Before I was afflicted I went astray, but now I keep your word…It is good for me that I was afflicted, that I may learn Your statutes."

Those who mourn are comforted because the Lord's anointed came into this world to carry our sorrows and bear our griefs (Isaiah 53.4). The punishment we expected for our sins which led us to mourn, was endured by Him on our behalf. "He was pierced through for our transgressions, He was crushed for our iniquities; the chastening for our well-being fell upon Him, and by His scourging we are healed" (Isaiah 53.4).

Those who mourn are blessed because as they endure the sorrow, grief and mourning of this life, they look forward to the next. When Jesus is revealed and we are fully released from our sorrows, we will rejoice with exultation (cf. 1 Peter 4.13). The weight will be completely removed when we finally enter our rest in the Lord.

Thinking about this, we already rejoice with joy inexpressible (1 Peter 1.6, 8), yet even in our present joy, we do not let go of the sadness that Jesus had to die to give us this joy. We mourn our sin. We mourn His death, even while we rejoice in the blessing it provides us.

Blessed are those who mourn, for they shall be comforted.

Responding to the Sermon

What is your initial response to mourning as presented in this chapter?

How do you believe we live out the paradox of rejoicing with joy inexpressible while mourning at the same time?

Meditating on the Sermon

What are some of the things for which you should mourn?

What did God have to do in order to provide the ultimate comfort for you, conquering the things you listed above? How does that increase your mourning? At the same time, how does it increase your joy? Meditate on this today.

Praying the Sermon

Holy God,

"My eyes are dry, my faith is old, my heart is hard, my prayers are cold." The words of this song too often reflect my life. Please, God, soften my heart that I may mourn and be blessed.

I have sinned against You over and again. My sins are ever before me. I have sinned, committed iniquity and acted wickedly. I have pursued the lusts of my flesh and my mind. I have followed after the course of this world and the prince of the power of the air. I have become by nature a child of wrath. I am sorry.

I am ready to fall and my sorrow is continually before me. I am full of anxiety over my sin. My eyes shed streams of water because I have not kept your law. I repent in dust and ashes.

Father, I am surrounded by sin. I groan and sigh because of the iniquity of this world. It seems like the days of Noah in which every intent of man's heart is only evil continually. Like Lot, I am vexed by the sinfulness of my neighbors. Help me be a light to them.

Oh, God, take note of my sorrow. Take account of my mourning. Put my tears in your bottle. Oh, God, hear. Oh, God, forgive.

Thank You for Jesus who has carried my sorrows and born my griefs. I rejoice with joy inexpressible because You have removed my sorrow through His. I will tell of Your wonderful greatness, I will praise Your name and speak of Your mighty deeds in the midst of the congregation and the world. You are righteous. You are holy. You are just. You are merciful.

I love You and I thank You for loving me.

Through Jesus who bears my sorrows and griefs I pray,

Amen.

Group Discussion

What are the most important lessons you have learned this week?

___

What questions do you have about what you have learned this week?

___

What practical improvement have you made in your life based on what you have learned this week?

___

What practical advice would you give others to accomplish what you have learned about this week?

With what issues do you need help or prayers based on what you have learned this week?

What do you expect to learn from this month long study of the Sermon on the Mount? How do you expect to be benefited?

What do you believe are the biggest obstacles to poverty of spirit and mourning? How can we overcome them?

The Gospel of the Kingdom

Week Two

Blessed are the gentle, for they shall inherit the earth.

Blessed are those who hunger and thirst for righteousness, for they shall be satisfied.

Blessed are the merciful, for they shall receive mercy.

Blessed are the pure in heart, for they shall see God.

Blessed are the peacemakers, for they shall be called sons of God.

Matthew 5.5-9

The Kingdom's Ladder:

Matthew 5.5

"Blessed are the gentle, for they shall inherit the earth."

Jesus the Gentle

No doubt, the first hearers of this Sermon were as shocked by this statement as they were by the Messiah who preached it. Blessed are the gentle? They shall inherit the earth? That is not the way it works. The earth goes to those who fight. It goes to those who step up to the plate, put themselves forward and trample all who get in their way. Success goes to those who climb the ladder kicking everyone else out of their way. Not so in Jesus' kingdom. The ladder of success in Jesus' kingdom goes to those who descend to gentleness.

This was not the kind of Messiah many were looking for. That was not the kind of Messiah many were hoping Jesus would be. They were looking for a Messiah who would assert his military prowess, gather the Jews to himself and begin a campaign of world domination. They were looking for a war hero like Saul, David or one of the Maccabees.

That, however, was not Jesus. Jesus did not come with violence and vengeance for His enemies. He came meekly and gently (Matthew 11.29; cf. 2 Corinthians 10.1). His triumphal entry into Jerusalem was not marked with military fanfare, parading to the king's palace in military procession on a gallant steed, receiving a crown of victory. Rather, He came in meekly, mounted on a donkey (Matthew 21.5; cf. Zechariah 9.9).

Jesus' meekness did not begin at age 30 when His ministry began. Rather it began when He came into the world. Philippians 2.5-8 says:

> Have this attitude in yourselves which was also in Christ Jesus, who, although He existed in the form of God, did not regard equality with God a thing to be grasped, but emptied Himself, taking the form of a bond-servant, and being made in the likeness of men. Being found in appearance as a man, He humbled Himself by becoming obedient to the point of death, even death on a cross.

In heaven, Jesus displayed His meekness. Instead of demanding He maintain His glorious divine form and demonstrating His equality with the Father, He let go of it and came into the world in the form of a man. Not only that, He came into the world as all men come into the world—a baby. I can hardly fathom the fact that deity resided in the manger in Bethlehem, babbling with infantile glee. Yet, there He was, God in the flesh.

His meekness continued. Though He certainly demonstrated His power, He never once demonstrated His power to get out of His Father's will, nor did He use His power to seek vengeance on those who annoyed or harmed Him. Instead, He graciously endured the beating, the mocking and the scourging. He went to the cross meekly as a sheep to the slaughter and did not even open His mouth (Isaiah 53.7). He could have called 12 legions of angels to His defense, yet, He didn't and He refused to allow His militant disciples to seek vengeance or violence on His behalf (Matthew 26.52-54). Instead He submitted to His Father's will as recorded in scripture.

While on the cross, He did not revile (1 Peter 2.23). Instead He blessed and prayed for His enemies saying, "Father forgive them; for they do not know what they are doing" (Luke 23.34; cf. Matthew 5.44). Why was He able to patiently endure this treatment? Why was He able to forbear these people and even want to forgive them? Because He trusted the Father. He committed Himself to the Father (1 Peter 2.23). Among His final words was a quote from Psalm 31.5, "Father, into Your hands I commit My spirit" (Luke 23.46). If vengeance needed to be taken, Jesus did not have to take it, the Father would. Why would Jesus need to assert Himself? His duty was to assert the Father and allow the Father to handle everything else.

What did Jesus receive for this lack of self-assertion? No doubt, He received beatings, mockings and death. But He also received a blessing. Psalm 2.8 promised He would receive the nations as His inheritance and the ends of the earth as His possession. Matthew 28.18 explains all authority has indeed been given to Him in heaven and on earth. Philippians 2.9-11 says God highly exalted Jesus, putting His name above every name. Every knee will bow to Jesus, whether of those on the earth, in heaven or under the earth. Every tongue will eventually confess Jesus is Lord.

Jesus was not the violent and vengeful Messiah. Rather, He was the meek and gentle Messiah. The worldly would say He failed because His gentleness led Him through great suffering. The spiritual recognize He succeeded because He was ultimately blessed beyond reckoning.

Jesus is the perfect example of this beatitude. If you cannot believe the gentle are blessed because they inherit the earth, look to Him.

Psalm 37: Gentleness Defined

This is the most difficult of the Beatitudes to grasp because we have such a hard time defining gentleness ("meekness" in some translations). We examine how it is used in other passages and note it is connected with humility, patience, kindness and forbearance (Ephesians 4.2; Colossians 3.12). Through this we begin to see a picture of what the meek look like and how they act.

We know it is contrasted with using the rod in 1 Corinthians 4.21. We know it is part of the fruit of the Spirit according to Galatians 5.23. We know it is the spirit with which we are to restore those who have fallen according to Galatians 6.1. We know it is the attitude with which the Lord's bond-servant is to correct those who are in opposition according to 2 Timothy 2.25. We know it is the attitude with which we are to receive the word of God according to James 1.21. We know true wisdom is demonstrated through gentleness according to James 3.13. But what is this meekness?

The best definition for meekness is found in Psalm 37, the psalm from which Jesus borrowed this beatitude. Psalm 37.11 says, "But the humble will inherit the land and will delight themselves in abundant prosperity." This entire psalm is a description of the meek who will inherit the land from God. From it we can learn Christ's definition of meekness. As you read it, remember the example Jesus established and how it exemplifies the teaching of this psalm.

Meekness is trusting the Lord (vss. 3, 5). As the proverbialist said, "Trust in the Lord with all your heart and do not lean on your own understanding" (Proverbs 3.5). The sinful assert their own will and way. The gentle submit to God because they trust Him. As Jesus was able to commit His spirit into the hands of the Father, even while at the hands of His enemies, the meek trust God through all things.

The meek do not sow their wild oats. Instead they cultivate faithfulness (vs. 3). They do good. The word translated "cultivate" in the New American Standard is actually the word for shepherd or pasture. They feed faithfulness. Thus, in keeping with Galatians 6.7-8, gentleness means sowing to the spirit and therefore reaping life. As Jesus was able to rebuff the advances of Satan in Matthew 4 by relying on God's word and not being fed by bread alone, the meek develop faithfulness to God, feeding the spirit and not the flesh.

Meekness means delighting in the Lord (vs. 4). Like the tree planted firmly by the waters in Psalm 1, the meek delight in the Lord's law. The meek are made happy by the Lord, His law and His things. They do not pursue their own course of happiness, delighting in the things of the flesh or of the world. Their joy and happiness come from the Lord. As Jesus said His food was to do His Father's will (John 4.34), the meek gain pleasure and satisfaction from the things of God.

The meek commit their way to the Lord (vs. 5). James 3.13-14 provides a great contrast to help us understand the meek and gentle. The passage says, "Let him show by his good behavior his deeds in the gentleness of wisdom. But if you have bitter jealousy and selfish ambition in your heart, do not be arrogant and so lie against the truth." The sinful and wicked are filled with selfish ambition. They pursue their own passions, putting themselves forward as something special. The meek and gentle commit their way to God. Their way is not about proving anything about themselves. Rather it is about letting people see God through them, bearing fruit that glorifies Him (Matthew 5.16; John 15.8). As Jesus was able to leave heaven and the glories of God (Philippians 2.5-11), enduring shame and reproach among men because He was going to live the Father's will, the meek do not assert their own way but that of God's.

According to vs 7, 34, meekness means waiting on the Lord and taking refuge in Him. This seems to be the heart of meekness within scripture. Instead of doing their own thing in their own time and expecting God to catch up, the meek wait for God. They seek His authorization and teaching before they step on to a path. They do not seek to protect or defend themselves by their own strength, but allow the Lord to do so. Thus they learn to turn the other cheek and go the extra mile (Matthew 5.39-42). If vengeance is to be taken, they commit themselves to the Lord to exact that vengeance. They wait on Him and take refuge in Him. As Jesus was able to hang on the cross in the face of His enemies without calling the vengeance of the angels upon them "but kept entrusting Himself to Him who judges righteously" (1 Peter 2.23), the meek entrust themselves to God, waiting on His time for reward and punishment.

The meek do not fret over those who are not meek seeming to get ahead (vss. 1-2, 7-9). The meek are pleased with the little they have now because they know the blessing of the Lord will come in His time (vss. 16-22). Though the meek may fall at times, they do not fall headlong because the Lord is holding on to their hand and they trust Him (vss. 23-26). As Jesus was able to endure all He suffered without fretting that it looked as though the Romans and Jews were getting the better of Him because He looked to the joy set before Him (Hebrews 12.2), so the meek endure. They do not worry over those living about us who are never molested, though in the wrong. The meek know judgment and reward are coming in God's time.

According to vs. 31, the meek and gentle have God's law in their heart. As Psalm 119.11 says, they treasure or hide God's word in their heart that they might not sin against Him. James 1.21 says we must with gentleness receive the word of God which is able to save our souls. The meek are quick to hear God's word, slow to speak their own mind against God's word and slow to anger against God and His word (James 1.19-20). Rather, we receive it submissively. As Jesus relied on the word of the Lord to overcome the devil (Matthew 4), the meek plant the seed of God's word deep in the soil of their heart so it will produce fruit.

Because they have God's word in their heart, we are not surprised to hear the gentle speak wisdom (vs. 30). The meek do not allow filthiness, silly talk or coarse jesting out of their mouths (Ephesians 5.4). Rather, they speak what is edifying, giving grace to those who hear (Ephesians 4.29). How could they do otherwise, they have filled their heart with God's Law and therefore, their mouth speaks God's utterances (1 Peter 4.11). As Jesus was able to answer with wisdom because He relied upon God and His word (cf. Luke 20.39-40), the meek learn to answer from God's word with wisdom.

Vs. 37 wraps up the description and definition of meekness and gentleness saying this person is one of peace. The wicked are the violent aggressors; the meek and gentle are the peaceful submitters. In the short run, it seems these meek and gentle will be overrun. They are, however, waiting on the Lord and will be avenged when the time is right for God. "He delivers them because they take refuge in Him" (vs. 40). As Jesus was one who would not cry out or raise His voice, one who would not break a bruised reed or extinguish a dimly burning wick (Isaiah 42.2-3), the meek is one who follows the course of peace with all men as much as it depends on him.

Considering all Psalm 37 says, what is meekness? Meekness is the attitude of heart so emptied of self it turns to the only source of strength and support it knows—God. Meekness is not living a weak life because it cannot be helped. It is a life of personal choice and strength held in check to follow the will of the One whose will is best. Meekness is displayed through voluntary obedience to the One whose will is right.

The Next Step

Gentleness is the next step in Jesus' overarching plan of salvation. It is the natural product of the first two beatitudes.

We began with the poor, broken, beggarly spirit, recognizing how vile and pitiful we were in comparison to the amazing holiness of God. Our sins have broken and killed us. Because of our own deaths we mourn. We rend our hearts in the presence of God, lamenting our iniquity.

However, if we stop there, we have yet to achieve the righteousness that comes from God through faith. Salvation will allude us if we halt our spiritual journey with remorse. Consider the example of Judas in Matthew 27.3-5. He felt remorse. Yet, he did not pursue his spiritual journey further. Instead, he hanged himself.

We must proceed to gentleness or meekness. That is, having come face to face with who we are in the presence of God and His people, we now refuse to follow our own strength, but instead willingly submit to the Lord's will no matter where it leads. In our relationships with others, we do not lift ourselves up as masters, because we know our utter worthlessness. Even when we need to correct others or restore them, we do not have them look to us but to God. We approach them with meekness and gentleness, knowing we are not different, but merely on a different leg of the same journey.

How can the man who is truly mourning his poverty stricken spirit really be anything but meek? Knowing I am broken, I do not rely on me. Knowing I am weak, I do not pass myself off as strong. Knowing I am sinful, I do not treat with harshness those who also sin. Knowing how much I need mercy, I treat others with mercy. Knowing how little there is in me worthy of defense, I do not put myself and my actions forward as defensible.

I am nothing. But God is everything. How could I do anything except simply and humbly submit to His will? The meek are on the next step of Jesus' plan to salvation because meekness is the attitude of spirit that is expressed through humble submission. It is not the action of one who cannot help himself. It is the action of one who does not want to rely on his own help. We could certainly go our own way. We could pursue our own appetites. But why? We have already seen where they lead.

Inheriting the Earth

The meek and gentle are blessed because they inherit the earth. To the Jewish minds first hearing this statement, Jesus' words were filled with meaning. Among the earliest promises to the fathers of the Jews was the land promise.

In Genesis 17.8, God promised Abraham the land of his sojournings.

The Israelites, for all of their national history, had been tied up in the land promised them. When they obeyed God they were blessed with the land. When they disobeyed God they were removed from the land. Each tribe was granted its very own land inheritance (except Levi whose inheritance was God). When they served the Lord meekly, their borders were extended. When they followed their own course, the borders were diminished.

Within the mindset of national Israel, receiving more inheritance seemed to be mostly about military conquest. Simply read Joshua and Judges to see this. However, in Christ's kingdom, it is not the militantly aggressive who receive the blessing, it is the meek and gentle. It is those who submit to God even when the wicked are trampling them underfoot.

We must not believe Jesus is actually addressing the Old Testament land promise to His New Testament citizens of heaven. Rather, He is borrowing the picture to make His point. As we have already seen from Psalm 37, even under the Old Covenant, receiving the land promise was really not about military conquest, but about humble submission to God. Under the New Covenant, that is going to be heightened. There is absolutely no sense of military conquest in spreading the Gospel of the Kingdom.

Rather, because we meekly submit to the Father, we can claim to be fellow heirs with Jesus Christ (Romans 8.16-17). Remember His inheritance from Psalm 2, as ruler of the nations? According to 2 Timothy 2.12, if we endure, we will reign with Jesus. We are sitting in the heavenly places with our Lord and Savior according to Ephesians 2.6-7.

Still, we wonder how we inherit the earth.

First, we inherit the earth because we have the proper relationship with the things of the earth. The natural man cannot truly understand this blessing and certainly not within the context of this sermon. Why? Because the natural man is enamored with the material things of the world. He is ever striving for more and never learning contentment. We, on the other hand, have our mind set on things above and not on things of the earth (Colossians 3.2). Thus our perspective of earthly things is in its proper place.

We recognize earthly things as mere resources to accomplish God's heavenly goals. Earthly things and material goods are not the score card by which we measure our worth and value. Whether we have a little or a lot, we are content (Philippians 4.12). Therefore, unlike the worldly, we are not owned by our possessions nor driven by the pursuit of material things. Rather, we own the earthly inheritance and are happy to use it to bless God and others (2 Corinthians 9.8).

Further, though we endure hardship, affliction and distresses we can say along with Paul in 2 Corinthians 6.4-10:

> But in everything commending ourselves as servants of God, in much endurance, in afflictions, in hardships, in distresses, in beatings, in imprisonments, in tumults, in labors, in sleeplessness, in hunger, in purity, in knowledge, in patience, in kindness, in the Holy Spirit, in genuine love, in the word of truth, in the power of God; by the weapons of righteousness for the right hand and the left, by glory and dishonor, by evil report and good report; regarded as deceivers and yet true; as unknown yet well-known, as dying yet behold, we live; as punished yet not put to death, as sorrowful yet always rejoicing, as poor yet making many rich, *as having nothing yet possessing all things.*

The entire passage is part of the meek inheriting the earth, but those final words drive it home. Even though it may look to the world as though we have nothing, we have all things. We have all we need. We have all we want. We are content because we have God who has promised to never leave or forsake us (Hebrews 13.5).

Second, we receive the inheritance within our present relationship with our brethren. According to Mark 10.29-30, in our gentleness we may have to abandon houses, farms and family for the sake of the Gospel of the Kingdom. Yet, we will receive "a hundred times as much now in the present age, houses and brothers and sisters and mothers and children and farms." When we meekly enter Christ, we enter His family. God's family takes care of its own. Just read Acts 2-4 to see this in action.

Third, we receive it in its ultimate fulfillment—heaven. The inheritance we most look for is not on this earth. Rather, it is "the new heavens and new earth," that is, the new order that will come when this world ends, burned up with all its works. As Jesus said in Mark 10.30, we receive eternal life in the age to come. Peter talked about our inheritance in 1 Peter 1.4 teaching us our inheritance is imperishable, undefiled, unfading and reserved in heaven for us. Those who meekly submit to the Father will mercifully receive heavenly real estate. We have a home in heaven through the blood of Jesus Christ.

Blessed are the gentle, for they shall inherit the earth.

Responding to the Sermon

What is your initial response to gentleness as presented in this chapter?

What do you think are the biggest obstacles to living meek and gentle lives? How can we overcome these obstacles?

Why does the world not understand the importance of gentleness?

Meditating on the Sermon

What are the differences between the world's common idea of who will be successful and powerful and the example of gentleness established by Jesus?

What changes do you need to make to follow Jesus' example of gentleness? Meditate on these things today.

Praying the Sermon

Sovereign God,

I am so weak and sinful. It is not in me to direct my steps, for what seems right to me leads to death. Be my ruler and my guide. Lead me in Your path for righteousness' sake. Fill my heart with Your word.

Forgive me. My sins rise up before me, hemming me in on every side. Wash me, purify me, cleanse me. Set me on the broad place that I may overcome.

Father, thank You for Your Son, who came into the world meekly and humbly. Thank You for His example of gentleness. Help me follow in His footsteps. Thank You for Your Word, which teaches me Your precepts. Your statutes are everlasting. They lead me into righteousness. Enlighten the eyes of my heart that I may have a spirit of wisdom and of revelation in the knowledge of Jesus Christ.

I humbly cast my anxieties before Your throne. Thank You for caring. Calm my heart and provide me with Your peace that passes understanding. Strengthen me to demonstrate peace to all men and to live peaceably with all men.

I love You, Father.

Through Your meek and gentle Son I pray,

Amen.

From Starvation to Satisfaction:

Matthew 5.6

"Blessed are those who hunger and thirst for righteousness, for they shall be satisfied."

The Hungry and Thirsty

Consider a time when you overslept and had to head out the door without breakfast. As lunch rolled around, your boss dropped an assignment on you due by the end of the day. You skipped lunch to get it done. As quitting time approached, you looked forward to finally getting something to eat, but then remembered you had to go pick up Junior from ball practice, rush Susie to Girl Scouts, grab some dry cleaning, go to the PTA meeting (or whatever you had to do that night). You finally got home around nine o'clock. What was the first thing you wanted to do? Imagine you looked in the pantry and the refrigerator and all the food was gone. What would you have done? Would you have said, "Oh well, I guess I'll just go to bed. Maybe I'll find something to eat tomorrow"? Or would you have hopped in the car and headed to the store or McDonald's?

If you are like me, you would have hit the road. You were hungry and you wanted food immediately. You would drive all over town to get it. Intriguingly, the word translated hunger in this verse is the same one used in the previous chapter to describe how Jesus felt after a forty day fast (Matthew 4.2). This is hunger.

I am reminded of the song we sing based on Psalm 42.1-2, "As the deer pants for the water, so my soul longs after You." The psalm is more explicit saying, "As the deer pants for the water brooks, so my soul pants for You, O God. My soul thirsts for God, for the living God." As the deer panting in thirst seeks out the water brook to refresh his beleaguered body, so do those responding to the Kingdom Gospel seek God's righteousness to refresh our beleaguered souls.

This is the picture in Matthew 5.6. Blessed are those who hunger and thirst for righteousness. Blessed are those who will do whatever it takes to get righteousness. Jesus hearkens back to this in Matthew 6.33 when He says, "But seek first His kingdom and His righteousness, and all these things will be added to you." We so hunger and thirst for righteousness that it is the number one priority in our lives.

Getting a perspective on this, remember (or watch if you haven't seen it) the final scene before the intermission in *Gone with the Wind*. The Civil War had wreaked havoc on Scarlett O'Hara's home. Their crops were devastated, their livestock all but gone. The survivors were faced with starvation. In despair, Scarlett runs out to the field and is able to dig up one potato. As the music begins to swell and emotions flow she cries out with a rabid look in her eyes, "As God is my witness, as God is my witness, they're not going to lick me! I'll live through this and when it's all over, I'll never be hungry again, no, nor any of my folk. If I have to lie, cheat, steal or kill, as God is my witness, I'll never be hungry again!" The second half of the movie is how she lived up to that promise. From that moment she was driven by whatever it would take to keep from being hungry. She did not care about her reputation. She did not care about propriety. She did not care about anything. She cared only about being satisfied.

That is the picture of our pursuit of righteousness. We must want righteousness so bad we can taste it. We must not care about our society's will. We must not care what our family thinks of it. We must not care about anything above our need and desire for righteousness. We will hunt it down and never let it go, as God is our witness.

"I Just Don't Know What I Want"

Have you ever said that? You have the munchies or your family is heading out to a restaurant, but you don't know for what you are really hungry. "I'm hungry but I just don't know what I want." That is truly an American problem. But it is not a kingdom citizen's problem. Jesus defined our hunger.

Notice what Jesus did not say. He didn't say we are to hunger for money and material goods. That was Scarlett O'Hara's hunger. That is the worldly hunger. In Matthew 6.32, Jesus talked about the hunger and pursuit of the Gentiles after material things. That is not our hunger.

Jesus didn't say we are to thirst for power. Remember the kingdom citizen is meek and gentle. We are not enamored with putting ourselves forward for the sake of selfish ambition and political power. Though we may strive to influence others for righteousness' sake, we are not out to influence the world for our sake. In fact, James 3.13-16 explains this thirst is earthly, natural and demonic.

Jesus didn't say we are to hunger for fame. As Matthew 5.16 says, we should want people to look to God, not us. We do not have to see our names in lights or headlines. We want people to see God in us.

Jesus didn't say we are to thirst for happiness. This brings us full circle to where we began with the beatitudes as we talked about receiving blessedness. We learned about Aristotle's determination that the ultimate end of every man's actions is happiness. We claimed God wants us to be happy, but we have to do it His way. In this beatitude we learn something amazing about the pursuit of happiness. That is, if our main pursuit is happiness we will always come up short. Rather, happiness and blessedness are the serendipitous byproduct of pursuing righteousness.

There is one more object Jesus did not teach here. This one is a bit surprising and the point we need to draw from it a bit subtle. It is important nonetheless. Jesus did not say we are to hunger and thirst for grace. How surprising is that?

Keep in mind we are making our journey through Jesus' plan of salvation. We began with a complete recognition of our utter unworthiness. We were starved beggars in spirit. But starved of what? Starved of righteousness. We became beggars in spirit because we recognized our own sin and unrighteousness. We mourned our death in sin, turning meekly and gently to the Lord's will to govern us. Now, in the moment we would expect Jesus to tell us to pursue the grace we need to be saved, He instead tells us to hunger and thirst for righteousness.

There is no doubt we must have grace to have righteousness. Apart from God's mercy we cannot be justified. But we are not to hunger and thirst for mercy, we are to hunger and thirst for righteousness. Jesus died, not merely to grant us mercy, but to make us righteous. Titus 2.14 says Jesus "gave Himself for us to redeem us from every lawless deed, and to purify for Himself a people for His own possession, zealous for good deeds." Jesus redeemed us from lawless deeds, not just to bestow mercy upon us, but to make us a pure people who can now be zealous for good deeds. Which is what we are hungering and thirsting for. We want purity. We want righteousness. We want to be devoted to good deeds.

The Righteousness for which we Hunger

While I have no doubt the kingdom citizen longs for the world to be governed by righteousness, within the context of the beatitudes, the meek, poverty-stricken, mourner is hungering for the solution to his own destitution. We are looking for personal righteousness within our own lives. We lost it and now we are willing to do anything to regain it.

As mentioned above, there is only one way to be righteous. God, through His mercy, must justify us. He must wipe away the sins which have made us destitute. This righteousness can only come through God's grace. Romans 3.23-26 explains that all of us have sinned, therefore God publicly displayed Jesus as a propitiation "so that He would be just and the justifier of the one who has faith in Jesus."

We see this hungering for righteousness in the life of Paul as described in Philippians 3.7-11. Paul abandoned his early life goals within Judaism and Pharisaism, counting as loss everything that had once been gain to him that he "may be found in Him, not having a righteousness of my own derived from the Law, but that which is through faith in Christ, the righteousness which comes from God on the basis of faith." Do you see what happened there? Paul was hungry for righteousness. After his meeting with Jesus on the road to Damascus, he realized Pharisaism was not the road to righteousness. Despite how much he had progressed and despite how much he had to lose personally among his Jewish peers, he abandoned it all. Why? Because he wanted righteousness more than he wanted anything else.

Within the meaning of this beatitude we find what we normally talk about when we speak of the plan of salvation. Righteousness, as seen in the passages above, comes to us by faith in Jesus. But, no doubt, that faith is accompanied with action and obedience or it is not saving faith. James 2.17 is abundantly clear. "Even so faith, if it has no works, is dead, being by itself." Then further in James 2.22, "You see that faith was working with his works, and as a result of the works, faith was perfected."

If we want the righteousness that comes from God through faith in Jesus, we have to have a living, active and obedient faith. As Paul said in Romans 4.12, if we want righteousness credited to us we have to believe like Abraham believed, but even more than that we have to "follow in the steps of the faith of our father Abraham." That is, we have to actively obey.

Certainly, the Paul who was hungering and thirsting after righteousness can establish the pattern for us regarding salvation. Having met Jesus on the road to Damascus, Paul traveled blindly into Damascus, fasting and praying for three days. But he still needed righteousness. He was still in his sins. Ananias came to him and said, "Now why do you delay? Get up and be baptized, and wash away your sins, calling on His name" (Acts 22.6). To receive the righteousness that comes from God on the basis of faith, we need to follow in the footsteps of men like Paul who we know received righteousness. We must obey in faith as Paul wrote in Colossians 2.12, "Having been buried with Him in baptism, in which you were also raised up with Him through faith in the working of God, who raised Him from the dead."

We cannot receive the righteousness that comes from God by faith in Jesus, apart from being buried with Jesus in baptism by faith. However, once that is accomplished, we who hunger and thirst for righteousness are not finished. We do not rest because we have received God's mercy and grace. Remember, we did not hunger for mercy and grace. We hungered for righteousness. Now that we have received mercy and grace through obedience to God's gospel, we follow the instructions of grace.

We read Titus 2.14 earlier. Now notice it in its larger context. Titus 2.11-14 says:

> For the grace of God has appeared, bringing salvation to all men, instructing us to deny ungodliness and worldly desires and to live sensibly, righteously and godly in the present age, looking for the blessed hope and the appearing of the glory of our great God and Savior, Jesus Christ, who gave Himself for us to redeem us from every lawless deed, and to purify for Himself a people for His own possession, zealous for good deeds.

God's grace instructs us to live righteously. That is what we hungered for, righteousness. Our hunger and thirst for righteousness does not stop the moment we have been justified by Jesus. It continues on as we grow in sanctification, becoming more and more like Him.

Paul talked about this in Romans 6. "What shall we say then? Are we to continue in sin that grace might increase? May it never be! How shall we who died to sin still live in it?" (Romans 6.1-2). We do not revel in God's grace believing it allows us to continue in sin. We revel in God's grace because it has set us free from sin allowing us to be righteous. Paul went on to say in Romans 6.12-14:

> Therefore do not let sin reign in your mortal body so that you obey its lusts, and do not go on presenting the members of your body to sin as instruments of unrighteousness; but present yourselves to God as those alive from the dead, and your members as instruments of righteousness to God. For sin shall not be master over you, for you are not under law but under grace.

We hunger and thirst for righteousness. Therefore, now that we have been forgiven and justified by the grace and mercy of God, we follow the charge of Paul to Timothy in 1 Timothy 6.11 and 2 Timothy 2.22. We pursue righteousness, faith, love, peace, godliness, perseverance and gentleness.

By pursuing this course, we do not believe we are earning anything from God. We know we are still unworthy slaves who are finally doing what we should have been doing all along (cf. Luke 17.10). Further, we know it was only by God's grace we were able to pursue the course of righteousness anyway.

Satisfied

Those who hunger and thirst for righteousness are blessed because they alone are satisfied. If we pursue righteousness like a starving man, God will grant us righteousness to our fill.

We must understand this. Only those who hunger and thirst for righteousness will be satisfied. No one else experiences true satisfaction.

Consider the Preacher of Ecclesiastes and his pursuit of meaning in Ecclesiastes 1-2. Nothing he pursued gave him satisfaction, whether wisdom, folly, pleasure, mirth, happiness, material goods, accomplishments…nothing. He declared life is vain. However, by the end of his book he determined man's important goal in life: "The conclusion, when all has been heard, is: fear God and keep His commandments" (Ecclesiastes 12.13).

Perhaps you have felt the emptiness inside, the poverty. No doubt you have because you have become poor in spirit. Perhaps you have wondered what can fill that gap. Do not pursue a course of rioting, partying, drunkenness, wealth, fame, pleasure or sin. Do not merely pursue mercy and grace. The hunger caused by your poverty must be one for righteousness. Only then will you be satisfied.

Lives of pure righteousness are difficult for us. We have down times when we have to go back to God penitently asking for mercy and then strive to live in righteousness again. No doubt the satisfaction of righteousness is not absolute while we live in this life. We do know, however, God has promised we will be conformed to the image of His Son (Romans 8.29). We know we will be like Him when He appears (1 John 3.2). We know we will be entering new heavens and a new earth where righteousness dwells (2 Peter 3.13).

Through God's forgiveness and grace we have a measure of satisfaction in righteousness even now, but in heaven we will be satisfied to the brim with righteousness. Our pursuit will have paid off. We will have been mocked and scorned by those who hungered and thirsted for other objects. But we will be satisfied while they will be in want. We will be given the one thing we want most—righteousness. But, of course, we have to want it most.

Blessed are those who hunger and thirst for righteousness, for they shall be satisfied.

Responding to the Sermon

What is your initial response to hungering and thirsting for righteousness as presented in this chapter?

What do you think you need to work on most right now in order to pursue righteousness like a starving person?

Meditating on the Sermon

How did Jesus demonstrate a life of righteousness?

If we hunger and thirst for righteousness, it stands to reason we are going to follow the advice of Philippians 4.8, meditating on what is true, honorable, right, pure, lovely, of good repute, excellent and praiseworthy. List some things that fit within those categories on the space provided on the opposite page and then meditate on those things today.

Praying the Sermon

Righteous and Holy God,

Forgive me, I have sinned. My unrighteousness is a blot on the beauty of Your world. Purify me and I shall be clean. Wash me and I shall be whiter than snow. Make me hear joy and gladness. Let the bones which You have broken rejoice. Hide Your face from my sins and blot out all my iniquities.

Create in me a clean heart and renew a steadfast spirit within me. Do not cast me away from Your presence and do not take your Holy Spirit from me. Restore to me the joy of Your salvation. Then I will joyfully sing of Your righteousness.

Father, please shepherd me in the paths of righteousness for Your name's sake. Gird me with strength and make my way blameless. Set my feet on high places and train my hands for the battle. Enlarge my steps under me that my feet may not slip.

Thank You, God, for Your Son, whose blood has cleansed me from unrighteousness, who has purchased me and redeemed me from my own lawless deeds. Purify me Father and prepare me to follow after the good deeds You prepared beforehand.

Father, I devote my life to You, presenting my members as instruments of righteousness and slaves of obedience. Forgive me when I fall from that commitment and lift me up.

I love You and I thank You for loving me.

Through Your Son I pray,

Amen.

God Helps Those Who Help Others:

Matthew 5.7

"Blessed are the merciful, for they shall receive mercy."

Not Just Forgiveness

In this beatitude, we see a shift. The first four led us down the road to righteousness. They took us from the sorrow over sin to the satisfaction of salvation. This beatitude shifts to expound the character of the Christian and their relationship with others. It tells us what the righteous do. Kingdom citizens are merciful.

What is mercy? Forgiveness, right? Not quite. For years I viewed mercy as essentially another word for forgiveness. Most of the time when we talk about seeking God's mercy, we mean we want His forgiveness. Therefore, I read this beatitude as another way to teach Matthew 6.14-15: "For if you forgive others for their transgressions, your heavenly Father will also forgive you. But if you do not forgive others, then your Father will not forgive your transgressions."

While forgiveness is certainly a form of mercy, it is not the extent of mercy. Look the word up in lexicons and concordances. You will find something similar to Bullinger's definition of "merciful"—"*actively* compassionate, not merely unhappy for the ills of others…but desirous of relieving them; not merely pity, but *beneficent aid promptly applied*" (emphasis mine, ELC).[12]

Mercy is the act of relieving the afflicted and suffering. Certainly, forgiveness is a form of that mercy. Having seen someone afflicted over their sins against us, we relieve their sorrow by forgiving them. However, that is not the only sense in which we show mercy to others.

Jesus told a story demonstrating the realities of mercy. A Jewish man was traveling the road from Jerusalem to Jericho. On his journey, thieves attacked and left him to die. By chance, a priest traveled that road, but seeing the wounded man he crossed to the other side. Later, a Levite also walked by, crossing to the other side. Did they pity the poor man? Probably. Did they help? No.

Finally, a Samaritan, a natural foe of this Jew, saw the dying man. Instead of passing by, he tended his wounds and carried him to an inn where he could recover. Further, he paid the inn bill and said he would pay whatever costs the wounded man incurred.

Jesus asked a lawyer, "Which of these three do you think proved to be a neighbor to the man who fell into the robbers' hands?" The lawyer responded, "The one who showed mercy toward him."

Jesus replied, "Go and do the same" (Luke 10.30-37).

We are to be like this Samaritan, merciful. Yes, we should forgive. But we have not become merciful people just because we offer some people forgiveness. We must be people who actively seek to relieve the affliction and sorrow of our neighbors, loving them as ourselves (Luke 10.27).

Be Merciful Not Pitiful

Another misconception believes this mercy is an attitude or a feeling. Not so; mercy is action. We are not to feel sorry for others, we are to actively provide relief. We are not to be filled with pity; we are to pour out mercy.

This is a repeated New Testament theme. Consider James 2. I have often wondered how James 2.1-11 leads into James 2.14-26. Understanding the Bible's teaching on mercy helps me see these two sections are tied together by vss. 12-13. "So speak and so act as those who are to be judged by the law of liberty. For judgment will be merciless to one who has shown no mercy; mercy triumphs over judgment."

James 2.1-11 spoke of the poor man who came into the synagogue of the Christians. Sadly, some Christians did not treat the poor with mercy, but with harshness. "Stand over there or sit down by my foot-

---

12. E.W. Bullinger, *A Critical Lexicon and Concordance to the English and Greek New Testament*, Zondervan, Grand Rapids, 1975, p. 495.

stool." Vss. 12-13 is hearkening back to that mistreatment of the poor who visit our assemblies. If we mistreat them, we are not being merciful and we will be judged.

That point segued to discussing the actions of faith, using mercy upon the destitute as an illustration in vss. 14-26. What good would it do to see a brother who was without clothing or food and say to them, "Go in peace, be warmed and be filled"? None. That was only pity. God doesn't want mere feelings and words, He wants actions. Instead of saying, "Go, be warmed and be filled," we should say, "Come inside, let me warm and fill you." We must actively pursue the relief of our brethren. We must be merciful.

Being Merciful

In James 1.27, we are told "pure and undefiled religion in the sight of our God and Father is this: to visit orphans and widows in their distress…" This is mercy—seeing the suffering widow and orphan and extending the hand to relieve their suffering.

Galatians 6.10 says, "So then, while we have opportunity, let us do good to all people, and especially to those who are of the household of the faith." We are to seek opportunities to do good, that is extend mercy to others around us. We should do this for all, but especially for those in the household of faith.

Perhaps the greatest passage demonstrating the importance of mercy is Matthew 25.31-46. In this picture of judgment, Jesus provided a dividing line between those inheriting the kingdom and those cast into the eternal fire.

The righteous inherit the kingdom because, "I was hungry, and you gave Me something to eat; I was thirsty, and you gave Me something to drink; I was a stranger, and you invited Me in; naked, and you clothed Me; I was sick, and you visited Me; I was in prison, and you came to Me" (vss. 35-36). "When did we do this?" the righteous asked. Jesus responded, "Truly I say to you, to the extent that you did it to one of these brothers of Mine, even the least of them, you did it to Me" (vs. 40).

What was the dividing line? Mercy. When we saw a brother or sister suffering, did we take action to relieve it? Or did we merely wish them well and send them on their way?

While we have learned forgiveness is not the entirety of mercy, we must not lose sight of forgiveness as mercy. The greatest mercy we can provide is to offer relief from sin through the message of the Gospel. In Matthew 9.36-38, we find Jesus' outlook on the people around Him.

The text says:

> Seeing the people, He felt compassion for them, because they were distressed and dispirited like sheep without a shepherd. Then He said to His disciples, 'The harvest is plentiful, but the workers are few. Therefore beseech the Lord of the harvest to send out workers into His harvest.'

We need to see the sinners around us in this light. We need to see them as suffering sheep, needing someone to guide them and get them out of the brambles and snares in which they led themselves. But it is not enough to get in our assemblies and pray with compassion. We need to get out into the fields and work with passion. We need to actively bring forgiveness through Christ to those still struggling in sin. We must not have mere pity for the lost, we must have mercy.

Being merciful takes three keys. 1) Observation. 2) Empathy. 3) Action. First, instead of navel-gazing myopically at our own lives and sorrows, we must take a look around. What are others going through? How can we help? Second, we must be able to place ourselves in their shoes. Empathy surpasses sympathy in that sympathy merely feels sorry for the sufferers; empathy puts itself in their place. Sympathy pities the sufferer, empathy suffers with them. Third, we must take action. We have not been merciful until we have acted to relieve the one suffering.

Receiving Mercy

The merciful are blessed, because they will in turn receive mercy. I am amazed at the Calvinistic teachers who turn this statement on its head. It does not say those who have received mercy will be merciful. It very clearly says those who are merciful are blessed because they will receive mercy.

How can we think about this beatitude without calling to mind the story of Matthew 18.23-35? The slave who owed the king an unthinkable amount had received mercy. His debt had been forgiven; his sentence to the debtor's prison had been removed. Yet, he did not have the same mercy on one of his fellow servants who owed him a trifling amount. When the king learned of his servant's unmerciful dealings, he removed the bestowed mercy and handed the servant over to the torturers until he should repay what was owed.

We received mercy to attain the righteousness taught in the last beatitude. That should spark us to extend mercy to others. If we do not extend it, we will not be blessed because we will not receive mercy and what mercy we have already received will be removed.

No doubt, we must extend forgiveness. As Luke 17.3 says, "If your brother sins, rebuke him; and if he repents, forgive him." If we desire forgiveness when we repent, we must extend forgiveness when those who sin against us repent. As we have already seen, Jesus teaches that very lesson later in the Sermon (Matthew 6.12, 14-15). Do we want others forgiven or do we want them to receive their just rewards? How often are we like Jonah who did not want to travel to and teach in Nineveh lest the men repent and God extend His mercy? How often do we want others to be judged for every little thing they have done to us? Yet, do we want that same treatment from God? If we want forgiveness, we must be actively offer forgiveness to others.

Beyond forgiveness, what about the mercy that seeks to relieve others of their affliction? We want that mercy, do we not? We who pray that God will heal our sicknesses, what have we done to visit mercy upon the sick? We who want God to provide our daily needs, what have we done to provide for others in need? We who want God to extend our lives, what have we done to make easier the lives of others? We who want God to help us overcome our sins, what have we done to help others overcome sin? When we are merciful, then we receive mercy.

What are we suffering? Poor health, financial need, psychological and mental illness, struggle with sin, etc? Do we see what this beatitude is telling us? Too often we go into our cocoons thinking if we don't provide for ourselves no one will. This beatitude is telling us that when we turn outward, seeking to provide mercy for others, seeking to actively relieve their suffering, then we will receive mercy. Then God will relieve our suffering. Our society says, "God helps those who help themselves." Jesus says, "God helps those who help others."

As Galatians 6.7 says, "Do not be deceived, God is not mocked; for whatever a man sows, this he will also reap." If we wish to reap mercy, we must sow mercy. God will treat us the way we treat men. Therefore, we must follow that Golden Rule. We must treat others the way we want to be treated (Matthew 7.12). We must be merciful.

How contrary this is to worldly thinking. The world believes the merciful will be used and abused. Jesus says, however, the merciful will be blessed with mercy. As Jesus said in Luke 6.38, "Give, and it will be given to you. They will pour into your lap a good measure—pressed down, shaken together, and running over. For by your standard of measure it will be measured to you in return."

Blessed are the merciful, for they shall receive mercy.

Responding to the Sermon

What is your initial response to being merciful as presented in this chapter?

What obstacles hinder mercy in your life? How can you overcome them?

How will being merciful make you different from those in the world?

Meditating on the Sermon

How did Jesus demonstrate mercy throughout His earthly ministry? How does He continue to demonstrate mercy?

For what do you want mercy? Upon whom can you show the same mercy? Spend some time meditating on these things.

Praying the Sermon

Almighty Father,

Be merciful to me the sinner. Forgive me as I have forgiven those who sin against me. Cleanse me of my sin and cause my soul to rejoice. Heal the bones which you have broken and make me to hear joy and gladness. Thank You for Your Son, whose blood cleanses me and whose mercy relieves me.

Strengthen me to be merciful. Open my eyes that I may see the needs around me. Open my heart that I may feel compassion and empathize with my neighbors. Open my hands that I may love them as myself, relieving them where I have resources and opportunity.

Father, forgive me for my times of selfishness. It is so easy to look at my problems and suffering. Help me open my heart to my brothers and sisters, to live with gentleness and kindness, bearing with them and forgiving them. Make -my heart tender that I may glorify You with all Your children.

I love You, Father. Thank you for loving me.

By the mercy of Your Son I pray,

Amen.

Undivided Devotion:

Matthew 5.8

"Blessed are the pure in heart, for they shall see God."

Purity

Pure gold. Pure silk. Pure water. What do those phrases tell us? The jewelry, the cloth and the drink are clean. They are 100% gold, silk or water. There are no mixtures, alloys or corruptions.

Undoubtedly, the first thing we think when we hear of the pure in heart is this picture of cleanliness. One author used the phrase "absolute innocence." We think of a heart that has no spot or blemish but is completely blameless, sinless and holy.

Yet, we recognize a problem. We do not have these kinds of hearts, and cannot on our own because we have already blown it. Our poverty of spirit has already recognized the absolute corruption we have allowed in our heart. We remember Proverbs 20.9, which says, "Who can say, 'I have cleansed my heart, I am pure from my sin'?" We can't do that. Thus, the desire for a pure heart drives us to Jesus Christ, seeking His grace and His mercy.

To be sure, there are passages speaking of purity with this exact picture in mind (cf. 1 Timothy 1.5). However, for two reasons I do not believe Jesus is speaking of this here.

First, the beatitudes have a consistent construction. Each of them describes something the kingdom citizen can do and the resulting action God takes to bless them. The kingdom citizens are poor in spirit. God blesses them with His kingdom. The kingdom citizens mourn. God blesses them with comfort. The kingdom citizens submit meekly. God blesses them with an inheritance. The kingdom citizens hunger and thirst for righteousness. God blesses them with righteousness. The kingdom citizens are merciful. God blesses them with mercy in return. If this beatitude is talking about something the kingdom citizen cannot do, the pattern is broken. Receiving the purity of heart that comes through the sacrifice of Jesus would be the blessing bestowed on the kingdom citizen, not the action the kingdom citizen takes in order to receive a blessing.

Second, the picture described above regarding seeking purity and going to Christ for mercy is the exact picture of the earlier beatitude about hungering and thirsting for righteousness. Because the kingdom citizen hungers and thirsts for righteousness, he cannot help but go to Jesus for grace and cleansing. Obviously, Jesus is allowed to repeat Himself, but in this progression of beatitudes, it doesn't make sense to do so. Jesus is not talking about purity in the sense of being cleansed and made righteous. That is the blessing we receive as we hunger and thirst for righteousness.

He is now talking about the character of the kingdom citizen. She now lives with a pure heart. But what does that mean? I believe Jesus speaks of the pure heart here in the same sense James would later write in James 4.8. "Cleanse your hands, you sinners; and purify your hearts, you double-minded." Jesus is speaking of singleness. The heart is not divided in two but is singly devoted to Jesus and the pursuit of God. In keeping with Hebrews 10.22 we must draw near to God with a sincere heart, free from hypocrisy and posturing.

Purity of Heart

> Woe to you, scribes and Pharisees, hypocrites! For you clean the outside of the cup and of the dish, but inside they are full of robbery and self-indulgence. You blind Pharisee, first clean the inside of the cup and of the dish, so that the outside of it may become clean also. Woe to you, scribes and Pharisees, hypocrites! For you are like whitewashed tombs which on the outside appear beautiful, but inside they are full of dead men's bones and all uncleanness. So you, too, outwardly appear righteous to men, but inwardly you are full of hypocrisy and lawlessness (Matthew 23.25-28).

In keeping with what we have learned about the purpose of the Sermon, this beatitude demonstrates an issue of righteousness that surpasses that of the Pharisees (Matthew 5.20). They were happy with outward service. As long as they could be seen technically obeying God's Law, they believed they were in fellowship with God. As long as they appeared righteous on the outside, the Pharisees were happy. But inside they were full of hypocrisy. Jesus cuts to the chase. The righteousness He desires comes from a pure heart, not a righteous appearing body.

How do we get this heart in line? We make it single, sincere and pure. We must not have a double mind, torn between two masters. Instead, our hearts must be singly devoted to God. As Elijah asked the Israelites in 1 Kings 18.21, "How long will you hesitate between two opinions? If the Lord is God, follow Him; but if Baal, follow him." If there is something else pulling on our heart, we have a double mind. We are impure and it will impact every aspect of our lives.

That is what happened to the Pharisees. They were filled with hypocrisy and lawlessness (Matthew 23.28). According to Luke 16.14, the Pharisees were lovers of money. We are not surprised then to see Jesus take up this theme later in the Sermon when He condemns having mammon as a master. The Pharisees' double-mindedness (trying to follow God and materialism) led them to extort widow's houses while making long prayers for a pretense (Matthew 23.14), lie, so long as they didn't use a particular verbal formula (Matthew 23.16-22), neglect justice, mercy and faithfulness (Matthew 23.23) and kill prophets, wise men and scribes (Matthew 23.34-35).

If our heart is not pure, singly devoted to God, we cannot maintain obedience to God. No matter what, sooner or later the two gods in our life will come to odds. Either Jehovah God will win out and we will become singly devoted in our hearts to Him or the other god will win and we will fall from our fellowship with Jehovah. That is Jesus' point in Matthew 6.24: "No one can serve two masters; for either he will hate the one and love the other, or he will be devoted to one and despise the other."

Psalm 73 began, "Surely God is good to Israel, to those who are pure in heart!" It proceeded to tell about Asaph's near descent into impurity. His heart became divided being lured by the lives of the arrogant and wicked who lived prosperously. In fact, at one point he wondered, "Surely in vain I have kept my heart pure" (vs. 13). However, upon coming in to the house of God and seeing the end of the wicked, he reversed his tune. Then he provided the greatest statement of pure, single-hearted devotion in the Bible. "Who have I in heaven but You? And besides You, I desire nothing on earth. My flesh and my heart may fail, But God is the strength of my heart and my portion forever" (vss. 25-26).

We need to be like David in Psalm 16.8, "I have set the Lord continually before me." Our mind's eye must be constantly focused on God and on His things (Colossians 3.2). We need to seek first the kingdom of God and His righteousness (Matthew 6.33). We need to dispose with the garbage anything that gets in the way of our pursuit of God (Philippians 3.7-14). We must attend our hearts to those things that are true, honorable, right, pure, lovely, of good repute, excellent and worthy of praise (Philippians 4.8). We must have pure hearts.

When we have this single-minded devotion, then our actions will line up with God's will. Obviously, there will be a growth process. As we add faith, knowledge, virtue, self-control, perseverance, godliness, brotherly kindness and love, our lives obviously do not completely match up with God's will. Otherwise there would be no room to add more (cf. 2 Peter 1.5-8). However, if we have this absolute and utter devotion to God in our heart, then the purity of our bodies and actions will follow. We will not be able to help ourselves but to delve into God's word to learn more about Him and His desires. We will not be able to help ourselves but apply what we learn to our lives. After all, our highest devotion is to Him. We want Him to be happy with us more than we want our own happiness. Our utter devotion will bring about utter obedience.

If we turn the tables, trying to clean up our act while our heart is split between two masters, we will be filled only with hypocrisy. We will be like the Pharisees. Sadly, Jesus pointed out that unless our righteousness surpasses theirs, we will not enter the kingdom of heaven (Matthew 5.20).

Seeing God

The pure in heart are blessed by seeing God. This calls to mind images of Moses in Exodus 33.18-23. Moses begged to see the glory of God. God explained that no one can see Him and live. Yet, He placed Moses in the cleft of the rock and allowed His glory to pass by. He covered Moses with His hand until He passed and allowed Moses to see His back, that is, to see the bearable part of His glory. What a powerful picture of reward that must have been for the Jews. How they must have looked to Moses with a slight amount of envy. Here was a man that got to see God. We can receive that very reward more fully. We are blessed because we see God.

While I certainly believe this blessing refers to seeing God one day. I believe it also refers to the fellowship we have with God even now. The word "see" is used here to refer to experience or relationship. For instance, in Acts 2.27, 30; 13: 35-36, the speakers explained that God would not allow His servant to see decay. That is, Jesus would not experience a decayed body because He would be resurrected. 1 Peter 3.10 speaks of seeing good days, which means they will experience good days. We will see God literally in heaven, no doubt, but we see God even now as we have fellowship with Him.

This drives home a point that must be noted through all these beatitudes. Some suggest these are merely icing on the cake. They suggest that not all Christians have these characteristics, but if you do, you get an added bonus. The blessing on the pure in heart is seeing God. The implication is no one but the pure in heart see God. No one but the pure in heart are in fellowship or in relationship with God. Therefore, this is not describing an elite Christian who goes the extra mile, this is describing the only Christian who is saved. Only those who are pure in heart are in fellowship with the Lord.

The pure in heart see God in five senses, experiencing Him and relating to Him.

First, the pure in heart see God by faith. Hebrews 11.27 describes Moses' escape from Egypt with the Israelites, saying, "By faith, he left Egypt, not fearing the wrath of the king; for he endured, as seeing Him who is unseen." The divided heart simply doesn't have the faith necessary to see God while in this life. The heart singly-devoted to God sees Him by faith. The divided heart has a portion that believes some desire or need will be filled by something other than God. The divided heart is not willing to put full trust in God because it is pursuing the course of another master. The divided heart, wanting fame, power, safety, happiness and pleasure, cannot see past this world. Only the pure heart can see God, see God's will and see the end God has promised for all things.

Second, the pure in heart see God through Jesus Christ. In John 14.8, when Philip said, "Lord, show us the Father, and it is enough for us." Jesus responded, "Have I been so long with you, and yet you have not come to know Me, Philip? He who has seen Me has seen the Father" (vs. 9). The pure in heart, through study of the Word, know Jesus. They have seen Jesus. As they grow in their knowledge of and relationship with Jesus, they are growing in their knowledge of and relationship with the Father. The divided heart does not see God in this way because it has so little time to get into the Word. They have their occasional forays, but will not consistently do so. It interferes too much with their other pursuits.

Third, the pure in heart see God through the revelation of the Spirit. 1 Corinthians 2.6-3.3 explains that the apostles and prophets of the New Testament were recording the work of the Holy Spirit. This Spirit knows the deep things of the mind of God. As stated above, the pure in heart will delve into these things to know and see God. The divided heart will not have the time. On those rare occasions that he does make time, he will not appreciate what he reads anyway, not appraising spiritual things because his mind does not ultimately value God's spiritual things.

Fourth, the pure in heart see God as a matter of perspective. Though I think Titus 1.15 uses "pure" in the sense of "clean" and not in the same sense Jesus does here in Matthew 5.8, the principle applies. "To the pure, all things are pure; but to those who are defiled and unbelieving, nothing is pure, but both their mind and their conscience are defiled." In like manner, the singly-devoted heart sees God in all things, while the divided heart cannot see God except in the most painfully obvious ways.

For instance, the divided hearts in Genesis 50 could only see their mean and hateful actions against Joseph as a boy. The pure heart, however, was able to see God in the big picture, saying, "You meant evil against me, but God meant it for good" (Genesis 50.20). The divided hearts in 1 Samuel 17 could only see a giant warrior no one could defeat. The pure heart, however, was able to see God's deliverance over one who mocked Him. The divided hearts of Daniel 1 could only see a tyrannical king who would kill them all if they didn't obey. The pure hearts were able to see an almighty God who would protect them if they obeyed Him above the king. The pure in heart look through the moment and beyond to the big picture. They can see God's handiwork, God's plans and God's opportunities in all that is around them.

Finally, the pure in heart will see God in heaven. 1 John 3.2 says:

> Beloved, now we are children of God, and it has not appeared as yet what we will be. We know that when He appears, we will be like Him, because we will see Him just as He is. And everyone who has this hope fixed on Him purifies himself, just as He is pure.

To be fair, the word translated "pure" in this text is different. Yet, we do see the hope of the Christian. We will see Jesus as He is. That is, we will see Him in His spiritual glory. We will see Him as God. We will be like Him in that we will be spiritual creatures who can endure the incredible glory of deity without perishing. But we will see Him in all His deity. We will see God.

Like the picture of worshippers in Revelation 4-5, we will be around the throne of God, gazing on the One sitting on the throne, the Lamb and the "seven Spirits of God." What a glorious hope the pure in heart have.

Blessed are the pure in heart, for they shall see God.

Responding to the Sermon

What is your initial response to purity of heart as presented in this chapter?

What are your biggest obstacles to a pure heart and how do you think you can overcome them?

How will being pure in heart make you different from the world?

Meditating on the Sermon

In the space provided, list Bible characters who demonstrated a singly-devoted, pure heart and how they demonstrated it.

_____

_____

_____

_____

_____

What caused their singled-hearted devotion? Meditate on these things today.

_____

_____

_____

_____

_____

Praying the Sermon

Almighty God,

Through Your pure hearted Son I ask You to forgive and cleanse me that I might present clean hands and a pure heart to You. Far too often my loyalties have been divided. I have pursued pleasure, power and personal importance. I have sought money, fame and accomplishment. Too often I have allowed other gods to compete with You and given them the victory. O God, hear. O God, forgive.

I present to You my heart, giving You my undivided attention and loyalty. I no longer desire what pleases me or makes me happy. I desire what pleases You and makes You happy. I will put nothing worthless before my eyes, instead You are ever before Me. Whom have I in heaven but You? And besides you, I desire nothing on earth.

You, great God in heaven, are my life and my support, the strength of my heart and my portion forever. You are my every waking thought. To You I will sing praises in the assembly and before mankind. I will ever seek Your will and way.

I love You, Father and I thank You for loving me.

Amen.

Lovely Feet:

Matthew 5.9

"Blessed are the peacemakers, for they shall be called sons of God."

Give Peace a Chance

You will not be shocked as I begin yet another look at another beatitude discussing how shocked the Jews must have been at this statement. Blessed are the peacemakers? They weren't looking for peace, they were looking for war.

They expected a militant Messiah who would ascend to the throne of David. They expected Him to be like David, a man of bloodshed (1 Chronicles 22.8). They expected Him to be a hero who gathered warriors to Him to conquer Rome and the rest of the Gentiles by force.

They expected to be a kingdom of soldiers, a military force to be reckoned with. They expected Jesus to say, "Blessed are the warriors," not "Blessed are the peacemakers."

With this statement, Jesus foreshadowed His stand before Pilate. "My kingdom is not of this world. If My kingdom were of this world, then My servants would be fighting so that I would not be handed over to the Jews; but as it is, My kingdom is not of this realm" (John 18.36).

This beatitude helps us understand Jesus' reaction when Peter drew his sword and cut off the slave of the High Priest's ear. "Put your sword back into its place; for all those who take up the sword shall perish by the sword" (Matthew 26.52).

This beatitude also helps us see the spirit of Christ when He rebuked the Sons of Thunder for wanting to call fire from heaven to consume an unreceptive Samaritan village. "You do not know what kind of spirit you are of; for the Son of Man did not come to destroy men's lives, but to save them" (Luke 9.55-56).

Sadly, too many continue to desire the military conquest of Christ. They misunderstand why Jesus came in the first place and they misunderstand why He will return. His kingdom is here and it is not a kingdom of warmongers who spread the gospel at the end of a sword. It is not a kingdom that keeps peace by the threat of the gun. The medieval Crusades were wrong. Any victories there were not God's blessings for faithfulness to Him, because His kingdom is for peacemakers, not warriors.

Thus Paul wrote, "For though we walk in the flesh, we do not war according to the flesh, for the weapons of our warfare are not of the flesh, but divinely powerful for the destruction of fortresses" (2 Corinthians 10.3-4). As he wrote in Ephesians 6.10-18, our enemy is spiritual, our battle is spiritual, our weapons are spiritual. Christ's kingdom does not win territory through conquest. It wins through peacemaking.

"Peace! Peace!"

God clearly can't stand for His people to misunderstand peace. He obviously hates for His people to proclaim peace when it is not really there. Read the contexts of Jeremiah 6.14; 8.11 and Ezekiel 13.10. Here the prophets and priests cried out, "Peace!" when there was none. Thus, if we miss what this peace is and act as though we have made it when we have not, we are going to be in trouble.

Jesus is not here talking about political peace between nations. World peace would indeed be a wonderful thing. Further, I am convinced if we were ultimately successful in the lives of all men in making the peace Jesus is talking about, we would have world peace. However, Jesus did not say, "Blessed are the diplomats" or "Blessed are the negotiators." He said blessed are the peacemakers.

Neither is He talking about a cold war kind of peace. For years the U.S. and the U.S.S.R. were at peace, but not really. They were not firing missiles. They were not deploying troops. But we who can still remember getting under our desks in air raid drills know there was no peace.

Jesus is not talking about appeasement and compromise. He is not talking about those of phlegmatic spirits who naturally despise confrontation, avoiding it at all costs.

He is talking about a peace that is not of this world (John 14.27), just as His kingdom is not of this world. He is talking about an active peace, that is, a peace that not only avoids confrontation but actively pursues benefit. The blessing for peacemaking is being called a son of God. It is no accident that Matthew 5.44-45 refers to those who love their enemies, praying for them and blessing them, as "sons of their Father who is in heaven." This is the peacemaking Jesus is talking about. Blessed are those who, through their love for others, even their enemies, pursue what benefits, builds up and edifies them (cf. Romans 15.1-3).

Peacemaking in Context

We might misunderstand the true nature of peacemaking in the beatitudes if we forget what we have already learned from the other beatitudes. We, who were once separated from God, mourned our spiritual death and meekly submitted to His will and way, being starved for the righteousness that only comes through God's grace and faithful obedience to His gospel. Having traveled that road, we could not help but grant mercy to others and singly devote our hearts to God and His will.

The peacemaking of this list is the natural byproduct of the previous two statements. Here we are people who have pure, single-hearted devotion to God and who want to extend mercy to all others as we want mercy extended to us. Think for just a moment. Into what do these two characteristics coalesce? Peacemaking. That is, as we extend mercy to men and extend our hearts singly to God, we cannot help but strive to bring these two together.

Please, take note that the characteristic is not merely being peaceable. It is not merely being peaceful. Rather, it is the making of peace. First, foremost and ultimately it is the making of peace between the men to whom we extend mercy and the God to whom we extend our hearts.

Meditate on Paul's words in 2 Corinthians 5.18-20:

> Now all these things are from God, who reconciled us to Himself through Christ and gave us the ministry of reconciliation, namely, that God was in Christ reconciling the world to Himself, not counting their trespasses against them, and He has committed to us the word of reconciliation. Therefore, we are ambassadors for Christ, as though God were making an appeal through us; we beg you on behalf of Christ, be reconciled to God.

How blessed are the ambassadors of reconciliation. How blessed are those who make the appeals of peace to their fellow man. Long before Jesus uttered this beatitude, Isaiah wrote, "How lovely on the mountains are the feet of him who brings good news, who announces peace and brings good news of happiness, who announces salvation" (Isaiah 52.7).

We have a message of peace, a ministry of reconciliation and how blessed we are when we fulfill our ministry.

What about My Neighbor?

We are absolutely supposed to seek peace between ourselves and our neighbors. Romans 12.18 says, "If possible, so far as it depends on you, be at peace with all men." Hebrews 12.14 says, "Pursue peace with all men." We are to strive for peace with all others.

Additionally, we are to strive to make peace between other men. Like Moses, who sought to bring peace between his fighting brothers (Acts 7.26), we should strive to make peace between others. As Paul did with Euodia and Syntyche, we are to encourage others to live in harmony.

What is the ultimate means by which we can accomplish this? Is it not through the Gospel of Jesus Christ? How did God bring down the dividing wall of enmity between the Jews and Gentiles? It was not through successful negotiations. It was not through weeks of peace accords with diplomats seeking a win-win compromise. It was by the blood of Jesus Christ (Ephesians 2.13-16).

Look to the 12 apostles. How could Simon the Zealot work with Matthew the tax collector? It was not because Jesus sat down as a third party mediator to resolve their differences. It was because the message of salvation in Jesus Christ produces peace between even those who disagree politically. I think Republicans and Democrats today might take a lesson from these two men. Is it possible that the goal of spreading the gospel is so outrageously important that it dwarfs the political differences we might have about how a nation is to be run?

I am not so naïve as to think that personal evangelism is the exact equal of all aspects of peacemaking. I do believe, however, that the foundation of peace is bringing the Gospel of peace to people. It is the foundation of reconciliation between men and God, between men and us and between men and other men.

The Practice of Peace

Making peace is not a passive responsibility, but is an active work. It is not enough for us to write books about making peace. It is not enough for us to conduct seminars about making peace. It is not enough for us to gather together and talk about the ways to make peace. We have to actually make peace. What must we be and do to make peace?

First, D. Martin Lloyd Jones is right when he says peacemaking is linked to meekness. "Before one can be a peacemaker one really must be entirely delivered from self, from self-interest, from self concern." He then made his statement more personal, "Before you can be a peacemaker you really must be entirely forgetful of self because as long as you are thinking about yourself, and shielding yourself, you cannot be doing the work properly." [13]

James pointed out that selfish ambition is antithetical to the peace of godly wisdom. "But if you have bitter jealousy and selfish ambition in your heart, do not be arrogant and so lie against the truth…For where jealousy and selfish ambition exist, there is disorder and every evil thing" (James 3.14, 16). He proceeded to say in contrast, "But the wisdom from above is first pure, then peaceable, gentle, reasonable, full of mercy and good fruits, unwavering, without hypocrisy. And the seed whose fruit is righteousness is sown in peace by those who make peace" (James 3.17-18). Notice how many of our beatitudes are bound up in godly wisdom. The major contrast, however, is between those who jealously pursue selfish ambition and those who sow and make peace.

As Romans 14.19 says, "We pursue the things which make for peace and the building up of one another." In context, Paul's point was pursuing peace means sacrificing our rights in order to help others go to heaven. If we want to be peacemakers, we have to be the meek and gentle who are devoid of selfish intent.

Second, though peacemaking does not equal peaceableness, we must be peaceable people. "The Lord's bond-servant must not be quarrelsome, but be kind to all, able to teach patient when wronged, with gentleness correcting those who are in opposition…" (2 Timothy 2.24-25). Some people are happy to take the Gospel with them, but only as ammunition for a fight. They do not view their prospects or contacts as needing freedom from the devil's entrapment. They view the prospect as the enemy who needs to be lashed with the flat side of the Spirit's sword. Like the Sons of Thunder who wished to call down fire on the unreceptive village, these quarrelsome evangelists are slow to give patient instruction and quick to call down the fires of hell on everyone else's head for not being at the same spot on the journey at the same time as they are. So important is peaceableness it is one of the qualifications for those who would shepherd a flock of the Lord (1 Timothy 3.3).

Third, we must love God and others. This may seem repetitive and obvious, yet sometimes we have to repeat the obvious. When the lawyer asked what was the greatest commandment, Jesus said the first was to love God and the second was to love our neighbors as ourselves (Matthew 22: 35-39). When we have this love for God and our fellow man, we will naturally want them to love each other. Of course, we have no trouble getting God to love men. It is the reverse that is the hard part.

---

13. D. Martyn Lloyd-Jones, *Studies in the Sermon on the Mount*, Eerdman's Publishing Comp., Grand Rapids, 1976, v I, pp. 122-124.

When we love God with all our heart, soul and mind, we want His will to be done. We want others to obey Him. We will not be able to help but try to get His message out to them. When we love our neighbors as ourselves, we will not be able to help wanting to bring the forgiveness and salvation offered through Jesus Christ to them. We will see them as "distressed and dispirited like sheep without a shepherd" (Matthew 9.36). We will want to bring the Good Shepherd to them and bring them to the Good Shepherd.

As we have previously noted, an extension of this love is seen in the Sermon on the Mount. Matthew 5.44-45 says, "Love your enemies and pray for those who persecute you, so that you may be sons of your Father who is in heaven." Luke's rendition of this says, "Love your enemies, do good to those who hate you, bless those who curse you, pray for those who mistreat you" (Luke 6.27-28). Seeking peace through love means doing good even to those who have not done good to us (cf. Romans 12.14-21). It means speaking with blessing to those who have cursed us (cf. Ephesians 4.29, 32; 1 Peter 3.8-12). It means praying for those who mistreat us. Can there be a greater example of that than Jesus on the cross crying out, "Father, forgive them; for they do not know what they are doing" (Luke 23.34)?

Finally, we must realize that the only peace that truly matters is the peace between God and His creation. Too often we substitute a semblance of peace between us and others for this peace. We look away from the sin of others because we do not want to rock the boat. We do not reprove and rebuke because we fear confrontation. We do not share the message because we fear rejection. We have, at best, a tenuous peace. We are walking on egg shells afraid that at any moment a bomb might be dropped that explodes the unspoken treaty we have established. You know the one I am talking about. It is the one that says you don't talk about religion in polite company. The one that causes us to tell our kids, "Don't say anything about church to them." That is not making peace.

In making peace, we will at times have to say hard things. We recognize by Paul's use of "if possible" that some will not let us be at peace with them no matter how hard we try (Romans 12.18). But we must strive to bring peace through the gospel. We cannot cry, "Peace! Peace!" when there is no peace. We must rather bring the Gospel into our lives and conversations that we might make peace between man and God. We must be ambassadors of reconciliation not diplomats of deception.

Sons of God

You have heard the expression, "Like Father, like son." The peacemakers are blessed because they, and only they, will be called sons of God. That is, when we are peacemakers we are like our Father who is in heaven. When we are peacemakers, people can use another common expression, "The acorn doesn't fall far from the tree."

Our heavenly Father is called the God of peace repeatedly. This title can be found in Romans 15.33; 16.20; Philippians 4.9; 1 Thessalonians 5.25 and Hebrews 13.20. He is called the God of love and peace in 2 Corinthians 13.11. Jesus was called the Prince of Peace in Isaiah 9.6.

God went so far to make peace with man that He sent His only begotten Son to die for the world, reconciling the word to Himself through the blood of Jesus Christ (Colossians 1.19-20). When we become true peacemakers we are going to look like that, willing to sacrifice ourselves in order to make peace between men and God.

But the great blessing is not just that we look like God. The great blessing is demonstrated in Romans 8.16-17, saying, "The Spirit Himself testifies with our spirit that we are children of God, and if children, heirs also, heirs of God and fellow heirs with Christ, if indeed we suffer with Him so that we may also be glorified with Him." The sons of God are the ones who receive the inheritance from God which is "imperishable and undefiled and will not fade away, reserved in heaven for you, who are protected by the power of God through faith for a salvation ready to be revealed in the last time" (1 Peter 1.4-5).

The peacemakers receive this blessing and this inheritance. Once again, we learn that these beatitudes do not describe the Christian "special forces" who go above and beyond the call of duty and therefore get an extra reward. This is the blessing we all want. This is the blessing of a home in heaven.

Blessed are the peacemakers, for they shall be called sons of God.

Responding to the Sermon

What is your initial response to peacemaking as presented in this chapter?

What obstacles hinder you from actively making peace? How do you think you can overcome those obstacles?

List some people with whom you should actively pursue making peace through means of the gospel?

Meditating on the Sermon

Reread James 3.13-18. How does God's wisdom contrast with man's?

How can the characteristics of godly wisdom be displayed in your life? Meditate on these things today.

Praying the Sermon

God of peace and love,

Thank You for Your Son, the Prince of Peace. Through Him I come to You in prayer. Thank You for Your envoy of peace, the Spirit, who revealed Your word, the means of reconciliation and peace between us. Help me understand it and apply it. Help me live it peaceably.

Forgive me Father, for I have too often been at war. I have been at war with You. I have been at war with Your word. I have been at war with Your children. I have been at war with those who harmed me. I have sought their harm and wanted them punished instead of seeking peace with them and for them. Help me want others to be forgiven as much as I want to be forgiven. Please forgive those who have harmed me and forgive me for harming others.

Please, guard my heart and mind with Your peace that passes all understanding. Stay with me through the storms and protect me from the tempter's snares. Help me live peaceably with all men, doing good, blessing and praying for them.

I love You, Father, and I thank You for loving me.

Amen.

Group Discussion

What are the most important lessons you have learned this week?

What questions do you have about what you have learned this week?

What practical improvement have you made in your life based on what you have learned this week?

What practical advice would you give others to accomplish what you have learned about this week?

With what issues do you need help or prayers based on what you have learned this week?

What do you believe are the biggest obstacles to accomplishing the beatitudes you have learned about this week? How can we overcome them?

How can a local congregation become a more active group of peacemakers?

The Gospel of the Kingdom

Week Three

If your right eye makes you stumble, tear it out and throw it from you; for it is better for you to lose one of the parts of your body, than for your whole body to be thrown into hell.

If your right hand makes you stumble, cut it off and throw it from you; for it is better for you to lose one of the parts of your body, than for you whole body to be thrown into hell.

Matthew 5.29-30

The World Strikes Back:

Matthew 5.10-12

"Blessed are those who have been persecuted for the sake of righteousness, for theirs is the kingdom of heaven.

"Blessed are you when people insult you and persecute and falsely say all kinds of evil against you because of Me. Rejoice and be glad, for your reward in heaven is great; for in the same way they persecuted the prophets who were before you."

Counting the Cost

I do not need to restate what kind of Messiah and kingdom the Jews had been looking for. They expected a kingdom that would put their enemies to flight. Yet, Jesus concludes His beatitudes by claiming His kingdom citizens would be blessed when they were put to flight.

According to Strong's Enhanced Lexicon, the word translated "persecuted" comes from the word meaning "to flee." Being persecuted means to be put to flight, to be chased down, to be pursued or hunted. Interestingly it is used in other texts to talk about how we should practice hospitality (Romans 12.13), pursue love (1 Corinthians 14.1) and press on toward our goal (Philippians 3.14).

Jesus provided a full picture of the Kingdom citizen. To this point, His descriptions have been shocking, but not overwhelmingly negative. If we open our eyes to our sinful condition and simply follow the natural path God's love and mercy provide for us, we will follow the other beatitudes. This one is the show stopper. It is tough to eat humble pie, begging for mercy and righteousness from God, but to do that while others are hunting us down with pitchforks and pickaxes is completely different.

The kingdom citizens are blessed people. They receive the kingdom, comfort, the earth, satisfaction, mercy, the ability to see God and the appellation "sons of God," but they also receive persecution. They will be hunted and chased, mocked and ridiculed, ostracized and cut off, insulted and reviled, beaten and killed by the people to whom they offer mercy and peace.

These final beatitudes encourage any who are interested in being a kingdom citizen to count the cost. Luke 14.27-28 says, "Whoever does not carry his own cross and come after Me cannot be My disciple. For which one of you, when he wants to build a tower, does not first sit down and calculate the cost to see if he has enough to complete it?"

Crucifixion is a hard thing for us in our enlightened society to picture. Recent movies notwithstanding, we have a tendency to water down the brutal nature of it. Thus, we may not get a full picture of Jesus' words when He described discipleship as carrying a cross. When Jesus' initial listeners heard this, they had a complete mental image. They did not picture a person under a great burden. Rather, they saw a person who had endured torment and agony in preparation for execution. They saw a person being resolutely forced to his death carrying the implement of his death on his back. This is what it means to be a Christian. We want to build the tower. We want to be a tower in the kingdom of God. We want the blessings. But are we willing to endure this blessing to get them? Can we possibly view this persecution as a blessing? Jesus wants us to count the cost of having the kingdom.

What Persecution

We have a tendency to hear persecution and think of Jesus on the cross and Stephen being stoned. However, persecution is not simply being put to death, but takes many forms. Persecution is connected to fleeing. It means to be pursued. The English words "persecution" and "pursue" even have etymological connections. "Pursue" comes from the Latin word *"prosequi,"* from which we also get "prosecute." "Persecution" comes from *"persequi"* which meant "to start a legal action."

Persecution is really any resistance intended to harm us because of our faith or make us flee from doing what our faith demands. In Matthew 5.11, Jesus mentions insult and slander as well as persecution. In Luke's parallel, Jesus spoke of being hated, ostracized and scorned (Luke 6.22). Persecution includes being disowned by family, being laughed at and made fun of for our decisions, being left out, being called names, being lied about, being threatened as well as being harmed physically, imprisoned or martyred.

We need to understand this. The texts here and in Luke let us know that if we are not being persecuted we are not being kingdom citizens. However, it does not say we are blessed only when we have been executed for our faith. It says we are blessed when we are persecuted.

The question for us then is does anyone hate us? Has anyone scorned or ostracized us? Has anyone tried to get us to turn from the path we believe is righteousness? Has anyone spoken ill of us? If not, Luke 6.26 provides an ominous warning. "Woe to you when all men speak well of you, for their fathers used to treat the false prophets in the same way."

What Have We Done to Deserve This?

Even apart from the Jewish mindset of a conquering kingdom, this statement is pretty shocking. Jesus has just described the best of people. These kingdom citizens are devoid of selfishness and arrogance. They put others before themselves. They extend mercy and peace to anyone who will accept it. They are transparently sincere, without guile or hypocrisy. Who on earth would want to harm these people?

This seems to be the question Peter asks in 1 Peter 3.13, "Who is there to harm you if you prove zealous for what is good?" However, he knew it would happen and followed that statement with, "But even if you should suffer for the sake of righteousness, you are blessed" (vs. 14).

Surely we will not be persecuted for mercy and peace? Surely it will not be for humility and gentleness? What have kingdom citizens done to provoke this kind of response from the world?

Jesus directly mentioned two reasons for persecution. The first was righteousness and the second was Him. Surely it goes without saying, we are not blessed if we suffer because of sin, stupidity or simply because that's life. Rather we are blessed when we are persecuted for the sake of righteousness or on account of Jesus.

Thus, those who hunger and thirst for righteousness will be persecuted for it. Those who pursue righteousness above all else will suffer. Paul told Timothy, "All who desire to live godly in Christ Jesus will be persecuted" (2 Timothy 3.12). Perhaps John 3.19-21 explains why this happens:

> This is the judgment, that the Light has come into the world, and men loved the darkness rather than the Light, for their deeds were evil. For everyone who does evil hates the Light, and does

not come to the Light for fear that his deeds will be exposed. But he who practices the truth comes to the Light, so that his deeds may be manifested as having been wrought in God.

We don't actually have to do anything to those who practice evil. However, as Matthew 5.14-16 says, we are the light of the world. When we are pursuing righteousness, the light of God shines through us and those who practice sin hate us. We don't have to say anything to them; we don't have to do anything to them. Our lives are a light that exposes their sin. They despise that and want to extinguish it.

Perhaps you have noticed all you have to do is tell people the things you do or don't do and see the defenses go up. This happens even among Christians. Talk to some Christians about the movies you won't watch and witness their temperature rise as they call you names or castigate your personal stance even when you made absolutely no judgment about their standards. If this can happen even among Christians who have slightly varying standards regarding entertainment, then just imagine how it can happen between people with completely different faiths. The fact is, people view any choices we make that are different from theirs as a judgment against them, whether we intend it that way or not. Thus, we will be persecuted.

The second reason for persecution was because of Jesus. In John 15.18, 20, Jesus said, "If the world hates you, you know that it has hated Me before it hated you…If they persecuted Me, they will also persecute you; if they kept My word, they will keep yours also." Jesus, belief in Him and obedience to Him simply attracts the ire of those who refuse to accept Him.

We know He is the stone of stumbling and the rock of offense. To the Jews, He is a stumbling block; to the Gentiles, He is foolishness. Those who follow Jesus are therefore seen as stumbling blocks and fools and then treated as such.

There is a third reason for persecution implied by Jesus' final statement on the matter. He said, "…for in the same way they persecuted the prophets who were before you." Why were the prophets of old persecuted? Because the prophets taught what the people didn't want to hear.

All people want blessing. They all want comfort. They all want mercy. They all want peace. The problem is, very few actually want it God's way. Most people do not want to hear God's way. Most people do not want to be restricted to God's path. Therefore, when we, in our attempt to make peace between our neighbors and God, teach them God's way, most will not like it. Like the prophets of old, we will teach what others do not want to hear. Many will persecute us for it.

We need to come into the kingdom with our eyes opened. Most people won't want to be in this kingdom with us and some of them will actively try to get us out. There is no way for us to teach what God wants and achieve universal popularity. God's children are not likely to be the most sought after speakers in the world. Our books will not likely make it on the best seller list. Our actions will not often be rewarded with honors of men.

But be assured, we will receive our reward.

Our Reward

In Matthew 5.10, Jesus brought His audience full circle to where He began. The persecuted poor in spirit receive the kingdom of heaven. Why this reminder? Because our minds are likely to think if we are being put to flight, we must not be in God's kingdom. After all, that kingdom is supposed to conquer and dominate all enemies. If we are being put to flight, it looks like God may not recognize us as His kingdom's citizens or maybe He has forgotten about us. Jesus wants us to know the persecuted are remembered. Persecution does not mean we haven't made the cut. On the contrary, persecution means we are in the kingdom.

Further, we have a reward in heaven, which I take to be distinct from receiving the kingdom of heaven. I believe being in the kingdom of heaven refers to being in the heavenly or spiritual kingdom Jesus was planning to establish on the earth (cf, Matthew 16.18-19). However, the reward in heaven is what is ultimately awaiting those persecuted poor in spirit who were part of Christ's heavenly kingdom on earth.

Our reward in heaven is great. Paul said, "For I consider that the sufferings of this present time are not worthy to be compared with the glory that is to be revealed to us" (Romans 8.18). Peter said our reward is "an inheritance which is imperishable and undefiled and will not fade away, reserved in heaven for you, who are protected by the power of God through faith for a salvation ready to be revealed in the last time" (1 Peter 1.4-5).

We must understand, there are basically only two rewards. We can, like the Pharisees, pursue the rewards here on the earth. We can pursue popularity among men, receiving accolades and honors from them (cf. Matthew 6.2, 5). Or we can pursue heaven. If we pursue the first, we need to enjoy the praises of men and their honors the short time they last, because that is all we get. The next life will hold nothing except torment for us. If we pursue the second, we will receive eternal reward that cannot be measured.

If you live for 100 years of peace and luxury, but endure eternity in hell, would it be worth it? However, if you live for 100 years of poverty, chased by the world from city to city, having no place to lay your head and finally ended it through painful martyrdom, but live for eternity in heaven with God, would that be worth it? As you, no doubt, have heard other people say, if we miss heaven, we have missed it all. By contrast, when we gain our great reward in heaven, we have gained it all.

Rejoice

Unlike the other beatitudes, Jesus included a response with this last one. When we are persecuted, we should respond with joy and rejoicing, instead of whining, complaining and asking, "What have I done to deserve this?"

That sounds odd. After all, we are talking about rejection, mockery, beating, imprisonment, death. None of these things sound very joyful. We do not rejoice at these things but at what they mean for us. We rejoice because these indicate we are right with God and have an inheritance awaiting us in heaven. According to 1 Peter 4.14, if we are sharing in the sufferings of Christ, we know the Spirit of glory and of God is with us.

Persecution is not just an indicator. Rather, the trials themselves are the tools God uses to help us receive our reward. James 1.2-4 says, "Consider it all joy, my brethren, when you encounter various trials, knowing that the testing of your faith produces endurance. And let endurance have its perfect result, so that you may be perfect and complete, lacking in nothing."

Have you ever done much working out? Building body muscle is a very interesting process. When our muscles are protected from harm, they do not grow. Instead, they atrophy and become useless. However, when we stress them through use, we break the muscle fibers. That sounds bad, but it is really a good thing. As the muscle heals itself and knits back all the broken and ruptured strands, it builds bigger muscle.

Building spiritual muscle is very much the same. We do not grow spiritually when our spirits are protected from harm. Rather, when we suffer trials and persecution our spiritual muscles are stressed, broken and ruptured. However, the endurance we develop causes that spiritual muscle to heal itself and grows back bigger than before. Thus, persecution is not just an indication of salvation, it is a tool God uses to help us be saved.

1 Peter 1.6-7 says:

> In this you greatly rejoice, even though now for a little while, if necessary, you have been distressed by various trials, so that the proof of your faith, being more precious than gold which is perishable, even though tested by fire, may be found to result in praise and glory and honor at the revelation of Jesus Christ.

Persecution is like the fire that refines the gold, removing impurities. It refines our faith, strengthening us in the kingdom of God and His righteousness. It really is a blessing.

Finally, trials, suffering and persecution are also an acknowledgment from God regarding His faith in us. They are an amazing testimony of what God thinks of us and therefore are an amazing confidence builder. 1 Corinthians 10.13 says God will not allow us to be tempted beyond what we are able to handle. Thus, when God allows us to undergo suffering and persecution, we know He is saying He believes we can handle that. He is showing how much faith He has in us. It is much like what He did behind the scenes with Job. "Have you considered My servant Job?" (Job 1.8; 2.3). God is putting us up and showing Satan, "Look, this one can stand up to what you throw at him."

For all of these reasons, we can now understand why the apostles could endure the beatings at the hands of the Jewish council, but walk away rejoicing that they had been considered worthy to suffer for Jesus' name (Acts 5.41).

We must mourn that we have sinned, but we can rejoice when we suffer persecution. Blessed are those who have been persecuted for the sake of righteousness, for theirs is the kingdom of heaven.

Responding to the Sermon

What is your initial response to persecution in the kingdom as presented in this chapter?

Why do so many fear rejection and persecution when Jesus said it was a blessing? How can we overcome our fear?

Meditating on the Sermon

How did Jesus establish the example of enduring persecution? How can we learn from His example?

What persecution have you endured? How did it help you grow? Meditate on these things today.

Praying the Sermon

Merciful Father,

Thank You for sending Your Son to endure the physical and spiritual agony of the cross. Thank You for letting Him endure the suffering that was rightfully mine. I am so sorry my sin led to that, but I rejoice that You were willing to provide for my salvation.

I know persecution lies in store for me if I serve You, living godly in Christ Jesus. Strengthen me to endure and grow through that persecution. Please, refine my faith that I might grow endurance. Allow endurance to have its perfect work in me, helping me be complete, lacking nothing.

Forgive me for so often avoiding any form of persecution by striving to fit in with the worldly crowd. Help me be different. Help me be Your light. Help me be Your salt. Help me stand up and be willing to endure, unafraid of those who can do nothing more than kill this worthless body.

Allow Your grace, mercy and benevolence to surround me, preparing me for the battle. Thank You for showing Your confidence in me by letting me endure suffering and persecution. Strengthen me to endure.

I love You Father and I thank You for loving me.

Through Your Son, my example in persecution, I pray.

Amen.

Anger Management:

Matthew 5.21-26

"You have heard that the ancients were told, 'You shall not commit murder' and 'Whoever commits murder shall be liable to the court.'

"But I say to you that everyone who is angry with his brother shall be guilty before the court; and whoever says to his brother, 'You good for nothing,' shall be guilty before the supreme court; and whoever says, 'You fool,' shall be guilty enough to go into the fiery hell. Therefore if you are presenting your offering at the altar and there remember your brother has something against you, leave your offering there before the altar and go; first be reconciled to your brother and then come and present your offering. Make friends quickly with your opponent at law while you are with him on the way, so that your opponent may not hand you over to the judge, and the judge to the officer, and you be thrown into prison. Truly, I say to you, you will not come out of there until you have paid up the last cent."

The Ancients Were Told

Jesus' audience had heard the law. Murder was wrong (Exodus 20.13; Deuteronomy 5.17). Those who murdered would be tried and condemned (Numbers 35.30-31). Since these statements were true under the Old Law and would be true for all times (cf. Romans 13.3-4), Jesus must not have had a problem with these statements all by themselves. The problem was with the reductionist mindset that ended with these statements.

There were two problems here.

First, the legalistic, line-drawing mindset of the scribes and Pharisees would reduce the first statement to mean as long as they didn't actually commit murder, they were fine. They could dream of murder. They could plan murder. They could speak slander and sedition. They could mar the reputation and ruin the livelihood of another. However, as long as no lifeblood had been spilt, all was good. No harm, no foul.

Second, the same reductionist mindset missed the real problem with breaking the law. If a person committed murder, they would be guilty before the court. Eternally there was little problem. They might be executed for their infraction, but their souls would be fine.

In other words, Jesus was not saying it is wrong to view murder as sin. It is. Jesus was also not saying the murderer should not be judged by the human court. He should. Jesus was saying that is not the whole picture. The kingdom citizen who lives according to the beatitudes does not end with these statements. The kingdom citizen is held to a higher standard, a righteousness that surpasses the legalistic, line-drawing Pharisees who seemed to be certain they could never do anything that would endanger their resurrected souls.

But I Say to You

Matthew 5.22 raises a question. Was Jesus merely establishing a new standard of lines to be drawn? "If you are angry, then it will be handled by the court (most likely a reference to the local courts of each town; cf. Deuteronomy 16.18). However, if you cross that line and call your brother a good for nothing, that will be handled by the Supreme Court (translating the term "sunedrion," a reference to the San Hedrin, the high council of the Jews at the time of Jesus). However if you go so far as to call your brother a fool, God will deal with that and cast you into hell."

It makes no sense for Jesus to remove one system of reductionary line-drawing and merely replace it with another. Instead, the point is if we sin so as to be guilty before man's court, how can we think we might possibly stand righteously before God's?

We also struggle with the fact that this passage seems to condemn anger while Ephesians 4.26 separates anger from the sin. Paul said we might be made angry, but we must refrain from sinning. Further, we have to deal with that anger quickly, not allowing the sun to go down upon it. How do these two passages coincide?

Some deal with this issue by noting the KJV translation of Matthew 5.22, which modifies "angry" with "without a cause." The problem with this, in my mind, is threefold. First, according to John Stott, though he believes this phrase helps us understand Jesus' meaning, he admits it is not found in the best manuscripts and is likely a later gloss. Therefore the more modern translations omit it.[14] Second, the word for being angry with our brother is passive. That means it is something being done to us. We are not simply angry but are being angered. Something has caused us to be angry. We cannot have something causing us to be angry and then told it is without a cause. Third, the immediate context leads us to believe Jesus is speaking against the anger that causes harsh words and eventually murder.

Therefore, I believe Jesus is rebuking any and all anger that is not properly dealt with. He is not saying any momentary anger is sin. Rather, He is saying exactly what Paul was saying. Anger not quickly and properly resolved, even if it never actually leads to murder, is condemned and liable to God's judgment.

What does the kingdom citizen do then when he is angered? Webster's defines anger as "a strong feeling of displeasure and belligerence aroused by a real or supposed wrong." When someone arouses this in us, we do not let it sit. We do not let it fester. We deal with it. Why? Because anger makes us liable to the court, to the supreme court, to God almighty. How can we allow that anger to settle in our hearts? How can we allow it to fester up in the form of harsh words? How can we allow it to explode with harmful actions? Instead, we will resolve the issue.

If we are still struggling with being easily provoked, then we need to deal with that within ourselves, removing the log that is in our own eyes, before trying to remove the speck in our brother's. We hope, of course, as kingdom citizens who are poor in spirit, mourning over our own sins, gently submitting to God and removing selfishness, we have learned to not be easily provoked (James 1.19). Therefore, if we are angered, it must surely be that someone has committed sin against us. Matthew 18.15 shows we must go to him in private. Of course, we do so with gentleness (Galatians 6.1) because we are the gentle (Matthew 5.5). We will do this quickly, not allowing the sun to go down on our anger. We will not wait, seething in our anger, claiming we will do nothing to resolve the situation because our brother is at fault. We will not wait for our sister's apology. We will go to them because we are merciful peacemakers.

The main thrust of Jesus' rebuttal to what His audience had been taught was that righteousness begins in the heart. As 1 John 3.15 says, "Everyone who hates his brother is a murderer; and you know that no

---

14. John R. W. Stott, *The Message of the Sermon on the Mount*, Intervarsity Press, Downers Grove, IL, 1978, p. 83.

murderer has eternal life abiding in him." The Law of Moses condemned hatred in Leviticus 19.17, saying, "You shall not hate your fellow countryman in your heart," yet whoever taught Jesus' audience must have had trouble applying that law to themselves.

As Jesus would later tell the Pharisees, if kingdom citizens want to have pure actions, they need to have pure hearts. Don't just clean the outside of the cup, clean the inside (Matthew 23.25-26). "Watch over your heart with all diligence, for from it flow the springs of life" (Proverbs 4.23).

Finally, Jesus drives home that our righteousness is not just about what we do with our hands, but also what we do with our mouths. In Matthew 12.33-37, Jesus explained that our words are a window to our heart. If we are good people with good treasure in our heart, we will not curse our brethren. We must understand that we will be judged by the words we speak. James would later write in his letter, which so often echoes the thoughts of the Sermon:

> But no one can tame the tongue; it is a restless evil and full of deadly poison. With it we bless our Lord and Father, and with it we curse men, who have been made in the likeness of God; from the same mouth come both blessing and cursing. My brethren, these things out not to be this way. Does a fountain send out from the same opening both fresh and bitter water? Can a fig tree, my brethren, produce olives, or a vine produce figs? Nor can salt water produce fresh.

The mouth that praises God in prayer and song, must not belittle and berate the man or woman God created. We must speak with humility, gentleness and mercy in the pursuit of peace.

When I Have Angered Others

The kingdom standard for relationships has implications beyond when we are angered. What happens when we have angered others? We might easily sit on our hands based on vs. 22 saying, "It is there job to deal with that. They aren't supposed to be angry." However, Jesus points out when we have angered others, it is our job to go to them, reconciling with them.

I find Matthew 5.23-24 to be one of the most astounding statements made in the sermon. When we read about this offering, we often jump to discuss issues of worship. Before going there, ask what was the main purpose of offering a sacrifice to the Lord? Was it not to bring reconciliation between the worshipper and God? When Jesus says the offending brother should leave his offering before the altar and first be reconciled with his brother, he is pointing out we have to be reconciled to our brethren before we can be reconciled to God.

This calls to mind Peter's words to husbands in 1 Peter 3.7, "You husbands in the same way, live with your wives in an understanding way, as with someone weaker, since she is a woman; and show her honor as a fellow heir of the grace of life, so that your prayers may not be hindered." Husbands who sin against their wives do no good if they end the day with a prayer of confession unless they have first repented and reconciled with their wives. The same is true for all Christians. There is no amount of worship or appeal for forgiveness that does us any good if we cannot humble ourselves and apologize to the ones against whom we sinned.

This will not be a problem for the poor in spirit. We have humbled ourselves before God almighty, we should be able to humble ourselves before our brethren. It is certainly no problem for the gentle who have removed from themselves any sense of spiritual self-promotion and self-protection. After all, what keeps us from owning up to our offenses other than foolish pride and the desire to act as though we do no wrong? If we have removed that, how hard will it be to admit it when we have done something wrong?

I remember one of the earliest times I dealt with this pride that doesn't want to apologize. I was a teenager. I had been sitting on the second row in the assembly with some other teenage boys. We were doing what teenage boys do—goofing around. As soon as the assembly was over, a sister approached us and rightly rebuked us for our behavior. That was Sunday night. On Monday afternoon, as my dad drove me home from school, we stopped by Mark White's house. He was the preacher. My dad made me go up to Mark's door on my own, knock on it, wait for him to get there and then apologize for being such a distraction while he was preaching. This was a nightmare. I begged and pleaded not to have to do that. I look back and wonder why. What was the big deal? I had done wrong. It was already known by everyone, including Mark. I was already convinced I wouldn't do it again. The apology was traumatic. Think about what an impression that made on me. It was nearly 20 years ago. Mark probably doesn't even remember it, but sometimes the memory wakes me up at night. Why was it so hard to apologize? Pride. Apologies take humility. They take verbal admission of wrongdoing. They take honest acknowledgment of fault and personal blame. It was a hard lesson. I didn't learn it completely that day and sometimes still have trouble with it. As much as I hated it then, I am glad my dad made me apologize. Mark, if you read this, I'm still sorry.

Debtor's Prison

As Jesus concluded His discussion of interpersonal altercations, He called to mind a very common picture in His audience's mind. Two men are going to court. Considering His final statement, it is likely a picture of debtor's prison. One man owes another man. Perhaps he thinks if he just waits it out and goes to court, the judge will side with him. If not, he will be thrown into jail and won't be able to leave until the debt is paid. Considering the fact he is in prison and can't work, that is going to be a long jail term.

Jesus points out a very practical lesson. There is only one sure way to keep from being thrown into jail. Reconcile with your opponent before you get to the judge.

How many people hold grudges, refuse to reconcile, acting as if they have no fault and are willing to just wait and let God decide? Jesus explains that is folly. He has explained if we are the ones angered, we should do something about it. He has explained if we did the angering, we should do something about it. How can we imagine that if we wait for the Judge's decision between us and our opponent that it will work out in our favor? Whether we are at fault or not we must reconcile with our opponent or we will be handed to the Judge, the Judge will hand us to the officer and we will be cast into the debtor's prison. The problem, of course, is we can in no way pay off our debt of sin.

Keep in mind what we have already learned about being peacemakers. God is not going to hold us accountable for those who refuse to allow us to be at peace with them. "If possible, so far as it depends on you," Paul wrote, "be at peace with all men" (Romans 12.18). The "if possible," demonstrates at times it will not be possible. Remember, the peacemakers are also the persecuted. Some will refuse to be at peace with us. We must simply make sure the lack of peace is not due to our actions or lack of repentance. We must be honest. Have we made every attempt to restore peace? Then we may return to our worship of God, making our offering to be reconciled with Him.

The ancients were told they shouldn't kill anyone. Jesus tells us, we must actively pursue peace with all men, whether they have offended and angered us or vice versa.

Responding to the Sermon

What is your initial response to this chapter about anger management and altercation response?

What hinders you from being at peace with others? How can you overcome that?

With whom do you need to make peace before worshipping God?

Meditating on the Sermon

Why do you think it is so important to God that we maintain proper relationships with one another before seeking forgiveness or worshiping Him?

What do you think can help you become less easily provoked and more ready to reconcile with others? Meditate on these things today.

Praying the Sermon

(Remember to reconcile with your brethren first)

Sovereign God,

Thank You for sending Your Son to provide reconciliation between us. I was at fault. I sinned and turned from Your way, but You took the step toward me, sacrificing Your Son that we might be reconciled.

Help me have that same mindset. Do not allow my relationships with my neighbors and brethren to hinder Your glory. Humble me and strengthen me to seek peace with all men. Forgive me for the times I have been at fault, offending and angering others. Help me reach out to them to be reconciled.

Father, when others refuse peace, help me have peace in my heart. Help me take courage and turn to You for solace and comfort. Please soften the hearts of those who refuse peace that we might glorify You together.

I love You Father and I thank You for loving me.

Through Your Son I pray.

Amen.

Marriage and Morality:

Matthew 5.27-32

"You have heard that it was said, 'You shall not commit adultery.'

"But I say to you that everyone who looks at a woman with lust for her has already committed adultery with her in his heart.

"If your right eye makes you stumble, tear it out and throw it from you; for it is better for you to lose one of the parts of your body than for your whole body to be thrown into hell. If your right hand makes you stumble, cut it off and throw it from you; for it is better for you to lose one of the parts of your body than for your whole body to be thrown into hell.

"It was said, 'Whoever sends his wife away, let him giver her a certificate of divorce.'

"But I say to you that everyone who divorces his wife, except for the reason of unchastity, makes her commit adultery; and whoever marries a divorced woman commits adultery."

Morality and Mental Purity

When we saw the statements about murder, we might have believed the legalistic line-drawing surrounding them was just a one issue deal. We now learn the Pharisaic righteousness had problems across the board. They wanted to get away with as much as they possibly could. Therefore, they read God's law to the letter. God's law said, "You shall not commit adultery," (Exodus 20.14; Deuteronomy 5.18). There you go. As long as we don't actually have sex with anyone other than our marriage partner, we are ok. After all, adultery is condemned, nothing else.

As with murder, we note adultery was unlawful under Moses' Law and Jesus knew it would be unlawful under His covenant (cf. Hebrews 13.4). Jesus was not at all upset by the statement itself and it still stands—You shall not commit adultery. The problem was the reduction down to that statement alone.

The command, "You shall not commit adultery," should in and of itself be seen as a restriction to all that leads up to adultery, including lustful thoughts. However, if the Jews couldn't see that, the tenth commandment should have established the point for them. "You shall not covet your neighbor's wife" (Exodus 20.18; Deuteronomy 5.21).

Jesus explained morality is not just avoiding illicit sexual intercourse, but is about maintaining total purity—spiritually, mentally and physically. Again, we must clean the inside of the cup that the outside may be cleansed also. Paul wrote in 2 Corinthians 10.3, 5, "For though we walk in the flesh, we do not war according to the flesh… we are taking every thought captive to the obedience of Christ." We are fighting a war in the heart. Satan knows He can get our bodies to follow where our minds lead. We must control our minds.

In 1 Thessalonians 4.3-5, 7, Paul talked about the moral purity kingdom citizens are to have, saying:

> For this is the will of God, your sanctification; that is, that you abstain from sexual immorality; that each of you know how to possess his own vessel in sanctification and honor, not in lustful passion…For God has not called us for the purpose of impurity, but in sanctification.

God's will for us is sanctification; that is, being set apart for holy use to His glory. He includes three aspects to that sanctification. First, we must abstain from sexual immorality. Second, we must possess our bodies in sanctification and honor. Third, we must avoid lustful passion.

Sadly, many today practice the same reductionism as the Pharisees with all three of these points. Some act as though as long as they don't actually have sexual intercourse they are free to hold, rub, touch, kiss or whatever else they may want to do. Sexual immorality is being involved in any activity that arouses or expresses sexuality and sexual desire with someone to whom we are not married and it is wrong.

With the second point, because Paul did not list any specific guidelines, some act as if we just can't really know how to possess, own or use our bodies in a holy manner. Thus, men and women wear such tight fitting clothes the bodies are more revealed than concealed. Men and women, who are not married, hold each other and move in sexually rhythmic ways on the dance floor and act as if the preacher who condemns that is legalistic. An increasing number of Christian teens wear revealing outfits, spread their legs for audiences to see and hold each other by the legs and rears for the sake of cheering on their school and those who question that are viewed as prudish. But think for yourself, when people witness us involved in these activities, are they likely to say, "There goes a holy child of God, set apart for His holy service"? Are we being a light to the world causing others to glorify God because of our good works?

With the third point, some act as if to say, "Just because I'm on a diet doesn't mean I can't look at the menu." They fill their minds with images that promote sexual thinking about those to whom they are not married. They scan the papers for underwear and swimwear advertisements, they walk the magazine aisles to catch glimpses of the scantily clad girls laying on muscle cars, they walk the mall to see the Victoria's Secret posters, surf the web for pornographic sites. All of these things feed their lustful passions but they justify it because at least they didn't commit sexual immorality with another person.

Immorality doesn't begin once we are alone with another person. It begins in our minds. We must, therefore, strive to live by Paul's teaching in Philippians 4.8, focusing on true, honorable, right, pure, lovely, excellent and praiseworthy things.

Allow me one quick side comment here. Please notice the difference between the legalism rebuked in the Sermon and legalism often condemned today. Today, the person who sees the commands not to murder or commit adultery as also limiting what we think and say would be called the legalist, line-drawers. Today, the people who urge more restriction and self-control are condemned as Pharisaical. I find it interesting that the legalism Jesus condemned was line-drawing that attached the most literal and absolute meaning to each word thereby providing more freedom than God intended. Today, the very mindset Jesus condemned is seen as tolerant, liberating and lovely by the religious masses. We must be careful. We are certainly not to force more restrictive lines on others than God intended. At the same time, we must understand the greater danger is legalistically allowing more freedom than God intended.

Amputation

On April 26, 2003, Aron Ralston was trapped between a rock and a hard place. Hiking and rock climbing alone in Eastern Utah, his right hand was crushed between a shifting boulder and the rock wall of the gorge he was navigating. Over a period of five days he made various attempts to free himself. He chipped away at the boulder. He tried to construct a pulley with his ropes to move the boulder. Nothing worked. When he ran out of the water supply he had been rationing, he was certain he was going to die. Knowing that no one knew where he was and that they would not find him any time soon, he tried one more desperate plan. He broke both the bones in his forearm. Then, using what was left of the dulled cutting tool with which he had been chipping on the rocks, he amputated his own right arm. He repelled down into the canyon and then hiked out to meet rescuers who had been looking for him. Nobody wants to lose an arm. However, when the choice is lose an arm or lose a life, the arm is not so bad.

If we would take such drastic measures merely to extend our temporal life a few years, how much more ought we do them to preserve our eternal life? Jesus said if our eye or hand makes us stumble, we should amputate them. We should throw them from us. It is better to lose a part of our body than for our whole body to be cast into hell. Many of us who struggle from day to day to lead pure lives might find immense success in our spiritual growth if we would merely undergo spiritual amputation.

To be sure, this is about spiritual amputation and not physical. Hands and eyes do not really make us stumble. The part of our body that has the biggest problem regarding purity is the brain. If we take Matthew 5.29-30 at its most literal regarding the part of our body that is the biggest problem, well… you see where that would lead.

Consider what these verses teach us to do. When we sin, we must not simply confess our sin, but consider what led to our sin. How did the fall begin? Do we see a pattern? Because Jesus made this statement in the context of sexual morality, I will keep my illustrations there, but the point applies to all sins from outbursts of anger to lying to gossip to stealing.

When you have fallen into sexual immorality, whether physically or mentally, ask how you got there? Where did it begin? Did it begin with a magazine ad? Did it begin with a song on the radio? Did it begin with unlimited access to the Internet? Did it begin with a character on a tv show? Did it begin with an emotional relationship at work? What led to the sin?

How many Christians have returned again and again to an affair with a co-worker after repeatedly repenting, mourning and committing themselves to sexual purity? What needs to happen here? A spiritual amputation. They need to quit the job. "But Edwin," someone will say, "I need the money. I won't be able to find another job that pays as well. And I have to eat. I have to have a roof over my head. If I give up this job, I will lose my house." This job is your hand caught between a boulder and a rock wall. It is killing you and destroying your eternal life. It is better for you to lose your house and even miss a few meals than to be thrown into hell.

How many Christian men, even preachers, have returned again and again to the sinful world of internet pornography after repeatedly repenting, mourning and committing themselves to purity? What is needed here? A spiritual amputation. At the very least they need to limit their internet access with strict filters and accountability parameters. They might even need to get rid of internet access entirely. "But Edwin," some will say, "there is a lot of good stuff on the internet. Plus, when I use those filters there are some good sites I can't access. After all, Biblical research and finding pictures for my PowerPoint presentations are so much easier with full internet access." But the internet is killing you and destroying your eternal life. It is better for you to lose access to the decent stuff, it is better for you to have to research the old fashioned way, it is better for you to have boring PowerPoint presentations than for you to be thrown into hell.

How many Christians have returned to lustful passions because of magazines, movies, tv shows or particular songs on the radio after repeatedly repenting, mourning and committing themselves to mental purity? What is needed here? A spiritual amputation. They need to discontinue their subscription to the magazine. They need to avoid those kinds of movies or stop watching that tv show. They need to quit listening to that song (perhaps even the entire cd or radio station). "But Edwin," some will say, "this is just entertainment. I can't live in a box. I have to live a little and have some fun. Aside from that, everybody is reading, watching and listening to these things. If I quit, I will be behind the times and look like an oddball." These things are killing you and destroying your eternal life. It is better for you to look like a behind-the-times oddball who can't join in on the conversations about the latest music, movies or magazines than for you to be thrown into hell.

Please notice the little word beginning both of the verses under consideration. Jesus began both statements with "IF." IF your eye causes you to stumble, tear it out. IF your hand causes you to stumble, cut it off. Jesus did not make a blanket statement for everyone to tear out their eyes or cut off their hands. Aron Ralston cut off his own right arm to survive. That doesn't mean all rock climbers have to cut off their right arms.

In our efforts to lead morally pure lives we all have different issues that cause us to stumble. I may have to spiritually amputate something you don't and vice versa. Just because our eye causes us to stumble doesn't mean everyone has to tear out their eye, nor should we try to make them.

Allow me to illustrate. When I first watched *CSI*, I became addicted. I loved the mystery. I loved the detective work. I loved watching how they figured out who was guilty. It was great. Then came *CSI: Miami*. It was awesome too. However, at some point I began to realize that the constant repeated themes of sexual crimes were starting to impact my mind. Many times, I was no longer being entertained by the detective work but being defiled by the immodestly dressed characters and caused to stumble in my mind because of the sexual themes. Eventually, I had to excise *CSI* and *CSI: Miami* from my life. Does *CSI* cause everyone to stumble? Probably not. Can I say that because it made me stumble and I had to amputate it everyone has to? Of course not. However, if it causes you to stumble, you need to get rid of it too.

We must be honest. It would have been pointless for Ralston to say, "I don't think the problem is my arm caught between these rocks. I'm not going to amputate." In the same way, it is eternally pointless for us to hang on to the very things that make us stumble.

When we think about Ralston's story, most of us wonder if we could do what he did. "I just don't think I could cut off my own right arm," many of us say. Sadly, there are too many Christians that say the same thing when they are faced with Jesus' words here. Let's buck up. Jesus will give us strength. Let's amputate what will destroy our eternal life.

Moral Marriages

With all we have learned about morality so far, we might say, "As long as we are married, everything is alright." In most instances, we would be right. However, in Matthew 5.31-32, Jesus explained that is not true in all cases.

It was said in Deuteronomy 24.1-4 that if a man found some indecency in his wife, wrote her a certificate of divorce, sent her away from his house, she became another man's wife and that man also wrote her a certificate of divorce or died, the woman's first husband could not marry her again because she had been defiled.

Do you see the first problem here? Deuteronomy 24.1-4 does not say, "Whoever sends his wife away, let him give her a certificate of divorce." Many read this passage as if it is the Old Law's legislation on how and when someone could divorce their spouse in Israel. It was not. This legislation actually assumed divorce took place sometimes. What it governed was when the divorcing Israelite husband could remarry his put away wife. The statement recorded in Matthew 5.31 demonstrates the same problem we have with the Deuteronomy passage today. It legalistically treats it as the law regarding when a person can divorce, how they should accomplish it and what the consequences are. As long as you live by the letter of that law, giving your spouse a certificate of divorce, you are ok.

Jesus explains that just wasn't so. Everything is not fine just because you have given your spouse a certificate of divorce when you sent them away. Jesus said, if you put your wife away (except if you are doing so because they committed sexual immorality), you are making them commit adultery. The most natural reason for this was women could rarely support themselves financially and had to remarry to survive. In like manner, in our society, most divorced people will remarry for all the same reasons that caused them to marry in the first place.

Similar to Jesus' statement, Moses had written that the first husband could not take the wife who had married again back because she had been defiled. The Hebrew word, *"tame'*," translated "defiled," is written in a passive and reflexive form. In other words, her defilement was something she had been caused to do to herself. Isn't that exactly what Jesus says about the man who simply decides to put his wife away? He makes her commit adultery. He makes her defile herself. Talk about being a stumbling block. Do you remember what Jesus said in Matthew 18.6? "Whoever causes one of these little ones who believe in Me to stumble, it would be better for him to have a heavy millstone hung around his neck, and to be drowned in the depth of the sea." Does that sound like it is alright to divorce your spouse for any reason?

Further, whoever marries the one who has been put away is also committing adultery. Notice there is no exception clause here. In other words, if you put your spouse away for any reason other than fornication, you are making them commit adultery. If you put them away because they committed sexual immorality, you do not make them commit adultery. However, if you marry the one who was put away, whether they were put away for fornication or not, you are committing adultery. In the Sermon, Jesus doesn't even get into the fact that if you divorce your spouse for any reason other than sexual immorality and you marry someone else you also are committing adultery (cf. Matthew 19.9).

What is Jesus' point? It doesn't matter if you went through proper legal procedures to send your spouse away. It doesn't matter if you went through the proper legal procedures to marry a divorced person. What matters is, with one exception, divorce leads to immorality for all who are involved. Don't do it.

Sadly, too many people miss the real point of these verses and others that talk about divorce. Many spend their time arguing over when it is proper to divorce and what are the proper procedures required. Does a certificate have to be filed or does a certificate even matter? Is it not really a divorce until a person really commits sexual immorality or is it a divorce when the certificate is given? We argue over these things trying to draw the fine lines of how far we are allowed to go and how much liberty we have to divorce and remarry. I fear we are following in the footsteps of our predecessors, the Pharisees. We must not lose sight of Jesus' main point. Marriage is for life. Divorce leads to immorality and we are not right to put that stumbling block before our spouse or anyone else who might marry our spouse. Jesus was saying, "What God has joined together do not let man separate." Don't divorce.

Yes, yes, I know there is one exception. Sadly, we have spent more time establishing the rules of the exception than propagating the rules of the rule. It is no wonder the Christian divorce rate is rising in lockstep with the world's. The fact is, if we constantly talk about how and when to end marriages, we are going to see more marriages ending. When we talk about how and when marriages can stay together, we will find a lot more marriages staying together.

Jesus' audience had heard they sinned only when they actually committed adultery. But kingdom citizens surpass the righteousness of the Pharisees, working to keep their minds pure, amputating anything that makes them stumble, striving to stay sexually pure through a lifelong marriage.

Responding to the Sermon

What is your initial response to morality as presented in Matthew 5.27-32 and this chapter?

Why is it hard to spiritually amputate things that cause us to stumble? What things do you need to spiritually amputate? Tell someone else about it and have them hold you accountable.

Meditating on the Sermon

This section in the Sermon is mainly about maintaining mental purity. What kinds of things must we meditate upon to help us maintain that purity?

Meditate on these things today.

Praying the Sermon

Holy God,

Forgive me, Lord. Extend Your mercy and cleanse my heart and mind. I have thought so many impure thoughts. Sadly, too many times my thoughts have become actions. Please forgive my immoralities and my mental impurities. Create in me a clean heart. Set a guard over my heart. Do not incline my heart to any evil thing.

Strengthen me to possess this vessel in sanctification and honor that I may glorify You in my body and my mind. I pray I will conduct myself in such a way that people around me will know I am Your child and they will see my good works and glorify You.

Strengthen my marriage. Do not let me be a stumbling block to my spouse. Make me a support and strength to my spouse, lifting my spouse up to glorify You.

Father, give me the courage, the strength and the humility to amputate everything that causes me to stumble. I want to go to heaven. I do not want to be thrown into hell. Help me sacrifice all things that hinder my spiritual growth. Make me willing and able.

I love You, Lord, and I thank You for loving me.

In Jesus' name I pray.

Amen.

Integrity Matters:

Matthew 5.33-37

"Again, you have heard that the ancients were told, 'You shall not make false vows, but shall fulfill your vows to the Lord.'

"But I say to you, make no oath at all, either by heaven, for it is the throne of God, or by the earth, for it is the footstool of His feet, or by Jerusalem, for it is the city of the great King. Nor shall you make an oath by your head, for you cannot make one hair white or black. But let your statement be, 'Yes, yes' or 'No, no'; anything beyond these is of evil."

The Ancients Were Told

Within our modern culture, Jesus' move from the permanence of marriage to the nature of vows and oaths is absolutely natural. One of the main problems plaguing marriage today is so few take their wedding vows seriously at all. With almost Pharisaic glee people constantly explain why they no longer have to live by the vows of their wedding ceremony. Their situation is an exception. Their spouse didn't live up to the rules. Their life is miserable. On and on the list goes as modern Pharisees explain why they don't have to keep that particular vow.

As with earlier statements, we at first wonder what is wrong with what the ancients were told. Is it not true that Jesus' audience was not to swear falsely and that it was to fulfill its vows to the Lord? Of course it was.

Now if a person sins after he hears a public adjuration to testify when he is a witness, whether he has seen or otherwise known, if he does not tell it, then he will bear his guilt—Leviticus 5.1

> You shall not swear falsely by My name, so as to profane the name of your God; I am the Lord.
>
> Leviticus 19.12

> If a man makes a vow to the Lord, or takes an oath to bind himself with a binding obligation, he shall not violate his word; he shall do according to all that proceeds out of his mouth.
>
> Numbers 30.2

> You shall fear only the Lord your God; and you shall worship Him and swear by His name.
>
> Deuteronomy 6.13

> You shall fear the Lord your God; you shall serve Him and cling to Him, and you shall swear by His name.
>
> Deuteronomy 10.20

> When you make a vow to the Lord your God, you shall not delay to pay it, for it would be sin in you, and the Lord your God will surely require it of you. However, if you refrained from vowing, it would not be sin in you. You shall be careful to perform what goes out from your lips, just as you have voluntarily vowed to the Lord your God, what you have promised.
>
> Deuteronomy 23.21-23

> But the king will rejoice in God; everyone who swears by Him will glory, for the mouths of those who speak lies will be stopped.
>
> Psalm 63.11

> Make vows to the Lord your God and fulfill them…
>
> Psalm 76.11

> When you make a vow to God, do not be late in paying it; for He takes no delight in fools. Pay what you vow! It is better that you should not vow than that you should vow and not pay.
>
> Ecclesiastes 5.4-5

> "Roam to and fro through the streets of Jerusalem, and look now and take note. And seek in her open squares, if you can find a man, if there is one who does justice, who seeks truth, then I will

pardon her. And although they say, 'As the Lord lives,' surely they swear falsely." O Lord, do not Your eyes look for truth?
Jeremiah 5.1-3

Listen to the word of the Lord, O sons of Israel, for the Lord has a case against the inhabitants of the land, because there is no faithfulness or kindness or knowledge of God in the land. There is swearing, deception, murder, stealing and adultery. They employ violence, so that bloodshed follows bloodshed.
Hosea 4.1-2

Then he said to me, "This is the curse that is going forth over the face of the whole land; surely everyone who steals will be purged away according to the writing on one side, and everyone who swears will be purged away according to the writing on the other side. I will make it go forth," declares the Lord of hosts, "and it will enter the house of the thief and the house of the one who swears falsely by My name; and it will spend the night within that house and consume it with its timber and stones."
Zechariah 5.3-4

Then I will draw near to you for judgment; and I will be a swift witness against the sorcerers and against the adulterers and against those who swear falsely
Malachi 3.5

The Israelites were indeed commanded that if they took an oath, it was to be by the Lord. They were told that they were not allowed to swear falsely in His name but were to fulfill their oaths to the Lord. Further, they were commanded to tell the truth if they were adjured, placed under oath, in court. They had no appeal to the Fifth Amendment.

Is it not also true under Jesus' covenant? Are Christians allowed to make false vows? Of course not. Must they fulfill their vows to the Lord? Of course they must (see Paul's example in Acts 18.18). Jesus, then, cannot be upset with the mere teaching of this statement. The ancients were in fact told to do this very thing by God, not man.

The Problem

Yet again the problem is the Pharisees' reductionist approach to God's Law. The issue is not with the statement alone, but how the Pharisees had abused this statement. In their legalistic, line-drawing, hair-splitting attempts to provide themselves with more liberty to act how they wanted, they turned God's commands regarding oaths and swearing into means by which they could rampantly tell lies.

In fact, they had developed strict guidelines about when they actually had to keep a vow or tell the truth according to Matthew 23.16-22.

> Woe to you, blind guides, who say, "Whoever swears by the temple, that is nothing; but whoever swears by the gold of the temple is obligated." You fools and blind men! Which is more important, the gold or the temple that sanctified the gold? And, "Whoever swears by the altar, that is nothing, but whoever swears by the offering on it, he is obligated." You blind men, which is more important, the offering, or the altar that sanctifies the offering? Therefore, whoever swears by the altar, swears both by the altar and by everything on it. And whoever swears by the temple, swears both by the temple and by Him who dwells within it. And whoever swears by heaven, swears both by the throne of God and by Him who sits upon it.

Do you remember what crossing your fingers behind your back meant on our childhood playground? We didn't have to actually do what we said we would or actually tell the truth if our fingers were crossed. "But you said…!" our friends would cry. "My fingers were crossed," was our smug reply. The Pharisees had merely worked out an elaborate formulaic approach to their oaths that amounted to nothing more than, "My fingers were crossed."

The Pharisees had missed the point behind all those statements in the Law. They had viewed those statements as legalistic claims explaining when an oath really mattered. They did not understand God's point to them was ALWAYS TELL THE TRUTH!

If they didn't get it from all the passages quoted above, they should have learned from passages like Proverbs 6.16-17, "There are six things the Lord hates, yes, seven are an abomination to Him: haughty eyes, a lying tongue…" And Proverbs 12.22, "Lying lips are an abomination to the Lord, but those who deal faithfully are His delight."

Thus, Jesus attacked the Pharisaic righteousness, which allowed lies. Their reductionism said it was only a false vow if they had made the vow to the Lord and not kept it. If they said the words "As the Lord lives" or "The Lord is my witness" or "I vow this to the Lord," they had to keep the vow because it was to the Lord. But if they merely vowed by heaven, earth, Jerusalem or the hair of their head, they did not have to keep the vow because it was not to the Lord. They could lie and say, "By heaven, earth and Jerusalem I swear this is so," and everything was alright, because it wasn't really a false vow. This reminds me of a scene in *Fried*

Green Tomatoes. In order to acquit one of the characters of a crime, the town's preacher was called to the witness stand. He refused to swear on the court's Bible and would only swear on his own. He then proceeded to tell what the movie's audience knew was a clear lie. How could he swear on the Bible and tell a lie? He didn't. He had wrapped what looked like a Bible cover around another book. The implication was if he had sworn on a real Bible, he would have been duty bound to tell the truth. However, he could swear and affirm he was telling the truth with his hand on another book and still be allowed to lie. How Pharisaical.

Jesus pointed out such formulas do not free His kingdom citizens from telling the truth or keeping their commitments. When we swear by heaven, we are swearing by the throne of God and therefore by the one who sits on the throne. When we swear by earth, we swear by the footstool of God and therefore by the One who rests on that footstool. When we swear by Jerusalem, we swear by the city of God's king and therefore by the one who established the city and His king. He further explained that we should not swear by the hair of our heads because we cannot change the natural color of our hair.

When we consider the argumentation of Jesus, we see He is not offering a prohibition of swearing in general. Rather, He is teaching that lying under any formula of words is a false vow and should not be done. Consider His points, if one were telling the truth, why would it matter if heaven were God's throne, earth God's footstool and Jerusalem the city of God's king? Why would it matter if the person couldn't change his hair color? Those issues only matter if the person is lying. The scribes and Pharisees had taught and practiced that it was only a false vow if it was made to the Lord. Jesus taught that all vows are made to the Lord no matter the verbal formula and therefore any lie is a false vow. He is prohibiting swearing falsely no matter what formula of words is used.

The Solution

Jesus highlighted the righteousness that surpasses the Pharisees' by saying, "Let your statement be, "Yes, yes' or 'No, no'; anything beyond these is evil" (Matthew 5.37). It is just that simple. We need to be people of our word. We need to exude integrity. We need to be people who do not have to shore up everything we say with oaths. We need to be people whose lives demonstrate faithfulness. If we say, "Yes," the answer had better be yes. Likewise if we say, "No." When we commit to an action, people should be able to rest their minds that the deed will be accomplished. We must not be people who lightly commit or over commit and then do not follow through.

My best friend in high school and my early college years was a great guy. He had one big problem. He lied. He lied a lot. It was a game to him sometimes. He would say he would do something and he wouldn't do it. He would say something happened a certain way and it hadn't. When he said something I couldn't quite believe, I forced him to swear on it. The only thing that really meant anything to him was music, so he would shore up anything he knew I wouldn't quite believe by saying, "I swear on a stack of 10 cds." The stack had to get progressively bigger to be sure he was telling the truth. Do you see the problem? My friend would not have had to take the oaths if he had just always told the truth. Oath taking is a direct result of lying. Let's face it. If people in our society were naturally honest, even the courts would not require oaths.

Sadly, my friend took a summer trip to France. Several of our friends gave him money to purchase souvenirs for them. He returned without souvenirs and a story of being robbed on the beach. While I do not think he would steal, because of his reputation, several of our friends thought him not only a liar but a thief. Dishonesty has consequences.

We need to tell the truth. We need to tell the truth always. We need to remove lies from us. We must live by Ephesians 4.25, "Therefore, laying aside falsehood, speak truth each one of you with his neighbor."

If we live a life where our friends and neighbors believe they have to force us beyond "Yes" and "No", we are leading evil lives. We are Christians. We are God's children. Everything we say reflects on Him.

The Mistake Repeated

I fear modern discussions of this passage are falling into the same trap into which the Pharisees fell. Too many today are missing the point of this passage making it little more than a seedbed for argument over oaths and affirmations in court.

Jesus was not regulating oaths. He was not laying down an absolute prohibition on swearing, oath-taking or vow-making. He was not claiming one could not be under oath in a court of law. He was teaching about honesty and faithfulness. He was pointing out that integrity matters.

Understandably, to many, this seems like the complete opposite of what Jesus said. Please consider the following.

First, when Jesus spoke again about oaths and the righteousness of the Pharisees in Matthew 23.16-22. He did not pronounce woes upon the Pharisees merely because they took oaths. Rather, he pronounced woes on them for their formulaic process by which they thought they could lawfully lie. His response to their sin was that they should be honest, not that they should cease from oaths. How can Matthew 5.33-37 correspond if it teaches it is wrong to take oaths at all?

Second, Jesus was placed under oath in a court of law. Matthew 26.63-64 says, "But Jesus kept silent. And the high priest said to Him, 'I adjure you by the living God, that You tell us whether You are the Christ, the Son of God.' Jesus said to him, 'You have said it yourself…'" Why did Jesus begin to speak after this adjuration, which means to be placed under oath? Because Leviticus 5.1 said the person placed under oath in court had to speak.

Third, God took an oath according to Hebrews 6.13-18. He certainly did not do so because His own dishonesty demanded it. He did so merely as a means to provide greater proof of His honesty to Abraham and his descendants. The point is, God, the one for whom it is impossible to lie, took an oath.

Fourth, Paul swore with God as his witness on multiple occasions. Romans 1.9; 2 Corinthians 1.23; 11.31 and Philippians 1.8 are examples. Let us not overlook these with statements about oath-like language. Would those who claim Jesus' words in Matthew 5.33-37 prohibit all manner of oaths claim we are allowed to use oath-like language, getting ever so close to taking an oath as long as we stop just short?

Finally, for those who will still cling to the prohibition saying, "But Jesus said make no oaths at all, He didn't say false oaths," allow me to point out Zechariah 5.3-4. In vs. 3, God said judgment would come upon those who swear. Left there, we might believe this was a prohibition against all swearing. However, even though God said He would judge those who swore, we learn in vs. 4 He was actually speaking about those who swore falsely. The same is true in Matthew 5.33-37. When Jesus condemned oaths and vow taking, He was not condemning any and all oaths and vows. He was condemning those who swore falsely believing their formula of words left them free to lie. The context, as demonstrated earlier, bears this out.

I fear if we reduce this text down to oath-taking instead of honesty, integrity and faithfulness, we may bear up wonderfully against the pressure in court to take oaths. We may know the proper formula for our words saying, "I affirm" instead of "I swear." But we may end up leaving room for the lying against which Jesus was really teaching.

Paul Earnhart's conclusion on this matter was excellent when he explained we can reconcile Paul's practice with Jesus' statement

> by realizing that Jesus is treating in this context the lying oaths of the Pharisees and not the solemn oaths of those who would tell the truth under any circumstances but find that at times others

are in need of special assurance. Each Christian must weigh this matter carefully, remembering that he is not compelled to swear, but that he is always compelled to speak the truth.[15]

Jesus' audience had heard as long as they didn't make their vow to the Lord, they didn't really have to keep it. Jesus' kingdom citizens, with righteousness surpassing that of the scribes and Pharisees, know we must always tell the truth. Our word is our bond without need for multiple phrases of assurance that we are indeed telling the truth this time.

---

15. Paul Earnhart, *Invitation to a Spiritual Revolution*, Published by Gary Fisher, Floyds Knobs, IN, 1999, p. 51.

Responding to the Sermon

What is your initial response to Jesus' teaching on honesty and oath-taking as presented in this chapter.

What do you think causes us to lie? How can we overcome lying?

Are there any commitments you "crossed your fingers" on and haven't fulfilled? If so, get busy and fulfill your word.

Meditating on the Sermon

What are the natural consequences to a dishonest life? What are the natural consequences to an honest life? Which consequences do you prefer? Meditate on these things today.

Praying the Sermon

Holy Father,

Thank You for being honest. I know You cannot lie and I place my trust in You and Your Word. Thank You for Your promises, in which I can rest my faith.

Father, help me be Your child. Help me put falsehood aside and speak truth to my neighbors. Help me live with integrity and character that my friends, family and neighbors can put their trust in me. Help me develop a reputation of honesty and faithfulness.

Forgive me, Father, because I have already fallen from this high standard. I have lied. I have deceived. I have betrayed confidences. I have fallen short on commitments. Strengthen me to overcome these failures and walk Your straight and narrow.

I love You Father and I thank You for loving me.

Through Jesus I pray.

Amen.

My Personal Space:

Matthew 5.38-42

"You have heard that it was said, 'An eye for an eye, and a tooth for a tooth.'

"But I say to you, do not resist an evil person; but whoever slaps you on your right cheek, turn the other to him also. If anyone wants to sue you and take your shirt, let him have your coat also. Whoever forces you to go one mile, go with him two. Give to him who asks of you, and do not turn away from him who wants to borrow from you.

The Chapter I Dread

We have arrived at the section to which most people want to skip when they confront the Sermon on the Mount. I must admit I have dreaded it. No matter what I say, someone will be upset and judge this entire book on whether or not I agree with what they already believe about this passage. However, I mostly dread this section because I know of all the points made in the Sermon this one most says what I do not want it to.

I cannot answer all the questions that have risen around these five verses and I do not intend to try. Though I would like to say I have these verses completely figured out, I cannot. I still have questions about them. However, what I am certain I do know about them challenges me more than the issues about which I have my doubts.

Before we consider the verses, we need to note some ground rules we should use as we strive to figure out how to apply these verses to our lives and to the questions we have about them. It seems to me many approach these verses with a completely different hermeneutic than they do the rest of the Bible.

First, with what other passage in scripture does any serious Bible student ever suggest the principle taught only applies to certain aspects of our lives? Yet sincere people strive to do so with this passage, compartmentalizing the individual's personal relationships from their relationship in the State. I cannot see how anyone can take any Biblical principle of Christian living, in this passage or any other, and then claim it only applies to our personal relationships. This applies to our conduct as a Christian whether it is displayed at home, among friends, with our neighbors, with our co-workers or with our brethren in Christ. This applies to our conduct in the way we serve God, His children, those in authority over us and even the State. However we serve the State, whether in the military, the police force, the political arena or merely as a concerned citizen these verses must govern our conduct.

Second, as much as I have wanted to in the past, we cannot apply this passage to religious persecution while disconnecting it from the evil others might inflict on us for non-spiritual reasons. Jesus did not say, "Do not resist a persecutor." He said, "Do not resist an evil person." Further, while the slap in the face may be religious persecution, the lawsuit to take our shirt is likely not. Even if we claim the lawsuit was spiritually motivated, the conscription to walk one mile was not. It was a matter of Roman law regarding the duty of all subject peoples. Additionally, the request for material goods is most definitely not an issue of religious persecution.

Third, whatever we determine this passage means, we may not dismiss possible interpretations by saying, "That is just not natural." That is the whole point of the Sermon. Nothing it suggests is natural. We must be honest enough to admit that if our only argument against a possible interpretation is, "It is just not natural," then our argumentation is not biblical. 2 Timothy 3.16-17 says the scriptures equip us for every good work. If we cannot go to the scriptures to equip us for what we propose, the "unnatural" argument, no matter how eloquently stated, does not provide biblical authority.

Fourth, we have to remember this Sermon is the Gospel of the Kingdom. It is Jesus' manifesto for His people, governing our lives as citizens in His kingdom. It is not Christ's constitution to govern earthly nations. Jesus never intended to establish another earthly kingdom. He never intended nations to be "Christian nations." We cannot take these verses and apply them as rules for nations or governments. We can only apply it to individuals and how they should react as Christ's kingdom citizens within those nations and governments.

Fifth, let us recognize from the outset that no matter how we answer questions about war and self-defense, none of Jesus' statements are universal absolutes. Jesus said, "Do not resist an evil person." Yet, James 4.7 and 1 Peter 5.9 both teach us to resist the devil. Ephesians 6.13 teaches us to resist in the evil day. Paul resisted Peter in Galatians 2.1, opposing him to his face. In Acts 13.8, when Elymas resisted Paul and Barnabas, opposing them, Paul and Barnabas certainly resisted back, striking the man blind. Therefore, however we answer the questions that arise, it is not enough to say, "Well the passage says, 'Don't resist an evil person,'" and leave it at that.

Finally, I must also state one of my biggest fears about this passage. I fear we spend so much time using this passage to argue about the war question, the self-defense question and the family protection question (questions about which only a fraction of us ever have to be practically concerned) that we never really apply this passage to our everyday circumstances. It will do us no good to conscientiously object to military service if we strive to cut off the person in traffic who cut us off first. It will do us no good to refuse to physically defend ourselves when mugged if we scheme to get back at the person who got the promotion we wanted. It will do us no good to allow our families to be ravaged by the attacker if we return insult for insult to our spouse every day. While the principles we discuss will impact our decisions on those "big questions," we must not lose sight of how these passages relate to our everyday behavior. That is the important point I want us to notice in this chapter.

The Ancients Were Told

Three times the ancients were told "eye for an eye and tooth for a tooth,"— Exodus 21.22-25; Leviticus 24.19-20 and Deuteronomy 19.16-21. The key to be noted in these passages is they were not about individual retaliation. They were about penalties to be applied by judicial courts. Further, they were not applied as harsh vindictive measures but as guidelines to make sure the punishment fit the crime. These measures protected the man who had merely knocked out another's tooth from being executed.

Considering the context of these injunctions, do we not see the point behind them also applies in the New? Consider Romans 13.4 and 1 Peter 2.13-14. Are not governing authorities still established to punish those who do evil? As they do so, is not the most appropriate limit of punishment making it fit the crime? Doesn't Paul's statement in Acts 25.11

demonstrate some crimes are worthy of death and some are not, thus establishing the punishment should fit the crime and not exceed it?

Once again, we see Jesus' problem cannot be with the statement itself. Jesus' own Father in heaven proclaimed this principle of criminal punishment. The problem is how this statement was abused by the scribes and Pharisees in their legalistic, line-drawing attitudes. In fact, they were much like people today. How many times have we heard someone say "eye for an eye, tooth for a tooth" to defend why he hurt someone who hurt him? We might have heard the similar expression—"tit for tat." That is the exact problem Jesus was addressing. The Pharisees and scribes had taken this God given legislation to the civil courts and applied it to their individual lives. Rather than allowing the civil courts to deal with personal hurts, they had used these passages to allow them their own personal vengeance. They allowed these passages to justify the very thing God wanted them to restrict.

I am concerned about us with this very problem. I am concerned about me. How many of our favorite movies and songs glorify the act of vengeance? I remember one of my favorite songs from my childhood, Kenny Rogers' "Coward of the County." The song talks about Tommy who was convinced by his dying father he didn't have to fight to prove he was a man. He lived by that principle for a long time. But then the Gatlin boys attacked and raped his girlfriend. Personally, I am certain Tommy had the right to restrain the Gatlin boys from such a sin and protect his girlfriend from such violent aggression. However, if he was in the act of protecting his girlfriend and restraining those boys from sin, was he allowed to do so with a spirit of vengeance? Furthermore, once the crime was committed, was Tommy allowed to inflict personal vengeance on those boys? As much as I personally want to say he was, Jesus said otherwise.

One of my favorite movies is *The Patriot*. However, since studying this passage more closely, I have had to rethink how glorious Benjamin Martin's (played by Mel Gibson) actions were. Interestingly, Martin initially rejected physical violence as a means for redress of grievances. However, when his son, Thomas, was killed by a malicious British colonel and another son, Gabriel, led away for unlawful execution, Martin, with the help of two younger sons, butchered an entire platoon of British soldiers. The end of that battle, a scene in which Martin continues to hack a dead British soldier repeatedly, demonstrates this was not a mere desire to protect his living son from unlawful execution. Nor was it a military action. This was vengeance. Then Martin signed up to fight in the war so he could exact retribution on the entire British army. The theme of vengeance was carried throughout the movie in every scene showing Martin melting his deceased son's toy soldiers to be the bullets for his gun. Whether or not the war which provided the backdrop for the movie is valid, Benjamin Martin's role within that fighting cannot be biblically justified. As much as I wanted to see Tavington get his just reward, Jesus explains it was not Martin's place to give it to him.

Whatever we might say about some of the big questions surrounding this text, Jesus is clear and other Bible passages support this same point. We are never allowed to exact personal revenge on anyone for any reason. Romans 12.17, 19 says, "Never pay back evil for evil to anyone… Never take your own revenge, beloved, but leave room for the wrath of God, for it is written, 'Vengeance is mine, I will repay,' says the Lord." I have become concerned about why I have been so entertained and moved by stories of vengeance. I have further wondered how my outlook, and the outlook of Christians in general, on what God allows and what is just naturally expected has been impacted by these glorified stories. Is our approach to this passage more based on godly principles or on Hollywood stories?

Kingdom Reaction

Jesus' reaction to this abuse of God's injunction went beyond restricting revenge and retaliation. He even restricted resistance. "I say to you, do not resist an evil person." We have already explained that this statement is not a universal absolute. This statement is not telling us we must let sin go unchecked and unaddressed. Additionally, Romans 13.2-4 demonstrates this passage must not be referring to government, which is specifically given by God the authority to resist and punish the evil person. Rather, it is mentioned in this context of taking personal vengeance. When someone mounts a direct and harmful action against us, however we might respond, we must never act out of personal vengeance. It is better for us to endure whatever they may dish out than to respond in kind or resist it.

Paul took this a step further in Romans 12.20-21 quoting Proverbs 25.21-22. "'If your enemy is hungry, feed him, and if he is thirsty, give him a drink; for in so doing you will heap burning coals on his head.' Do not be overcome by evil, but overcome evil with good." Peter explained we were called for this purpose, that we not return evil for evil or insult for insult but give a blessing instead (1 Peter 3.9).

Usually, when we discuss this passage, we speak in big terms. We think about war and self-defense. But in reality, Jesus' illustrations are rather small. They demonstrate His main point is about how we deal with it when what we view as our rights are violated. What happens when someone violates our personal space? How should we react? Look at each example separately and briefly.

Turning the Other Cheek

What do we do when someone physically violates our personal space? Someone has slapped us on the right cheek. How should we respond? The natural reaction is to slap him back. The world's reaction is to seek retribution. Our reaction is to turn the other cheek.

The biblical context demonstrates this statement is no universal absolute. It does not mean we are never allowed to defend ourselves from all violent aggression. Jesus demonstrated this when He made a change in how He sent out His disciples in the world by saying the one who has no sword should even sell his outer garment to buy one in Luke 22.36. Those swords were not to be used as means of aggression (cf. Matthew 26.52). And they must certainly not be used in a spirit of vengeance or retaliation. That is the whole point of the passage we are studying now. Those swords were for self-defense. This passage also does not mean we are forced to absolutely stand by and receive physical harm. The number of times Christians fled instead of sticking around to receive more persecution in Acts should demonstrate that.

However, we must be careful we do not so limit this statement that it has no meaning. While this passage may allow for self-defense, we must recognize that the attitude that says, "Try something with me and see what happens," or "Let someone break into my house; I'll break their neck," violates Jesus' teaching here.

Further, this picture of being struck on the right cheek is not strictly about physical aggression. A normal attack made with the right hand would strike a person on their left cheek. This is a backhand, an almost universal symbol of insult and challenge, not of violent aggression. How do we handle it when someone challenges and insults us? Do we step up to the plate and issue an insulting rebuttal? Do we follow their lead and walk into a duel? No, kingdom citizens overcome evil with good. Instead of reaching out to slap our offender's cheek, we offer them the other also. We make ourselves vulnerable.

For us, this is more a verbal problem than a physical one. How many homes are filled with insult after insult? How many times do we get into arguments with our co-workers and lash out with repeated insults and barbs? How many times do we get cut off in traffic and we respond with rude gestures, name-calling and insults? How many times has someone treated us rudely and we said, "I just got tired of taking that"?

Jesus said to turn the other cheek. Take the insult without retaliation.

Give Your Coat Also

In Exodus 22.26-27, God restricted the Israelites from taking a man's outer garment, his cloak, or coat as the NASU translates Matthew 5.40. However, Jesus said if someone was pressing suit against us and wanted our shirt, we should give him our cloak as well.

As above, this is not a universal prohibition of asserting our civil rights. Paul appealed to his Roman citizenship to keep from being beaten in Acts 22.25. He further made use of his civil rights when he refused to go to Jerusalem but appealed to Caesar in Acts 25.11.

This is merely a further illustration that kingdom citizens are not out to protect their own. We are devoid of selfish desires and in order to be gentle, merciful, peacemakers, we would rather suffer wrong and be cheated than seek retaliation. In fact, we would rather bend over backwards, giving more than is asked to reconcile with this person who believes he has a suit against us.

This should be especially applied in our relationship with other Christians. Paul said it is better to be wronged and cheated than to further such disputes between Christians (1 Corinthians 6.7).

The Extra Mile

Roman law allowed soldiers to force subject peoples to carry burdens for them a distance of one mile. It did not matter what the individual was doing. It did not matter where they were going. If the soldier called them to carry the burden, the person had to. Obviously such a chore would be odious to anyone so conscripted. It was, no doubt, most often met with complaining and murmuring.

How should the kingdom citizen act when his personal space was violated in this way? Without grumbling and complaint, they would carry the burden and then go another mile. So unconcerned with protecting their own space and time, the kingdom citizen gave themselves into the service of others.

I can't help but think about the times my wife has asked me to get something out of the attic or do some other chore for her. Of course, this is not an issue of governmental oppression, but if I should go the second mile in that situation, how much more in my relationship with my wife? Instead of complaining and grumbling, I should joyfully serve her no matter how it impacts me and I should finish with, "Anything else, dear?" (Remind me not to let her read this chapter.)

How should we apply this on the job, with our neighbors and with our brethren? Instead of being so caught up in preserving our space, our time and our rights, we are to be servants who go the extra mile. Please do not say, "Well, I'll go two miles because Jesus said I had to, but don't expect me to go 2½."

Give to Those Who Ask

Again, Jesus' final illustrations to give to those who ask and to not turn away from those who want to borrow are not absolute. 2 Thessalonians 3.10 explains that a person unwilling to work should not eat and we are not to enable such laziness by heeding their requests for our food. Further, it is only logical that we are not to honor any requests that further sin. We must not heed the drug addict's request for money to get his next fix.

I believe this passage is actually in juxtaposition to a situation found in the Old Testament. In Nehemiah 5, Nehemiah was trying to lead the Israelites to rebuild Jerusalem's walls. In the midst of this work there was an outcry from some of the people that their brethren had loaned them money at such interest they could not pay it back and must go into slavery. Nehemiah rebuked the usurers and they agreed to give back what they had taken from their needy brethren and not expect payment.

The world's approach to someone's need is to take advantage. "Certainly, I will loan you money, but you must pay me with so much interest." The kingdom citizen is not out to protect his own personal space or property. He is not out to gain advantage on the back of those who are in need. Rather, he is happy to use the possessions with which God has blessed him to serve others. A great example of this is seen in Acts 4.36-37 when Barnabas sold a tract of land and used the money to provide for others.

Are we willing to use our blessings to help others? Or do we hoard them, reserving them for our own personal use? After all, they are ours, the asker has no right to them.

A Big Risk

I don't like this passage. I find it hard to follow. Why? Because it is a big risk. If I offer my other cheek, the offender may slap it as well. If I offer my coat as well as my shirt, the plaintiff may take them both. If I go the second mile, the oppressor may want me to go more. If I give to him who asks, he may ask again.

Our society says, "Fool me once, shame on you. Fool me twice, shame on me." Jesus tells us to open ourselves up, to be vulnerable. We have to understand this. No one ever went to hell for being taken advantage of. But people will lose their souls if they cannot lower their defenses and open themselves up to people, overcoming evil with good, refusing revenge, retaliation and even resistance.

Jesus' audience had been told they could seek personal retribution with God's blessing. Jesus told His audience they should meekly endure what the evil people inflict and offer a blessing in return instead of more evil.

Responding to the Sermon

What is your initial response to Jesus' teaching on retaliation and resistance as presented in this chapter?

Why do we so wish to pursue retaliation and revenge? How can we overcome that seemingly natural desire?

Meditating on the Sermon

As mentioned in the first chapter of this book (p. 18), Jesus did not just ask these things of us, He exemplified them. How did Jesus exemplify this teaching of non-resistance and gentle peaceableness?

Into what situations in your present life do you need to apply this teaching and Jesus' example? Meditate on these things today.

Praying the Sermon

Merciful God,

There is perhaps no part of this sermon that I need help with more than this one. Please strengthen me to obey it. Help me be willing to void myself of self-interest. Help me be willing to pursue only what glorifies You and serves Your children.

I thank You, Lord, for treating me in this way. I have sinned against You. I have rebelled against Your will. I have trampled underfoot Your covenants and laws. I have spit in Your face. Yet You did not seek vengeance and retaliation. You sought reconciliation. You provided a blessing. You sent Your Son to die to save me from my sins. Thank You. Please forgive me.

Help me be Your child, living as You have lived, acting as You have acted. Help me live in this manner today. When men insult and offend me, help me offer a blessing instead. When people seek to take advantage of me, help me willingly offer myself in their service. Help me do this at home, at work, at school, in the neighborhood and in Your church.

Help me love as You have loved.

I love You, Father, and I thank You for loving me.

In Jesus' name I pray,

Amen.

Group Discussion

What are the most important lessons you have learned this week?

_____

_____

_____

_____

_____

What questions do you have about what you have learned this week?

_____

_____

_____

_____

_____

What practical improvement have you made in your life based on what you have learned this week?

_____

_____

_____

_____

_____

What practical advice would you give others to accomplish what you have learned about this week?

With what issues do you need help or prayers based on what you have learned this week?

How can we make righteousness an issue of the heart every day in our lives?

Why is the world so opposed to Jesus' standards of righteousness? How can we best demonstrate these standards to them?

The Gospel of the Kingdom

Week Four

Seek first His kingdom and righteousness, and all these things will be added to you.

Matthew 6.33

Love's Response:

Matthew 5.43-48

"You have heard that it was said, 'You shall love your neighbor and hate your enemy.

"But I say to you, love your enemy and pray for those who persecute you so that you may be sons of your Father who is in heaven; for He causes His sun to rise on the evil and the good, and sends rain on the righteous and the unrighteous. For if you love those who love you, what reward do you have? Do not even the tax collectors do the same? If you greet only your brothers, what more are you doing than others? Do not even the Gentiles do the same? Therefore you are to be perfect, as your heavenly Father is perfect."

You Have Heard

Jesus' final rebuke against the scribes and Pharisees' legalistic, line-drawing, loophole finding approach to God's law was a very natural progression from his last statement. Leviticus 19.18 says, "You shall not take vengeance, nor bear any grudge against the sons of your people, but you shall love your neighbor as yourself; I am the Lord." Refraining from vengeance was linked with loving your neighbor. Having explained the extremes to which His kingdom citizen's go to refrain from retaliation and vengeance, Jesus continued to further define love and whom we should love.

"You shall love your neighbor," is clearly found in the Old Testament. However, "hate your enemy" is not. Perhaps the scribes and Pharisees justified this hate for enemies from the imprecatory Psalms, in which the psalmist called down the wrath of God on His enemies. Perhaps they garnered it from the numerous wars God commanded. If so, both cases fall short of justifying this sort of statement.

The psalms actually demonstrate a very important point. We have enemies who anger us. Instead of taking our anger to the enemies in vengeful hatred and retaliation, we take our emotions to God. We vent our emotions by expressing them to Him, leaving room for His vengeance if it is appropriate. But the Psalms do not command us to hate our enemies. The Old Testament wars were not an expression of the Jews' hate for their enemies. Rather, they were an expression of God's judgment on sinners. God demanded these wars not because the foreigners were the enemy, but because they were rebellious and sinful. In fact, when these wars led Jonah to hate the Assyrians so much he did not want them forgiven, God rebuked Him.

Sadly, however, I do not think the scribes and Pharisees had such a noble reason for claiming they were to hate their enemies. Consider the lawyer and his question about the Law and love in Luke 10.29. He had recognized the greatest commands to be loving God and loving his neighbor. But then he asked, "And who is my neighbor?" This question demonstrates the mindset of the scribes and Pharisees. They had not looked to other passages to justify hating their enemies. They had once again taken a plain passage and reduced its meaning. Since the text says "love my neighbor," we are allowed to hate everyone who is not our neighbor. If you can't prove someone is my neighbor, don't expect me to love them.

When the lawyer asked this question, he wasn't expecting Jesus' answer. He expected something similar to "The Jews are your neighbors." Or "Everyone who lives within a Sabbath day's journey is your neighbor." Jesus' story of the Good Samaritan basically said the person near you right now, no matter who she is, is your neighbor. Love her and do good to her.

Additionally, if the scribes and Pharisees had simply read Exodus 23.4-5, they would have seen their interpretation of "Love your neighbor" was faulty. "If you meet your enemy's ox or his donkey wandering away, you shall surely return it to him. If you see the donkey of one who hates you lying helpless under its load, you shall refrain from leaving it to him, you shall surely release it with him." This command is similar to the one given in Deuteronomy 22.1-3 about the neighbor's animals. Even in the Old Law, God demonstrated His children should love their enemies and do good for them.

Love Your Enemies

Jesus has built His way up to the greatest challenge of the Sermon. In fact, it must be viewed as the central point, considering the place we know love holds in the scheme of God's commands (cf. Matthew 22.36-40). Everything else in the Sermon will rest on how well we submit to this challenge.

This is the "agape" love we have heard so much about in sermons and Bible class lessons. It is the love that seeks what is best for the loved without regard for what the one loved has done or offers. It is unconditional. It is the love God has for us because He is love (1 John 4.8). He does not love us because we are pretty, smart or wealthy. He does not love us because we first loved Him. He loves us because He is love. That is the love for which we strive.

I am sure you have studied this love before and know about Paul's description of it in 1 Corinthians 13.4-7:

> Love is patient, love is kind and is not jealous; love does not brag and is not arrogant, does not act unbecomingly; it does not seek its own, is not provoked, does not take into account a wrong suffered, does not rejoice in unrighteousness, but rejoices with the truth; bears all things, believes all things, hopes all things, endures all things.

The truly hard part about this is Jesus is telling us to act this way toward our enemies. We are supposed to be patient with people who are impatient with us. We are supposed to be kind to people who are unkind to us. We are to refrain from jealousy and arrogance in relation to those who are jealous or arrogant. They will behave unbecomingly, seek their own, be easily provoked and keep score, but we must not respond in kind. They will rejoice when we are in unrighteousness, but we must rejoice only in truth and righteousness. They will abandon us in all circumstances and believe the worst about us at all times, but we must still believe the best about them and be there to help them bear their heavy loads. We must love those who do not love us.

Luke's rendition of this principle says more, "Love your enemies, do good to those who hate you, bless those who curse you, pray for those who mistreat you" (Luke 6.27-28). Love, then, is not merely an emotion. Rather, it is an attitude in action. Loving others means doing good to them, blessing them and praying for them.

Obviously, Jesus' work on the cross stands out as the supreme example of this love. However, it is so grand we have a hard time believing we can ever measure up to that. Consider another demonstration of Jesus' love. In John 13.1, we see Jesus on the night of His arrest. The text says, "Having loved His own who were in the world, He loved them to the end." Then it relates His washing of the disciples' feet. What most amazes me about this good done to His disciples is who was included. That He washed the ignorant, arrogant, rash and often unbelieving disciples' feet in general is amazing. But there was also Peter, who argued with Him right on the spot in front of the other apostles and who was going to deny Him three times that very night. Jesus loved Him and washed His feet anyway. However, the greatest demonstration was Judas Iscariot. The very heel lifted up against Him (John 13.18) was washed by Him. That is loving our enemies.

Having said the above, we do need to realize love is an action based on an attitude. Consider 1 Corinthians 13.3: "If I give all my possessions to feed the poor, and if I surrender my body to be burned, but do not have love, it profits me nothing." Paul said it was possible to give all his possessions to feed the poor and do so without love. That means we can do good to someone without loving them. Keep this in mind. It provides little benefit for our souls if we do good to others through clinched teeth all the while hating them. We must work on our hearts. Granted, I agree that emotion will often follow action. Therefore, even when we don't feel like it, we should do good. Further, as Jesus goes on, we should pray for our enemies. It is hard to hate a person with whom we are empathizing in prayer. If we go through the mental work to see where our enemy is and what needs he has, our hearts open up to him. Please understand this love is an attitude in action. We need both the attitude and the action.

Sons of God

Jesus said we are to love our enemies "so that you may be sons of your Father who is in heaven." There are two sides to this statement.

First, as we learned in our study of being peacemakers (Matthew 5.9; Chapter 10), when we love others we look like God. It calls to mind the phrase "like Father, like son." We demonstrate a family resemblance when we love because we are love.

God demonstrates this love when He sends the sun and rain on all people alike. The sun and rain continue the cycle of life, providing for the growth of crops and food. While God uses the patterns of weather as a means of judgment at times, the general rule is the blessings of weather fall on the good and the evil alike. God sends blessings even on the evil and unrighteous. When we, with impartiality, do good to all those with whom we have opportunity, we look like God.

Second, the text says, "So that you may be..." This unconditional love is the condition for being children of God. If we do not love in this way, we demonstrate we are not God's children. If we are not His children, we do not have the inheritance He offers. We do not inherit the earth or receive the kingdom.

This is not a teaching for the Green Berets in the Lord's army. This is not the Special Forces. This is the requirement for every child of God. We must love our enemies as God loves His enemies. Then and only then do we show we are His children.

With whose family do we bear resemblance? Even the tax collectors loved those who loved them. Even the Gentiles greeted their brethren. God has called us to be different from the world (Romans 12.2). The tax collectors and Gentiles were seen as the lowest of the low by the Jews. The Gentiles were obviously outside of a relationship with God. They were not a part of the chosen people. But tax collectors might even be worse. They were Jews that knew better, but had compromised with the Gentiles becoming the Roman government's agent to take away the Jews' money. Even these despicable lowlifes loved their friends and greeted their brothers. Whom do we look like—the sinners of the world or God?

Perfect

The word translated "perfect" in Matthew 5.48 is also translated "complete" (Matthew 19.21; Colossians 1.28) and "mature" (1 Corinthians 2.6; Ephesians 4.13). Some, noting the different uses of this word, have softened this verse. No doubt, they mean well. After all, none of us want to leave the impression that if we fall short of personal perfection we are not children of God.

However, when I consider the place of love in the grand scheme of things as demonstrated by Matthew 22.35-40, I fear the distinction between "perfect" and "mature" is overstated in regards to this passage. Jesus said the greatest commandment was to love God. The second was to love our neighbor. Then He concluded by saying, "On these two commandments depend the whole Law and the Prophets." In other words, as we grow in love, we grow in our ability to keep God's commandments. When we love God, we keep His commandments. When we love others we keep God's commandments toward them. 1 John 5.2-3 says, "By this we know that we love the children of God when we love God and observe His commandments. For this is the love of God, that we keep His commandments; and His commandments are not burdensome." What does this mean other than as we grow in love for God and others, especially our enemies, we are becoming perfect as God is perfect, holy as God is holy? As love grows, we increase our victory over sin.

Does this mean we will become perfectly sinless before we die? I doubt that. 2 Peter 1.5-8 demonstrates love is a never-ending growth process. It must be ours and it must be increasing. Peter left no room for people who finally loved as much as they possibly could. Jesus' point is not that we must reach a state of perfection to enter heaven. Rather, His point is merely this is how we become like our Father. The more we love the more we are like Him. The more we love the more holy we are. The more we love the more perfect we are.

Let us never forget, however, no matter how much we grow in love, we have already botched the perfect life heaven mandates. Though we grow in love, we are only doing what we ought always to have done (cf. Luke 17.10) and we still stand in need of God's forgiveness by the blood of Jesus Christ. We cannot earn our salvation by our growth in love. We can merely grow to be more like our Father.

Jesus' audience had been told they could pick and choose whom they would love. Jesus told His audience they must love all men, even their enemies if they wanted to be God's children.

Responding to the Sermon

What is your initial response to Jesus' teaching on loving our enemies as presented in this chapter?

What obstacles keep us from loving our family? …friends? …brethren? … enemies? How can we overcome those obstacles?

Is there an enemy you need to learn to love? What steps will you take?

Meditating on the Sermon

What kind of actions measure up to the standard of love set in 1 Corinthians 13.4-7? How can you improve in those actions across the board? Meditate on these things today.

Praying the Sermon

Loving Father in Heaven,

Thank You for loving me. Thank You for sending the rain to water the crops that produce food for my family and me. Thank You for causing the sun to rise, which continues the cycle of life and provides beautiful days of enjoyment for me. Thank You for allowing me a job. Thank You for giving me the mental faculty and physical ability to provide for my family and myself. Thank You for allowing me to breathe in and out all day long. Thank You for the food I have eaten every day of my life. Thank You for the home in which I live, the car I drive, the clothes I wear. Thank You for the appliances which make my life easier, my refrigerator, my stove, my microwave.

Most of all I thank You for Your Son, whose blood has cleansed my iniquities. Thank You for Your patience allowing me time to repent and grow. Thank You for Your Spirit who has revealed Your word. Help me follow Him.

Strengthen me to love as You have loved me. You sent Your Son to die while I was Your enemy. You sent Your word while I was in rebellion. Help me love others with that unconditional nature. Help me do good to, bless and pray for those who abuse and mistreat me. Help me remember this principle of love within my family where it is so easy to get lax and forget.

I love You Father and, again, I thank You for loving me.

Through Your loving Son I pray,

Amen.

Secret Service:

Matthew 6.1-18

"Beware of practicing your righteousness before men to be seen by them; otherwise you have no reward with your Father who is in heaven. So when you give to the poor, do not sound a trumpet before you, as the hypocrites do in the synagogues and in the streets, so that they may be honored by men. Truly I say to you, they have their reward in full. But when you give to the poor, do not let your left hand know what you right hand is doing, so that your giving will be in secret; and your Father who sees what is done in secret will reward you.

"When you pray, you are not to be like the hypocrites; for they love to stand and pray in the synagogues and on the street corners so that they may be seen by men. Truly I say to you, they have their reward in full. But you, when you pray, go into you inner room, close your door and pray to your Father who is in secret, and your Father who sees what is done in secret will reward you.

"..."

"Whenever you fast, do not put on a gloomy face as the hypocrites do, for they neglect their appearance so that they will be noticed by men when they are fasting. Truly I say to you, they have their reward in full. But you, when you fast, anoint your head and wash your face so that your fasting will not be noticed by men, but by your Father who is in secret; and your Father who sees what is done in secret will reward you."

A Day in the Market

It's market day. As the sun rises into the sky, you brave the crowds and walk into the square looking to purchase some food. As you pass a bread stand, your attention is grabbed by a man standing in long robes on the corner. The tassels on his robe drag the ground and you notice a phylactery, a small scroll of scripture, on his head. Even across the clamoring crowded street you can make out what he is saying as he looks to heaven with his arms outstretched.

"Oh God, I thank you that I am not like these. I fast twice a week. I pay tithes of all I get. I am no adulterer, I have never murdered or stolen anything. God, I thank you that I am not a Gentile or a Samaritan…" The prayer goes for a long time. When it is done, another onlooker praises the man, "Rabbi, you are indeed holy. We all look up to you."

You turn back to your shopping. However, while you examine a piece of fruit, the sound of a trumpet startles you. As you accidentally drop the pitcher you were planning to use to fetch water on your way home from the market, you turn to see what is going on. Everyone in the street turns with you. All eyes are riveted on a trumpeter dressed in servants' garb and a robed, tasseled and phylacteried man standing next to him. At just the moment when it seems everyone in the crowd is finally looking, the Pharisee hands a small bag, presumably filled with money, to a lame man who has been begging in the street. You watch while several men praise the benefactor for his generosity and tell the blind man how lucky he is this righteous servant of God passed by today.

While eating your fruit, you continue down the marketplace hoping to find a new pitcher. As you peruse the pitchers and other pottery inside a shop, you notice a man who looks deathly ill. His face is pale. His visage disfigured. He looks as if he can hardly walk without leaning on something. You politely ask the man, "Are you alright? Do you need me to fetch you some water? Can I get my mule and allow you to ride it home?" The man straightens up, looks scornfully at the remains of your lunch and curtly replies, "No. I'm fine. I am fasting. Some of God's children do that twice a week you know."

The scene is really quite ludicrous. Yet, this is the picture Jesus paints for us in Matthew 6.1-18. Having addressed the attitudes and teachings of the Pharisees' substandard righteousness, He now addresses the unrighteous nature of their "righteous" actions. The Pharisees and scribes appear to lead holy lives of generosity and spiritual endeavor. But they do not. They are hypocrites basking in their own vainglory.

In Matthew 23.5-7, Jesus said of the scribes and Pharisees,

> They do all their deeds to be noticed by men; for they broaden their phylacteries and lengthen the tassels of their garments. They love the place of honor at banquets and the chief seats in the synagogues, and respectful greetings in the market places and being called Rabbi by men.

The scribes and Pharisees, despite their pretense, were really unconcerned with God's glory. They were concerned with their own. They fasted, they prayed, they gave alms to the poor without thought for the God they were supposedly honoring. They wanted to be seen. They wanted men to praise them. They wanted other men to hear men praising them. They wanted accolades, medals and certificates. Perhaps that is why their main response against Jesus and the apostles was jealousy (Matthew 27.18; Acts 5.17; 13.45).

Jesus said of them, "Truly they have their reward in full." That is, they had better enjoy those kind words of honor because that is all they are getting for their hypocrisy. They will not receive the kingdom. They will not receive God's comfort. They will not inherit the earth. They will not find satisfaction. They will not attain mercy. They will not see God. They will not be called sons of God. They will not receive a great reward in heaven. They will have eternity in hell to try to gain some sense of satisfaction from the honors they received from men on earth (cf. Matthew 23.15).

Are there those who act like this today? Are there those who want to be seen of men? How many preachers fall prey to this? They do not preach to glorify God and turn people to Him, they preach to hear the compliments as people leave the building. How many others let it be known how much they have prayed and how many studies they have conducted? How many "accidentally" let the word slip about how they helped a brother or sister financially?

One of my big concerns is about the people I hear say, "I had to leave that big church and get in a smaller one. I just didn't get to lead singing or wait on the table very much over there. I like smaller churches because there is more opportunity for me to work." While there are some who legitimately work with smaller churches to help build them up, what lies behind the idea of wanting to get to be publicly used more? For too many, it is a desire to be seen praying, waiting on the table or leading singing. The person could do far more good if he wasn't so worried about praying publicly and spent more time on his knees in private prayer for the congregation. He would do far more good if he wasn't so concerned with being seen around the Lord's table and spent more of his time generously and quietly providing for his needy brethren's tables. We need to be wary of our own motivation if we are too infatuated with public service. The greatest work each congregation needs is not done on the stage but behind the scenes.

Jesus began this section saying, "Beware of practicing your righteousness before men to be noticed by them; otherwise you will have no reward with your Father who is in heaven."

Serve in Secret

As the preacher shook hands with those departing from the assembly, he saw one rare face. Deciding to motivate the brother, he asked, "Are you in the Lord's Army?"

"Absolutely," came the reply.

"Then why don't I see you very much," the preacher challenged. The man warily looked to his right and left, leaned in to the preacher's ear and whispered, "I'm in the Secret Service."

God certainly doesn't need that kind of secret service. However the first half of Matthew 6 is devoted to encouraging us to serve God in secret. The point of this secret service is not to hide what we are doing from men. After all we are supposed to be exposed lights. Rather, it is to keep us from practicing our righteousness so we can be noticed, seen and honored by men.

How easy it is to get caught up in the accolades, wanting to see our names in lights, on billboards and in the headlines. But Jesus says we are to refrain from such desires. Instead, when we give to the poor, we should not let our left hand know what our right hand is doing. When we pray, we should go into our closets, close the door and pray to our Father in secret. When we fast, we should act like nothing out of the ordinary is happening and not let anyone know what is going on.

Granted, we need to know Jesus is using hyperbole here. Even Jesus prayed with others (see Luke 9.28). The point is not so much about what other people see but about why we let them see it.

James 3.13-14 says, "Who among you is wise and understanding! Let him show by his good behavior his deeds in the gentleness of wisdom. But if you have bitter jealousy and selfish ambition in your heart, do not be arrogant and so lie against the truth." According to this passage we demonstrate our wisdom by showing good deeds done in the gentleness of wisdom. However, we must not have selfish ambition. We are not political crowd pleasers looking for man's approval. We are not trying to put ourselves forward in the eyes of men. Therefore, we are happy to do

God's will in secret, working behind the scenes. If our preaching trip is not mentioned in our home congregation's announcements, it does not bother us. If we are never asked to lead a prayer and no one ever knows how much we pray on our own, we are just as happy. If someone else is given public accolades for a work and our involvement is overlooked, we don't get upset. We don't have a problem with secret service.

When service is public, it is for a specific reason. Matthew 5.16 says, "Let your light shine before men in such a way that they may see your good works and glorify your Father who is in heaven." They can't see God, but they can see us, His children. They can see Him through us. Or can they? John 15.8 says, "My Father is glorified by this, that you bear much fruit and so prove to be my disciples." We prove to be Jesus' disciples when we bear fruit to God's glory, not our own.

Allow me one aside that is related but not a direct part of Jesus' teaching. In this sermon, Jesus is focused on us directing the glory and honor to God. I think it is also good to notice our relationship with our brethren. According to Romans 12.10 we are to "give preference to one another in honor." According to 1 Corinthians 12.22-24 we are charged to bestow more honor on those we might believe are less honorable because those who are more honorable do not need the excess honor. Finally, remember Philippians 2.3-4 explains we should put others before ourselves pursuing their needs and what they find important above our own needs and desires.

We must not do our good works to hoard the honor and accolades. Rather, we should direct people's attention to God and to bestow their honor on others who need it more than we do.

Our Reward

This is really an issue of comparative rewards. Which do we want more? Do we want man's praise while here on the earth? Or do we want God's praise on the Day of Judgment? Is man's praise here and now worth missing out on God's praise then? Or is the reverse the case?

I believe Hebrews 11.16 offers the greatest compliment and honor anyone could receive. "But as it is they desired a better country, that is, a heavenly one. Therefore God is not ashamed to be called their God; for He has prepared a city for them." I want to hear that when I stand before God. I want to hear Him say, "I was not ashamed to be called your God, Edwin."

Of course, to hear that, I must not be ashamed of my Father but openly confess my faith in Him with my words and actions (see Matthew 10.32-33). At the same time, I must serve God to be seen by God, not men. When I shift from honoring and glorifying God before men to wanting men to honor and glorify me, then I have lost my reward with the Father.

One of the great assurances Jesus offers in this section is our Father does see us in the secret places. Psalm 139.7 says, "Where can I go from Your Spirit? O where can I flee from Your presence?" While there may be a frightening side of that, there is also a comforting one. We cannot hide our wickedness and unrighteousness from God no matter how secretive we are. At the same time, nobody can hide our obedience and righteousness from God. He sees. He knows. He will not forget. We do not have to worry that our deeds have to be displayed in lights to receive God's reward. God sees even what is done in secret and He will reward.

God's rewards are greater than all man can offer. According to 1 Peter 1.4, God's reward is imperishable, undefiled, and will not fade away. It is reserved in heaven for us. The rewards of men perish with the using. They become corrupt and defiled. They fade in the memories of men with time. Sometimes they are even lost. But God's reward is there waiting for us, if we will only bear fruit that glorifies Him, not seeking the praises and honor of men.

The scribes and Pharisees could not wait for their reward. They worked to be seen by men. Though they argued with the Sadducees about whether or not there was a resurrection, they lived as if the greatest reward was here and now. We must live otherwise. We must live so men can see the glory of God, being happy to serve secretly even if we are never once praised by men. If we do, God will reward us and He will reward us far greater than we deserve.

Responding to the Sermon

What is your initial response to the secret service Jesus taught as presented in this chapter?

Why is the praise and honor afforded by men so appealing and inviting? How can we avoid that desire for present accolades?

How can we overcome the jealousy this desire for honor causes?

Meditating on the Sermon

What do you envision the eternal reward of heaven being like? How does it exceed anything man can offer you? Meditate on this today.

Praying the Sermon

Almighty God,

Through the blood of Your Son I humbly bow before You, begging Your forgiveness. I have too often thought too highly of myself. I have too often wanted men to think of highly of me. I have wanted the praise of men and have performed righteous deeds before them seeking my own glory and not Yours. I am sorry, Father. Please forgive me. Cleanse me of my sin and help me stand up against the tempter. Set me on my feet that I might fight for Your glory in the battle.

Give me the strength to do Your will without the need for man's rewards. Help me be happy behind the scenes when necessary. When in public, help me work so You will be glorified and not me. Help me point people to You. You are the awesome God and I cannot act except by Your grace and mercy. Yours is the kingdom, the glory and the power; not mine.

Strengthen me also to prefer Your children in honor. Help me divert the honor to those who need it more. Help me be unconcerned with getting credit and only concerned with accomplishing Your work.

You are awesome and greatly to be praised. Your lovingkindness, Your mercy, Your grace is forever. Thank You.

I love You, Father. Thank You for loving me.

Amen.

Pray This Way:

Matthew 6.7-15

"And when you are praying, do not use meaningless repetition as the Gentiles do, for they suppose that they will be heard for their many words. So do not be like them; for your Father knows what you need before you ask Him.

"Pray, then, in this way:

Our Father who is in heaven,
Hallowed be Your name.
Your kingdom come
Your will be done,
On earth as it is in heaven.
Give us this day our daily bread
And forgive us our debts, as we also have forgiven our debtors.
And do not lead us into temptation, but deliver us from evil.
For Yours is the kingdom and the power and the glory forever.
Amen.

"For if you forgive others for their transgressions, your heavenly Father will also forgive you. But if you do not forgive others, then your Father will not forgive your transgressions."

Avoid Meaningless Repetition

In the midst of Jesus' discussion of Secret Service, He segued into a more detailed discussion about prayer. The first point he made was not to pray like the Gentiles. They thought their prayers' effectiveness was increased based upon the number of words they said. Therefore, they packed their prayers with meaningless repetition.

Please carefully attend to the word "meaningless." Jesus did not condemn repetition but *meaningless* repetition. See Jesus' prayer in Gethsemane as recorded in Matthew 26.39. "My Father, if it is possible, let this cup pass from Me; yet not as I will, but as You will." How long did it take you to read that? 10 seconds? However, notice vs. 40. When Jesus found His inner circle sleeping He asked, "So, you men could not keep watch with Me for *one hour*?" (emphasis mine—*elc*) Matthew had only provided a summary of Jesus' hour long prayer. Jesus basically said the same thing over and over again for an hour. He may have used different words and different phrases, but He spent a whole hour making one plea. "Let this cup pass from Me; yet not as I will, but as You will." Then He turned around and had two more prayer sessions just like this first one (vss. 42, 44).

There are some prayers so meaningful and so important we cannot help but pray them over and over again. This is called importuning God. Not only is Jesus not condemning this, He actually advises it in Luke 11.5-8 when he told the story of the neighbor who got out of bed because of the persistence of the one knocking on his door. Jesus is not condemning repetition. He is condemning meaningless repetitions.

The problem is the Gentiles did not expect to be heard based on what was in their heart or the attitude prompting their prayer. They expected to be heard only because they said a lot. Therefore, instead of giving thought to their prayers, they simply said the same things over and over again.

I call to mind the prayer of the Hare Krishna. Those who worship Krishna believe they can be brought to peace and spiritual awareness by the mere repetition of the prayer:

Hare Krishna Hare Krishna

Krishna Krishna Hare Hare

Hare Rama Hare Rama

Rama Rama Hare Hare

This prayer merely contains three names applied to the god of the Hindu—Krishna, Hare and Rama. There is no thought. There is no meaning. It is nothing more than a chant addressing what they believe to be god by name. They expect to receive spiritual blessing by repeating this over and over again.

Among "Christian" culture, this can be seen in the many jokes told about Catholics. How many times have we heard the joke that a priest told his parishioner to say three "Hail Marys" and five "Our Fathers" in penance for some sin? I don't know if that sort of thing happens for real in the Catholic confessionals or not, but the jokes demonstrate the issue. The issue here is not about the thought behind prayer. It is not about the meaning of the prayer. It is about getting through the repetitions. If we say the prayer so many times, we think we will be heard. This problem was also seen in the recent craze surrounding the prayer of Jabez. The suggestion was that merely repeating that prayer would cause wonders. Jesus condemns that idea.

Our prayers should come from our heart as a natural response to the awesomeness of God. We will not be heard in secret if we are merely going through the motions by rote. We will only be heard if our words are backed with meaningful intent, even if we are repeating a prayer that is written as we often do in songs or as Jesus did when He quoted Psalm 22 in prayer.

Jesus' Example Prayer

In the context of Matthew 6.7-8, we realize Jesus is not providing us with a prayer to be repeated endlessly. Rather, He is providing a guide map regarding the meaning that ought to be in our prayers. Sadly, too many Christians spend their time arguing over whether or not we can say this prayer based on the statement "Your kingdom come" and miss the importance regarding the meaning that ought to be in our prayers.

Our Father who is in heaven

The term "Father," as used here, is not just the title of the one to whom we pray. It is a description of the relationship we must have if we want to pray. God must be our Father. This is more than physical paternity. The Father is the one who nourishes, strengthens and provides for. The Father is the one who supports and maintains. Finally, the Father is the one who is in authority. If we desire to pray, we must find our sustenance and support in God. Further, He must be our final authority. What He says goes. We cannot come to God in prayer if we are not willing to accept His final answers in all aspects of our life.

Note that Jesus did not say, "My Father." While that is certainly a lawful address in our prayers (see Romans 8.15), Jesus' particular address here indicates a relationship with the Father entails a relationship with His children. I am well aware there are numerous egregious errors accomplished by organized churches today. However, we must not throw the baby out with the bathwater. If we do not want a relationship with

God's children through His church, then we cannot have a relationship with our Father. When we pray this way, we are acknowledging we cannot call God "Our Father" if we are not willing to be part of the "Our."

Our Father is in heaven. We are on earth. What an admission. God is not one of us. He is not just one of the guys. We cannot, as so many want to suggest today, just come into God's presence snapping our fingers under His nose and acting as though anything we say and do in prayer is alright because He is one of our buds. Ecclesiastes 5.1-7 warns that God's residence in heaven means we need to take care how we approach Him. Our prayers need to be offered with care, not carelessness. I appreciate the well-intentioned prayer advice offered by many today saying we can talk to God in the same way we would our best friend. They simply want to encourage prayer. However, our best friend is from the earth, not heaven. We must not talk to God that way. Rather, we need to talk with thought, reverence and honor. We need to approach prayer with caution.

Further, acknowledging God's residence in heaven acknowledges His superiority. He doesn't think like us. His ways are not our ways (Isaiah 55.8-9). If we pray to Him now in basically the same way we did before we became Christians, we have not fully grasped the significance of our Father's residence in heaven. We must not come to Him as the natural, worldly man would. We must come to Him based upon His word.

Finally, acknowledging God's residence in heaven demonstrates that God's power transcends what we can imagine. It is an admission at the beginning of the prayer that our God is beyond us. His power surpasses even our greatest request. Therefore, our prayers cannot manipulate Him. We are not even trying to come to Him to manipulate Him to our will, we know it cannot be done. When communicating with people on earth, we can often hide our true intention, but not so when we communicate with our God in heaven. He sees what is done in secret. He knows before we even ask. We must come to Him in openness and honesty seeking His will through prayer and not our own.

Hallowed be Your name

"Hallowed" means to sanctify or set apart as holy. God's name is to be extolled. God's name is to be highly esteemed. God's name is to be honored. "Your name" is used by metonymy to mean more than the appellation by which we address God. It refers to everything God is. Thus, we are praising and honoring God.

What a great profession this is. What a humbling profession. Our name is not to be hallowed. God's name is to be hallowed. Our prayer is not about glorifying us or setting our will on high. It is about glorifying God and setting Him on high. As the Psalmist said, "Not unto us, O Lord, not unto us, but to Your name give glory." This is more than a trite phrase of praise; this is the mission statement for every Christian. Our job is to bear fruit glorifying God (John 15.8).

We must certainly recognize we cannot utter this prayer in our prayer closets if we utter God's name vainly in the world. However, there is more to it. We who wear the name of God must go beyond just refraining from taking God's name in vain. We must live in a way that glorifies God at all times if we wish to utter this prayer.

Your kingdom come, your will be done on earth as it is in heaven

Regrettably, many Christians get snagged on the phrase "Your kingdom come." Certainly, if Jesus was modeling a prayer for the start of God's kingdom on earth, we could not utter that prayer today. His kingdom has been established (see Colossians 1.13). However, I believe the statement "Your will be done on earth as it is in heaven" is a further explanation of what He meant by "Your kingdom come."

This is not merely a prayer for the establishment of the kingdom, but for the progress and growth of it. It is a prayer that God's rule permeate the earth as it permeates heaven. As Luke 17.20-21 demonstrates, the kingdom of God is not one of land and continents, but of the hearts of men. This is a prayer that God's rule infiltrate the hearts of all men and affect their actions such that God's will be done all over the earth. We can and must pray for that.

That being said, if we are praying for God to have complete control down here, where should the answer for such a prayer begin? Matthew 6.33 says we should seek first God's kingdom and righteousness. Thus, if we are going to pray this prayer, we had better let God start with us. We must allow His rule to take over our hearts and His will to take over our actions. If we are not willing to obey God, how can we pray that His will be done?

Further, this prayer is not just about us. It is about the whole world. We are saying we want God's will to rule in the hearts of everyone on earth. If we really mean that, we will do something about it, getting this gospel of the kingdom out to others, making peace between God and as many as we possibly can.

Offering this prayer is not about getting God to do something for us. It is about getting us to do something for God.

Give us this day our daily bread

This prayer is more than a passing request for our physical needs. In this prayer, we acknowledge our physical needs can only be fulfilled by God. Yet, it goes deeper. As we rely on Him, we are saying all we want is what God feels is all we need. This is an abbreviated form of the plea of Agur, the son of Jakeh, in Proverbs 30.8-9. "Give me neither poverty nor riches—feed me wit the food allotted to me; lest I be full and deny You, and say, 'Who is the Lord?' Or lest I be poor and steal, and profane the name of my God."

Most of us would pray that God not let us be poor. But how many of us would do so out of concern for God's name? On the other side, how many of us are willing to say, "God, give me just enough. I don't want too much." How many of us could say we have a concept of what too much would even be? Consider 1 Timothy 6.8 in this context. How many of us would be content if God decided all we needed was food and covering?

Further notice that this prayer is not just for my daily bread, but our daily bread. This prayer is not just for myself but for my brethren as well. Do you remember the teaching of James 2.15-16? When we pray for God to feed and clothe our destitute brethren, our faith must be accompanied by action. It does us no good to say, "Be warmed and filled." We must be willing to be part of the answer. Do you realize what this means? It means if we are going to pray this prayer, we are agreeing to be God's tool by which He blesses others who are also praying this prayer.

And forgive us our debts, as we forgive our debtors

In addition to praying for physical needs, Jesus teaches us to pray for our spiritual needs. Our greatest spiritual need is forgiveness. Of course, to be able to pray this prayer, we must recognize we have sinned. We must not be like the Pharisee of Luke 18.11-12 who seemed not to recognize his own sins.

Interestingly, this prayer doesn't say, "Forgive us our sins." It says, "Forgive us our debts." This prayer does not acknowledge a mistake in judgment, a character flaw or a natural human deficiency. It acknowledges that we owe God and we cannot pay what we owe. We need grace and forgiveness. Since we are asking for forgiveness, we acknowledge we are asking for something we do not deserve. We cannot demand it. We could not be upset if God refused. Further, when God forgives as He has promised (1 John 1.9), we cannot become arrogant. We do not suddenly become worthier or better than anyone else just because God has forgiven us.

Finally, this prayer comes with a qualification. In fact, this qualification is so important, it is the only part of the prayer on which Jesus made further comment in the Sermon. "For if you forgive others for their transgressions, your heavenly Father will also forgive you. But if you do not forgive others, then your Father will not forgive your transgressions" (Matthew 6.14-15). Do we really want God to deal with our sins the way we have dealt with the sins of others?

And do not lead us into temptation, but deliver us from evil

This statement is the most difficult part of this prayer for me to understand. I struggle with understanding why we would ask God not to lead us into temptation when we know full well He tempts no one (James 1.13-14). However, there are two passages in the Psalms that help me.

Psalm 119.33-40 and Psalm 141.3-10 both contain similar statements. In the context of these psalms, we see a picture that says, "God, left to myself, I know I am going to fail. Please, lead me so I do not fall prey to the traps laid by the evil one. Help me understand Your word. Have Your children rebuke me when I am falling. Do whatever it takes to keep me from destroying myself."

We all intellectually know we want to avoid sin. None of us wants to experience the ultimate end of our sins. Yet, despite that, left to our own guidance we will inevitably fall. The only way to escape temptation is to let God lead us. Remember, with every temptation God provides a way of escape (1 Corinthians 10.13). However, to take it, we have to give up leading ourselves and let God lead us in His paths of righteousness. We are praying for more than just a viable escape route. We are praying for God to guide us along that path. We are praying for God to open the Red Sea before us and lead us away from the army of the evil one.

No doubt, we cannot pray this prayer of deliverance apart from the rest of this prayer. Without the "Our Father," without the "hallowed be Your name," without the "Your will be done," without the "forgive us our debts," we could not possibly expect God to provide deliverance. But in the context of this entire prayer and what we are saying when we pray this way, we can have faith God will deliver. He knows how to deliver the godly from temptation (2 Peter 2.5-10).

For Yours is the kingdom and the power and the glory forever. Amen.

In all honesty, there seems to be good reason behind why many translations leave this part of the prayer out of this passage. The earliest manuscripts do not include it. The parallel passage in Luke 11.4 does not include it. It may very well be an interpolation added in for some reason by some later scribe. Whether or not that is the case, this statement certainly corresponds with the entire tenor of scriptural teaching on prayer.

Consider the similar prayer offered by David in 1 Chronicles 29.10-12.

> Blessed are You, O Lord God of Israel our Father, forever and ever. Yours, O Lord, is the greatness and the power and the glory and the victory and the majesty, indeed everything that is in the heavens and the earth; Yours is the dominion, O Lord, and You exalt Yourself as head over all. Both riches and honor come from You, and You rule over all, and in Your hand is power and might; and it lies in Your hand to make great and to strengthen everyone.

This principle really is the basis for everything else in the prayer. Why should God's name be hallowed? Why do we want God's will to govern the earth? Why do we ask for daily bread, forgiveness, leadership and deliverance from God? Because God is the sovereign ruler of the universe. We want to submit to His rule. He can accomplish all we ask. He will accomplish all He has promised. Finally, the glory belongs to Him and not to us. Therefore we pray.

Allow me to boil down what I have learned most from Jesus' example prayer. Most of the time, we study prayer hoping to learn how to pray the right way in order to get what we want. Regrettably, we too often take a formulaic approach. We believe we can start with a healthy layer of Praise, add the appropriate amount of Confession, pour in a heaping amount of Petition, that has been strained of Selfishness and then add Faith until God finally gives us what we want. It does not work this way. Rather, to get what we want. We must not pray by formula. Instead, to get what we want through prayer, we must learn to want what God wants and pray for that. When we are transformed by the renewing of our mind to want what God wants, we will always get what we want through prayer. That is the crux of this example prayer.

Responding to the Sermon

What is your initial response to prayer as presented in this chapter?

What are your biggest hindrances to prayer? What are your biggest hindrances to praying the things mentioned in Jesus' example prayer?

How can you overcome these obstacles?

Before you move on to the meditation for today, pray right now.

Meditating on the Sermon

Why does God deserve our prayer?

Why do we need to pray to God? Meditate on these things today.

_____

_____

_____

_____

_____

Praying the Sermon

Our Father who is in heaven, Hallowed be Your name.

Your kingdom come, Your will be done, on earth as it is in heaven.

Give us this day our daily bread.

And forgive us debts, as we also have forgiven our debtors.

Lead us not into temptation, but deliver us from evil.

For Yours is the kingdom and the power and the glory forever.

Amen.

Membership Has Its Privileges:

Matthew 6.19-23

"Do not store up for yourselves treasures on earth, where moth and rust destroy, and where thieves break in and steal. But store up for yourselves treasure in heaven, where neither moth nor rust destroys, and where thieves do not break in or steal; for where you treasure is, there your heart will be also.

"The eye is the lamp of the body; so then if your eye is clear, your whole body will be full of light. But if your eye is bad, your whole body will be full of darkness. If then the light that is in you is darkness, how great is the darkness!"

Is He Talking to Us?

Jesus is still explaining the righteousness that surpasses that of the scribes and Pharisees. Luke 16.14 says, "Now the Pharisees, who were lovers of money, were listening to all these things and were scoffing at Him." However, at this point in the Sermon, He steps on our modern American toes more than in just about any other place.

Let us be careful as we read this section and the next. It is too easy to read a Bible passage, which should humble us and cause us to change, in such a way as to believe it isn't asking anything of us. The fact is, not a single Pharisee had the wealth and luxury we have. They did not have cars to drive all over the country. They did not have a closet full of clothes to change based on what they were doing that day or how they felt. They did not have a dishwasher, air conditioner, microwave oven or refrigerator. They had no computers or entertainment centers. They did not have plasma televisions, cell phones, i-pods or Blackberries. I fear we pander to the god of mammon without even knowing it at times.

How many cannot help in the work of the church because of their work on the job? How many have no time to teach others or even learn to teach others because they have to work overtime or have an extra job to pay credit card bills? How many have a huge mortgage, two car notes, multiple credit card bills and a bass boat payment, but only drop a few dollars in the congregational collection every week because they can't make ends meet? How many turn a deaf ear to the needy because they have to make sure their retirement is funded before helping someone else have a meal today?

Paul told Timothy in 1 Timothy 6.10 that the love of money is the root of all sorts of evil. Yet I have never met anyone who believed they loved money enough to violate this passage. We must be careful as we read this text. Jesus might very well be talking to us. We had better pay attention if He is.

Where Do You Bank?

"Membership has its privileges." American Express coined that phrase and it has been stolen and used by banks and other organizations ever since. "When you bank with us," they want us to know, "we take care of you." These promises and guarantees are good, insofar as they go. But they are nothing like God's promises. They rest on nothing so solid as God.

"Don't store up treasures on earth," Jesus said. Allow me the obligatory caveat. Jesus was using a figure of speech known as ellipsis. That is, to heighten the impact of His message, he left out understood words. Jesus did not mean it is wrong to have a savings account. He also did not mean it was wrong to own anything. Numerous passages demonstrate that. Proverbs 13.22 says, "A good man leaves an inheritance to his children's children." (My friend, Gary Kerr, told me he thought it was funny that it is always our children and grandchildren who remind us of this verse.) Proverbs 21.20 says, "There is precious treasure and oil in the dwelling of the wise, but a foolish man swallows it up." In Acts 5.4, when Peter addressed the lie of Ananias and Sapphira, he explained they were not obligated to sell their land and when they sold it they were not obligated to give away all the money. It was theirs to use as they saw fit.

1 Timothy 6.17-19 provides a great explanation of Jesus' point.

> Instruct those who are rich in this present world not to be conceited or to fix their hope on the uncertainty of riches, but on

God, who richly supplies us with all things to enjoy. Instruct them to do good, to be rich in good works, to be generous and ready to share, storing up for themselves the treasure of a good foundation for the future, so that they may take hold of that which is life indeed.

It is not wrong to have riches. If in your pursuit to serve God excellently as you provide for your family God has blessed you with riches, then enjoy them. If we supplied the understood words of Jesus' ellipsis the text would say, "Do not primarily store up treasures on earth, but more importantly store up treasures in heaven."

Sin begins when we trust in those riches as though they are what protect us or as though they can actually provide some eternal benefit. Ours is a society that lives by the fallacy exposed in Ecclesiastes 10.19. "Money is the answer to everything."

How can we be protected from criminals? Buy a security system. How can we be protected from ill health? Buy expensive supplements and don't forget to buy insurance. How can we be cared for in our old age? Have an IRA, 401(k), retirement plan and buy long term care insurance. Some emergency comes up. Have an emergency fund. There is nothing wrong with these things necessarily. However, we are quickly getting to the point where we are trusting in wealth. When our riches don't hold out, we rely on the government to take everyone else's riches to bail us out. Sadly, many people even believe the answer to their sadness is money and material goods. "I could be happy if I only had that house, that car, that computer, that new carpet, etc."

Here is the problem. When we put our faith and trust in material things, it will fail. Material goods pass. They cannot last forever. Our luxury cars break down and no matter how we care for them, given enough time they will rust away. The foundation of our house shifts. The roof leaks. The landscaping falls apart. Nothing lasts. In a moment of identity theft, our life's savings, our retirement account and our emergency fund can all be wiped out. While the bank may not be able to hold the credit card debt against us in these thefts, they will not refill our savings account. After a house fire, no amount of insurance can give us back all we had in that home. When our lives are bound up in earthly banks, we are asking for trouble. Membership in earthly banks has privileges, but not very good ones.

There is a bank where deposits don't go away. No one can steal our identity and take over our account there. Our savings will not decline. Our retirement will not fade away. Our possessions will not perish. The bank of heaven is not insured by the FDIC. It is insured by the very power of God. As we have noticed in previous chapters, the reward we gain there is reserved, undefiled, unfading and will not perish (1 Peter 1.4-5). Membership truly does have its privileges.

We need to use the material goods with which God blesses us here to store up treasures there. The passage we read above in 1 Timothy 6.17-19 said we must do good works, be generous and ready to share. We should be ready to do that whether we have a lot or a little. As one person said, "It is not what you would do if a million were your lot, it is what you are doing with the dollar and quarter you've got." In fact, just today I heard a story that illustrates this generosity even in the poor. A friend of mine worked at a homeless shelter on Monday nights in New York. The first night she was there a woman asked her if she owned a cat. She did, its name was Lily. The homeless woman said, "I used to have a cat. Her name was Kathryn Grayson. When I was evicted from my apartment, I had to let my cat be put to sleep. I saw a cat tonight in the alley and it looked like it was starving. It reminded me of my old cat. So I took my last dollar and bought a can of cat food, but when I got back to the alley, the cat was gone. Would you take it and let your cat have it?" That is generosity. That is not putting your hope in earthly treasures.

"But, Edwin," someone will say, "if I keep giving away, I won't be able to have some of the things I have worked for and a have right to." Hebrews 13.16 says, "And do not neglect doing good and sharing, for with such sacrifices God is pleased." Doing good and sharing is a sacrifice. It costs us something. But it is the kind of sacrifice God wants us to make.

Consider the parable of the unrighteous steward in Luke 16.1-9. There are many things we question about this parable, but Jesus' conclusion is actually pretty clear. We are supposed to use the stewardship He has granted us over material things in such away that others will be able to receive us into heaven. There are three things we need to notice from this parable. First, we do not own anything. We are just managers of blessings from God. God does not own 5% or 10%, He owns 100%. Therefore, we must use it all to His glory and not our own. Second, we must use this stewardship to build eternal dwellings in heaven. We must not be so worried about our homes down here. Instead, we need to focus on building a heavenly home. Third, we must use this stewardship so others can welcome us into that eternal dwelling. That is, we must use our material goods in a way that gets other people to heaven as well. Or I guess we could just go buy a new truck. It is really up to us.

Here is the deal. We can spend our material goods on that which perishes with the using, rusts and rots away and will be burned up in the Day of Judgment anyway. Or we can invest our material goods in ways that will pay eternal dividends. The choice is ours to make. We must choose wisely.

Our Heart and Our Treasure

Proverbs 4.23 says, "Watch over your heart with all diligence, for from it flow the springs of life." As Jesus said, where our treasure is, our heart will be. Colossians 3.2 says, "Set your mind on things above, not on things that are on the earth." When we value and esteem the material things of the earth, finding our sense of worth from what we own, our heart will be on the earth. When we value and esteem the spiritual things of heaven, finding our sense of worth from God and His blessings, our heart will be in heaven.

Cyprian, a third century Christian wrote,

> A blind love of one's own property has deceived many; nor could they be prepared for, or at ease in, departing when their wealth fettered them like a chain. Those were the chains to them that remained—those were the bonds by which both virtue was retarded, and faith burdened, and the spirit bound, and the soul hindered…If rich men did this, they would not perish by their riches; if they laid up treasure in heaven, they would not now have a domestic enemy and assailant. Heart and mind and feeling would be in heaven, if the treasure were in heaven; nor could he be overcome by the world who had nothing in the world whereby he could be overcome. He would follow the Lord loosed and free…But how can they follow Christ, who are held back by the chain of their wealth? Or how can they seek heaven, and climb to sublime and lofty heights, who are weighted down by earthly desires? They think that they possess, when they are rather possessed; as slaves of their profit, and not lords with respect to their own money, but rather the bond-slaves of their money.[16]

Those who focus on the material treasures and have their heart firmly planted on the earth are like the Laodiceans of Revelation 3.17: "Because you say, 'I am rich, and have become wealthy, and have need of nothing,' and you do not know that you are wretched and miserable and poor and blind and naked." If our hearts are wrapped up in this world, we are of all men most to be pitied, because the rewards of this world are all we will receive. We can enjoy them for a time, but be prepared; they won't make it into eternity (2 Peter 3.10).

---

16. Cyprian, *Treatise III: On the Lapsed*, sections 11, 12. The Ante-Nicene Fathers, Eerdmans Publishing Com, Grand Rapids, 1997, v 5.

Consider the great example of Moses, who, according to Hebrews 11.24-26, abandoned the riches of Pharaoh's house. Yet he did so looking to a reward that was greater. Because he valued God and God's things, his heart was in heaven. Because his heart was in heaven, he was able to give up all that might keep him from heaven. This is the same heart that drove Paul, in Philippians 3.7-11. What he valued most was knowing God and attaining the resurrection. Therefore, he was willing to give up his standing among the Jews. He was willing to give up his place among the Pharisees. He was willing to give up everything else so long as he would gain eternity.

The real point behind Jesus' teaching in this section of the Sermon can be summed up by His words in Matthew 16.25-26. What is our soul worth to us? What will we give in exchange for our soul? What is eternity in heaven worth to us? Is it worth our house, our cars, our gadgets?

Having said all this, God has not left us without enticement. He has asked us to give up all things for Him, but He has also promised us great things. In Matthew 19.29, Jesus said, "And everyone who has left houses or brothers or sisters or father or mother or children or farms for My name's sake, will receive many times as much, and will inherit eternal life." Let your heart be there. Let your heart be focused on eternal life.

A Good Eye

Jesus' teaching about our eye is confusing at first. We typically think of the eye as something that looks outward. Jesus, however, spoke of it as something going inward. The eye is the lamp that brings light to the whole body. This hearkens back to Matthew 5.14-16. We are supposed to be the light of the world. We are supposed to let our light shine in such a way that others may see our good works and glorify God. However, it seems if our eye is unhealthy, we cannot be the light because our body is plunged in darkness and how great is that darkness.

What is up with this metaphor? What is Jesus saying? He is actually drawing on the real life experience of something akin to cataracts. Cataracts are actually dead cells trapped in the "bag" that contains the lens of our eye. As those dead cells increase, they begin to blur our vision. As our vision blurs, the input to our brain is hindered. As our vision gets worse and worse, our ability to act, walk and move is hindered. We may be able to "get along alright," but we cannot get along as well as when we had clear eyes.

Jesus borrows this picture to make a spiritual point. Just as what enters our eye affects our behavior physically, it also affects our behavior spiritually. When our eyes are focused clearly on what is right and good (perhaps here we should think "mind's eye," but not necessarily), then our body will do what is good. Our body will be filled with light and we will be the light of the world. However, if our eyes are clouded and unclear, that is, if they are not focused on what is good, but are distracted by what is bad, then darkness will enter our body and our spiritual activity is hindered.

Allow me to illustrate. A few weeks ago I went on a white-water rafting trip. Before we began, our guide gave us some instructions. She explained that her main job was to help us stay in the boat. One of her instructions was about leaning in. If she shouted, "Lean in! Lean in! Lean in!" we were to lean toward the inside of the boat, touching our shoulders to the person next to us. She said the most important part of obeying this directive was to look into the bottom of the boat. Why? Because our head is the rudder for our body. If we leaned in but kept looking out, our body would likely follow our head into the river and they would have to fish us out. That is the very point Jesus is making. Our head is the rudder for our body. Where we are looking is where we are headed. If we want to go to heaven, we have to look to heaven.

This proceeds from Jesus' statement about our treasures and values because we look at what we value. Why do we steal a final peak at our children as they sleep in bed before we hit the sack? Because we value them. Why do we look at beautiful art or jewelry? Because we value them. Why do some people travel hundreds of miles to visit museums or halls of fame? Because they value them. A friend of mine traveled to Franklin, Tennessee earlier this year in order to preach a gospel meeting. While here, he made sure to take the hour and half journey to Bowling Green, Kentucky. He was 85 miles away from Bowling Green but wanted to get there. Why? Because he valued something there—the Corvette plant and museum. Why are we willing at times to go multiple hours out of our way on journeys to see friends? Because we value those friendships. We look at what we value. It is not wrong to value any of these things. It is wrong, however, when we value these things more than we value God's kingdom and righteousness.

Allow me to share a very practical look at Jesus' point. Have you been in this situation? I want to get out of debt and save money. But one day while picking up an affordable new movie at *Best Buy*, I decide to walk over to the laptop section, the handheld pc and palm section or the big screen TV section. I have no intention of buying. In fact, I am very well convinced that buying would not only be financially bad but also spiritually bad because I know it would be poor stewardship to place another one or two thousand dollars on a credit card. So, I look at the gadgets, drool a little while and then leave. But what entered my brain through my eyes now starts to play on me. I remember the features list and begin to think about all the things I could do. That laptop would be useful when I am traveling. The palm organizer would really be good for me because of my busy schedule. It would probably make me more efficient so that I won't be writing these chapters the day of the deadline. That wide screen television would really be great to have so other Christians could come over to watch appropriate movies. "Nope, I can't buy those," I tell myself. "But look at this, there is *Best Buy* again. I'll just run in and look at those bad boys again. I'm not going to buy anything though. I'm just going to look." Then my brain works a little more. Then I go back and look a little more. Finally, I am convinced. I have to have it. Nothing can stop me. I buy it, putting hundreds, if not thousands of dollars on a credit card that I cut up a few weeks ago. How did it all start? With my eyes. My vision was clouded by material things and the spiritual issue of stewardship was lost.

This same thing could happen in any area of life. Nobody ever committed adultery with a woman they never looked at. Nobody ever went into a bar or took a drink of alcohol they never saw. Nobody ever bought a lottery ticket they didn't look at. On the list could go. It begins with the eyes. Then our brain starts to work. The more we look, the more our vision of heaven and godly things blurs, the more our body and our actions are darkened until we are no longer the light of the world. Our eyes are the rudder for our body. Where they go, our body follows.

We have to keep our eyes clear and focused on heavenly things. That is where the real treasure is. That is where the real value is. Don't be duped by the devil's deceptions. He promises big, but he can't deliver. Store up treasures in heaven. The world may think we are poor, but membership in our heavenly bank has real privileges, eternal privileges.

Responding to the Sermon

What is your initial response to Jesus' teaching on what is really important as presented in this chapter?

Why are we so easily allured by earthly treasures? How can we overcome that?

Meditating on the Sermon

With what spiritual blessings does God bless His children while still in this life?

Why is heaven greater than any possible earthly blessings? Meditate on this today.

Praying the Sermon

Holy God,

I need Your forgiveness. My eye has been clouded and distracted by so many things on this earth. Houses, cars, clothes, gizmos, gadgets, appliances, computers, televisions and so much more have attracted my attention. I have worked for those too often while leaving Your work undone. Please forgive me. Cleanse my heart and make me single-minded. Clear my eye and direct my attention to You and Your heavenly reward.

Father, You are greater than all. Your reward is greater than all. Heaven is Your throne, the earth is Your footstool. I want to be around Your throne. I want to look for that better city, that heavenly kingdom. My heart longs for it. Help me look past the momentary pleasure. Help me overcome the temptations and sin to look elsewhere. Help me look to You and Your will.

Thank You for the home in heaven You have reserved for me. Strengthen my faith that I may enter that home. Help me always look to the reward.

I love You, Father, and I thank You for loving me.

Through Jesus I pray,

Amen.

Money Talk:

Matthew 6.24-34

"No one can serve two masters; for either he will hate the one and love the other, or he will be devoted to one and despise the other. You cannot serve God and wealth.

"For this reason I say to you, do not be worried about your life, as to what you will eat or what you will drink; nor for your body, as to what you will put on. Is not life more than food, and the body more than clothing? Look at the birds of the air, that they do not sow, nor reap nor gather into barns, and yet your heavenly Father feeds them. Are you not worth much more than they? And who of you by being worried can add a single hour to his life? And why are you worried about clothing? Observe how the lilies of the field grow; they do not toil nor do they spin, yet I say to you that not even Solomon in all his glory clothed himself like one of these. But if God so clothes the grass of the field, which is alive today and tomorrow is thrown into the furnace, will He not much more clothe you? You of little faith! Do not worry then, saying 'What will we eat?' or 'What will we drink?' or 'What will we wear for clothing?' For the Gentiles eagerly seek all these things; for your heavenly Father knows that you need all these things. But seek first His kingdom and His righteousness, and all these things will be added to you.

"So do not worry about tomorrow; for tomorrow will care for itself. Each day has enough trouble of its own."

The Competition

Money must be a major problem. I understand money itself is not the problem. I know the Bible doesn't say money is the root of all kinds of evil, but the love of money. However, when Jesus preached this Sermon and made the point about two masters, He could have picked anything under the sun as the competing master. In fact, He could have picked the sun. However, He chose money.

In Colossians 3.5, Paul said greed amounts to idolatry. In Ephesians 5.5, he wrote a covetous person is an idolater. The United States stamps every piece of currency printed with the words "In God We Trust." Sadly, for many people, even Christians, the god in whom they trust is the one on which this statement is printed.

Satan is using money and material goods to cloud our vision and our devotion to the Lord. When Jesus explained the Parable of the Sower in Matthew 13.22, He said the seed among the thorns represented those who heard the word, but allowed the worry of the world and the deceitfulness of wealth to choke out the word. Worldly worries and wily wealth made the seed worthless and unfruitful.

When prosperous Americans read these passages, the first thing we want to do is let everyone know it is fine to be rich. I know it is fine. It does concern me, however, that instead of initially trying to find out what this passage really does mean, we always feel the need to defend our own prosperity first. Our next step with the passage is rarely to find out what it means, but to also point out that this passage doesn't mean we should go hungry. After all, we have to live and have a place to do so. Surely we have to eat and have clothes on our back. Even Dave Ramsey seems to say the four walls of food, clothing, housing and transportation have to be taken care of first. God can't possibly be telling us to put our daily necessities behind anything else. Frankly, I am not so sure that is the case.

We just have to be honest. There is a cosmic competition going on and we are the prize. God and wealth are vying for our loyalty and only one can get it. We may try to balance both for a while, but it can't remain that way for long. Many people want to go to heaven, but they don't want that endeavor to get too much in the way of the rest of their life. Many people want to serve God but make sure they get to taste of everything this world has to offer along the way first.

The story is told of a very wealthy man who died and approached the gates of heaven lugging an extremely heavy bag. Peter met him at the gate and said, "I'm sorry sir, but your name is not written in the Book of Life. You may not enter." The man stammered, "But wait, look what

I have in the bag. That ought to count for something." Peter opened the bag and pulled out a handful of golden coins. With a smile he exclaimed, "Oh, look! Pavement!" For all the value we place on money God doesn't place any eternal value on it. Psalm 49 demonstrates this, putting money squarely in its place, saying, "No man can by any means redeem his brother or give to God a ransom for him—for the redemption of his soul is costly, and he should cease trying." We can follow wealth as our god, but it will not help us on the Day of Judgment. As the bumper sticker says, "He who dies with the most toys is still dead."

We need to remember what Jesus said as the rich young ruler walked away sorrowing, "Truly I say to you, it is hard for a rich man to enter the kingdom of heaven. Again I say to you, it is easier for a camel to go through the eye of a needle, than for a rich man to enter the kingdom of God" (Matthew 19.23-24). We can make all the caveats and demonstrate all the exceptions, but this is the rule. This should concern us. Go back to the last chapter and remember the description of our wealth. This rich young ruler probably had nothing on most of us. By the very nature of our prosperous society, we are in negative straits when it comes to salvation. We had better proceed with caution and make absolutely sure we have no other gods before us. We can't serve two masters.

The Bottom Line

Could Jesus be more shocking? For all of us who have said, "Come on, I at least have to take care of food and clothing first," Jesus responded, "Don't worry about what you will eat, drink or wear."

This is another one of those passages with which we struggle. As we try to delineate what it doesn't mean, we sometimes run the risk of ruling out any meaning at all. These verses certainly are not giving an absolute prohibition of any thought or concern given to any issue. 1 Corinthians 12.25 says every member should have the same "care" for one another, translating the same word used in our present text. In Philippians 2.20, Paul said Timothy was unmatched in "concern" for the Philippians, again translating the same word. In 2 Corinthians 11.28, Paul said he experienced daily "concern" for the churches, using a related word.

Further, we really cannot take this passage to mean we are to have absolutely no thought for the care of our bodies. Ephesians 5.28-29 would be putting wives into tight spot if that were the case, teaching their husbands to have absolutely no thought for them whatsoever.

The point of this passage is, however, that our driving thought every day is not about how we are going to eat, drink or have clothes. Our priority is not our physical necessities. When we tally in our physical needs on the ledger with God's kingdom and righteousness, God's kingdom and righteousness come out on top.

The bottom line for any business is to make sure income exceeds outgo. In a financial sense, as stewards we hope that is the same principle with which we govern our families. However, there is a sense in which that is not true. The bottom line for Jesus' kingdom citizens is not really about income or outgo at all. It is about following the rule of God and seeking His righteousness above all other things no matter how it affects our income or outgo.

Remember in the beatitudes we learned we are to hunger and thirst for righteousness. Here Jesus explains our hunger for righteousness should outweigh even our hunger for food. As Jesus exemplified in John 4.34, our food should be to do the will of God.

Seeking first God's kingdom and righteousness means our number one priority, the driving value of our life, is to accomplish the will of God. If that costs us money, we don't worry about it. If it means we miss out on material pleasures, we don't get concerned about it. If it means we miss a meal, we don't spare a thought for it. We are unconcerned with even our physical needs, let alone our desires and luxuries, if they conflict with accomplishing the will of God.

The gospels provide a great story to illustrate this principle. In Luke 10.38-42, Jesus was teaching in Mary and Martha's home. Martha was busy with the hostess responsibilities while Mary sat at Jesus' feet. Martha had finally had enough of Mary's apparent lack of concern regarding the household chores. She asked Jesus, "Lord, do You not care that my sister has left me to do all the serving alone? Then tell her to help me." Jesus responded, "Martha, Martha, you are worried and bothered by so many things; but only one thing is necessary, for Mary has chosen the good part, which shall not be taken away from her."

Jesus' word for "worried" is the same one He used in Matthew 6.25. She was eaten up with concern about unimportant things. But only one thing is necessary—seeking God's kingdom and righteousness. By sitting at the feet of the Master, Mary was pursuing with priority the kingdom of God and His righteousness. That would not be taken away from her. The clean house Martha was preparing would just have to be cleaned again when Jesus and His disciples left.

This demonstrates Satan's plan for us. He really doesn't care if we seek God's kingdom and righteousness. Martha certainly sought them. He only cares that we don't seek them first. He is happy when we spend our days anxiously worrying about our food and clothing budget. He doesn't mind if that is the only thing between us and God. It only takes one thing. At least, that's what Jesus told the rich young ruler in Luke 18.22, "This one thing you lack…"

Please understand that this is not talking about prioritizing our daily schedule. This does not mean we are free to live how we want as long as we get our prayer and Bible study out of the way first thing in the morning. This means every decision of every day should be made with the pursuit of God's kingdom and righteousness in mind. God wants to be our Prime Mover. When we make God our Prime Mover, we don't have to worry about anything else.

God Will Provide

While we seek first God's kingdom and righteousness, we don't need to worry about our needs. Instead, we can toss our worries and anxieties over to God. 1 Peter 5.6-7 says we should humble ourselves before God "casting all your anxiety on Him, because He cares for you." Philippians 4.6 says, "Be anxious for nothing, but in everything by prayer and supplication with thanksgiving let your requests be made known to God."

Jesus said if we truly seek first the kingdom of God and His righteousness, God will cover the food, drink and clothing. This principle goes back even to the Law. Leviticus 26.3-4 says, "If you walk in My statutes and keep My commandments so as to carry them out, then I shall give you rains in their season, so that the land will yield its produce and the trees of the field will bear fruit." He goes on to provide many descriptions of how He will provide if they will simply obey.

Pointing to the sky, Jesus illustrated, "See the birds. They don't worry about what they are going to eat and drink and they are all fed." Pointing to the ground around the disciples, He said, "See the lilies. They don't toil and spin, but they are more beautifully clothed than even Solomon." His point was if God will do this for what is unimportant to Him, how much more will He feed and clothe us who are important to Him.

He also drove home some points of logic. "Isn't life more than food and the body more than clothing?" Of course they are. It is harder to give life than to provide food. It is harder to create a body than to make clothing. Who gave life and provided our bodies? Was it not God? The same God who could create the body from the dust of the earth and breathe into it the breath of life can make sure we have food and clothing.

The question is not whether God can do it. The question is how large is our faith. Is our faith large enough to trust God and therefore seek first His kingdom and righteousness even when it seems doing so will keep food and clothing from us? Or will we continue to hang on to that little need to worry about the physical necessities first?

Sadly, I think a greater problem for many is not that they disbelieve He will provide the necessities. Rather, they know He didn't promise the luxuries. How many place the kingdom of God and His righteousness after the luxuries they want so much in order to keep up with their friends in the world? Allow me to share a great passage I use to help me control my coveting and greed issues. Psalm 73.25 says, "Whom have I in heaven but You? And besides You, I desire nothing on earth." If we can just get that verse down, we will do alright.

No Worries

Jesus concludes this section of the Sermon saying, "So do not worry about tomorrow; for tomorrow will care for itself. Each day has enough trouble of its own."

That is really the problem for us, isn't it? We have all eaten today. We all have clothes today. But what about tomorrow? What about next week? …next month? …next year? What about when we are old and ready to retire? What will we do then? If we spend too much of our time seeking the kingdom of God and His righteousness now, we may not have enough savings to take care of us then.

Jesus said we have too much to deal with today to spend our time worrying about that. Additionally, there is no amount of worry in the world that will increase our life by even one hour (Matthew 6.27). We can worry all we want about our retirement, but the worry won't make our retirement any better or any longer. In fact, the worry might decrease it a bit. Time wasted on worry is not spent doing God's will.

Jesus' point is if we spend our time today doing what God wants, then when tomorrow comes, spend that day doing what God wants, God will take care of us. One of my favorite church building marquees is the one that said, "We don't have to worry about tomorrow, God is already there." Too many of us spend so much time regretting the past and worrying about the future we don't use today to glorify and serve God. That only provides us with more regrets and worries for the future.

Live today. Serve God today. Do what you can right now. Let God worry about tomorrow. He is the only that can see that far ahead anyway.

Responding to the Sermon

What is your initial response to Jesus' teaching on money and the kingdom as presented in this chapter?

What things do you find yourself worrying about? What has your worry ever accomplished regarding any of those things?

What must you do to improve your seeking of the kingdom of God and His righteousness first?

Meditating on the Sermon

How has God taken care of you already in this life?

Why are God's spiritual blessings greater than any of the earthly distractions around us? Meditate on these things today.

Praying the Sermon

Loving Father in heaven,

Your name is to be hallowed and praised. You, who have created all things and provided for all Your creatures, are worthy of glory and honor.

Thank You for the food I have eaten today and every day. Thank You for the clothes I am wearing today and have always worn. Thank You for the roof over my head. You have provided excellently.

I have not always honored You from these blessings. Please forgive me. Sometimes I have sought more for the blessing than for You, the blessing giver. Please forgive me for that. Help me seek You, Your righteousness and Your kingdom first.

Grant me peace that passes understanding, Father, as I cast my cares upon You. I know You will provide and care for me. Thank You.

I love You, Father and I thank You for loving me.

In Jesus' name I offer this prayer,

Amen.

Group Discussion

What are the most important lessons you have learned this week?

What questions do you have about what you have learned this week?

What practical improvement have you made in your life based on what you have learned this week?

What practical advice would you give others to accomplish what you have learned about this week?

With what issues do you need help or prayers based on what you have learned this week?

Why are we tempted to keep our service secret in all the wrong places and public in all the wrong places? How can we overcome that temptation?

What are the biggest issues we face with money today? How can we use money properly in our service to the Lord?

The Gospel of the Kingdom

Week Five

Enter through the narrow gate; for the gate is wide and the way is broad that leads to destruction, and there are many who enter through it.

For the gate is small and the way is narrow that leads to life, and there are few who find it.

Matthew 7.13-14

Righteous Judgment:

Matthew 7.1-6

"Do not judge so that you will not be judged. For in the way you judge, you will be judged; and by your standard or measure, it will be measured to you. Why do you look at the speck that is in your brother's eye, but do not notice the log that is in your own eye? Or how can you say to your brother, 'Let me take the speck out of your eye,' and behold, the log is in your own eye? You hypocrite, first take the log out of your own eye, and then you will see clearly to take the speck out of your brother's eye.

"Do not give what is holy to dogs, and do not throw your pearls before swine, or they will trample them under their feet, and turn and tear you to pieces."

The Final Chapter

Many authors struggle (this one included) with the final chapter of Jesus' Sermon on the Mount. Granted, Jesus did not present this teaching in chapters and Matthew did not originally write it as such, but the chapter break is here because these final paragraphs seem to be a completely different section of teaching. At first, they appear to be disjointed admonitions pieced together and tacked on to the end of the Sermon. This has caused some authors to assert these paragraphs were not originally part of the mountainside message. They suggest Matthew merely added these other teachings of Jesus on the end of this address to provide a fuller picture of His teaching.

Their assertions do not threaten the nature of the gospel. We have already admitted none of the gospels were intended to be moment by moment, action by action, word by word biographies of Jesus. Rather, they are thematic presentations of who Jesus is so we might believe on Him and, through that, have life everlasting. While their suggestions do not really do great harm to the text, I think they are unnecessary. When we keep in mind the Sermon is founded upon the major premise that "unless your righteousness surpasses that of the scribes and Pharisees, you will not enter the kingdom of heaven" (Matthew 5.20), this final chapter actually has a great unity.

The first section regarding judgment, hypocrisy and giving what is holy to the unholy, clearly fits within the theme of rebuking the scribes and Pharisees for their substandard righteousness, which we will discuss further within this chapter. The remaining sections provide great closure on this matter of entering the kingdom. The Sermon began, "Blessed are the poor in spirit for theirs is the kingdom of heaven." That theme was carried out when the blessing was reiterated for those who had been persecuted for the sake of righteousness. It resurfaced in Matthew 5.19 as Jesus described who would be least and who would be greatest in the kingdom. Then, within the model for prayer, Jesus brought the kingdom back to light again as He taught us to pray for the coming of the kingdom into the entire world. Finally, His most recent admonition to seek first the kingdom of God and His righteousness carries on the theme. Why is it surprising to see a series of paragraphs all addressing how to seek and enter the kingdom based on what has been heard in this Sermon? These are not disjointed paragraphs tacked on by a disorderly redactor. These are an appropriate conclusion for this teaching. We must read them as such, keeping them in the context of the Sermon itself first and within the biblical context second.

Judge Not

I have heard someone suggest that while John 3.16 used to be the Bible's most well known passage, Matthew 7.1 has surpassed it. Everyone under the sun turns to Matthew 7.1 to rebuke anyone who tries to obey Hebrews 10.24, stimulating them to love and good works. No matter how closely someone might attempt to obey Galatians 6.1, gently restoring the one caught in a trespass, they might be confronted with this verse. "Who do you think you are? Jesus said don't judge. You have no right to talk to me about this."

The struggle we have is that the word "judge" can convey a wide spectrum of meaning. It can mean anything from discerning to decision making to condemning. Jesus is not prohibiting all judgment. He commands us to judge with righteous judgment in John 7.24. He is most certainly not prohibiting discernment. Hebrews 5.11-14 demonstrates we must discern between good and evil. He is also not prohibiting decision making. We see the apostles and other Christians in Jerusalem working through the judgment process in Acts 15 as they strived to figure out if the Spirit wanted Gentiles to be circumcised. In Acts 15.19, James said, "Therefore it is my judgment that we do not trouble…" Additionally, Jesus cannot be prohibiting all kinds of judgment regarding people. In Acts 16.15, Lydia spoke to Paul and Barnabas saying, "If you have judged me to be faithful to the Lord, come into my house and stay."

What most people want this passage to say is that Jesus prohibits us from declaring any work anyone else committs as wrong. Further, that He prohibits us from suggesting someone is unholy, unrighteous and in danger of losing their soul. Actually, what most people want it to say is, "You are not allowed to say anything I am doing is wrong or that I am unholy, unrighteous and in danger of losing my soul." However, Jesus cannot have meant this either. If for no other reason, He cannot have meant this because the world would be all too happy to hear that. If Jesus' Sermon is anything, it is displeasing to the world. Further, this cannot be true because in the immediate context Jesus commands His citizens to judge. They must judge when someone is a swine or a dog who has no appreciation for the holy and spiritually valuable. Finally, in 1 Corinthians 5, Paul, by inspiration of the Holy Spirit, commanded the Christians to judge an unrighteous brother and deliver him to Satan. He further said the church must judge those who are within. While God judges those who are without. Of course, to obey Paul, we have to make judgment regarding who is within and who is without the body of the Lord.

To understand Jesus' teaching on judgment, we must keep it in the context of the surpassing righteousness theme. Look at the scribes and Pharisees. How did they judge? In Luke 18.11-12, we see the judgment of the Pharisees. "God, I thank You that I am not like other people: swindlers, unjust, adulterers, or even like this tax collector. I fast twice a week; I pay tithes of all that I get." In Matthew 23.4, we see the judgment of the scribes and Pharisees. "They tie up heavy burdens and lay them on men's shoulders, but they themselves are unwilling to move them with so much as a finger." In John 8.1-11, we see the judgment of the scribes and Pharisees. They tried to act like they were obeying the Law as they sought Jesus to stone the woman caught in adultery. But where was the man? How did these Pharisees know about this sin? They did not have righteous judgment here. They had hypocritical judgment.

They did not leave because they knew they weren't sinless in general but because they knew they weren't sinless in this particular situation. This is the kind of judgment Jesus condemned.

Additionally, a look at Luke's parallel helps us understand. In Luke 6.35-38, we see this as part of Jesus' teaching on love:

> But love your enemies, and do good, and lend, expecting nothing in return; and your reward will be great and you will be sons of the Most High; for He Himself is kind to ungrateful and evil men. Be merciful, just as your Father is merciful.
>
> Do not judge and you will not be judged; and do not condemn, and you will not be condemned; pardon, and you will be pardoned. Give, and it will be given to you. They will pour into your lap a good measure—pressed down, shaken together, and running over. For by your standard of measure it will be measured to you in return.

Jesus was condemning the hypercritical, hypocritical judgment of those who set themselves up as the standard. He was condemning those who would put themselves in the seat of God as though we are able to make up the laws by which people will be judged. He was further condemning the judgment more concerned with putting people in their place than trying to help them get to God's place.

Once, as Jesus was traveling to Jerusalem, He passed through Samaria. When a certain village there refused to receive Him, James and John stepped up to the plate. "Lord, do You want us to command fire to come down from heaven and consume them?" Jesus rebuked them saying, "You do not know what kind of spirit you are of; for the Son of Man did not come to destroy men's lives but to save them" (Luke 9.51-56). This is the kind of judgment Jesus condemned, the one that is all to happy to rain the fires of hell on the heads of those we view lower than us instead of reaching out the helping hand to lift others up.

Let us not misunderstand. Some have a tendency to believe we have only violated this passage if we judge others for the exact same sin we have committed. Not true. When we want to bring the fire of hell on someone because they have not attained our standards, God will bring upon us the fire of hell because we have not attained His standard.

We must learn to be like our Master, who is the judge according to John 5.22. Yet Jesus said in John 12.47, "I did not come to judge the world, but save the world." Here is the one who is the judge, yet His goal was not to judge and condemn people, but to save them. We must have that mindset as well. Our desire is not to judge and condemn people, but to save them. Thus, when we have judged that they are caught in sin, we strive to restore them with a spirit of gentleness (Galatians 6.1). Even when we, within the congregational context, have to discipline a brother or sister, we do not treat them as an enemy but admonish them as a brother (2 Thessalonians 3.15).

That some try to use Matthew 7.1-2 to suggest we can establish our own rules and all that matters for our heavenly journey is how sincere we are is simply laughable. Considering the Biblical context it is almost unworthy of even receiving rebuttal. However, to be biblically sure, notice 1 Corinthians 4.4. Paul said, "I am conscious of nothing against myself, yet I am not by this acquitted; but the one who examines me is the Lord." Paul explains we are not judged by our own standards but by God's. Jesus' point within the Sermon's context is when we hold people to standards higher than God's we will be held to higher standards. Further, when we seek to judge people rather than extend mercy to them, helping them be saved by God's grace, God will seek to judge us rather than extend mercy to us, saving us by His grace.

Discern good from evil. Judge when others are violating God's will. But do not do so as a means to wreak vengeance or punishment on others but as a means to know when to come alongside someone and help them grow in Christ.

Spiritual Ophthalmology

Jesus' picture in Matthew 7.3-5 is admittedly funny. It is a word picture equivalent of what we might find on the editorial page of any local newspaper lampooning the hypocrisy of the scribes and Pharisees. Can you imagine sitting in the doctor's chair, awaiting eye surgery? The nurse has already applied the local anesthetic and the doctor comes in. He is wearing robes with long tassels and a phylactery on his head. Out of his eye protrudes a six foot log. He can hardly enter the door. He is bumping equipment and can't even see to get his gloves on let alone do the surgery. That is Jesus' picture.

Performing this kind of surgery is dangerous. You are more likely to gouge out the other's eye than safely remove the splinter. The same is true spiritually. When your vision is unclear spiritually, you are not likely to perform this spiritual procedure with the gentleness requisite to the operation. You will end up doing more damage to the patient than he has already endured.

One mistake with this passage is to assume the speck represents a sin in our brother's life while the log represents the same sin in larger proportions in our own lives. While that would be included, the picture is not limited to that. The speck in the brother's eye is anything that is harmful to his vision. Think about the times you have gotten a speck in your eye. Think of the pain, the irritation, the inflammation and the hindrance to every walk of life. I remember once when a small bug flew into my eye while I was driving. If I hadn't been able to remove it quickly, I would have had to pull over. The speck in my eye hindered my ability to drive. In fact, I was probably only saved from wrecking by the fact that no other cars were near my swerving vehicle. The log is anything blocking our perception of the real issue. It may be our own sin. It may be our improper attitude and motivation. It may be our own arrogance and pride. It may be our preconceived notions about the person involved. It may be our lack of knowledge regarding the situation. It may be our lack of knowledge regarding the scripture. It may be our lack of prayer for God's strength and guidance. Anything impeding our ability to perceive the real problem regarding our brother's speck could be that log.

I don't think we should miss the connection between this verse and the passage we studied in Matthew 6.22-23. When the eye is clouded and blocked we are not the light of the world. Our body is darkness. Therefore our actions will not be right. That is why we must remove the log from our eye before we proceed to remove the speck from our brother's. If we are walking in darkness, we cannot be the light this brother needs to overcome his problem.

Having said all that, we must clearly point out that Jesus does intend for us to remove the speck from our brother's eye. We are not to leave our brother in that pained and detrimental situation. I remember a time when my family and I were sitting at the dining room table. Suddenly my daughter, Tessa, started screaming. She was grabbing at her eye and shaking her head. Something had gotten into her eye. Marita looked at me with a "Do something" plea in her face. What would you think of me if I had said, "I'm sorry. I can't do anything about that because I don't have my glasses," and then just turned back to my lunch? The obvious solution would be to get my glasses and do something about it. As ludicrous as my scenario is, allowing a brother with a spiritual speck in his eye to just go his own way is worse. That has eternal consequences. The obvious solution is to do whatever it takes to clear our vision, become the light of the world and then help our brother with his speck.

Too many Christians sit back being of little use to their brethren spiritually, always claiming they have things in their own life to take care of first. Jesus' command to us is to get those things taken care of so we can be of positive use in the kingdom, not constantly castigating people to hell but continually calling them back to God's path, bearing their burdens along the way.

The Counterbalance

For the first time in the Sermon, Jesus provides His own counterbalance. We have repeatedly pointed out that the Biblical context demonstrated Jesus' words should not be taken to their absolute and literal extreme. Jesus apparently felt His words about removing specks needed an immediate counterbalance.

While our goal is to help others remove the speck from their eye, we must recognize there are some who simply do not want any help. Even when our vision is completely clear, there are some who don't want us getting our helpful fingers near their eyes.

Call to mind the story I told you about Tessa on the previous page. I didn't actually make any silly excuses. In fact, I always wear my glasses. Instead, I immediately started trying to help. The problem was, she would not keep still. She smacked at my hand and shook her head. I grabbed her, picked her up and then pinned her on the sofa. I had Marita hold her arms and sit on her legs while I held her face. Forcing her eye open with one hand, I removed the speck with the other. In that fit, she didn't want any help. It was ok in this situation because I was an adult; she was a child. But imagine if she were a full-grown adult. At some point, in her pain over her eye, if I had kept attempting to help, she would have turned on me and in a blind rage harmed me.

This is Jesus' final picture in this scene. It is a picture of a man or woman who cannot appreciate the help we are offering. They are like wild dogs that could not care less whether the meat offered to them came from the garbage can or from the sacrificial altar. They are like pigs who might mistake a pearl for an acorn and upon discovering their mistake, in hungry rage, charge the one who gave them the useless pearls.

We are commanded to teach others with patience (2 Timothy 4.2). We are commanded to restore them with gentleness (Galatians 6.1). But with some, there will come a time when we must shake the dust from our feet and allow their condemnation to rest on their own heads (Luke 9.5; Acts 13.51; 18.6).

It does us no good to continually strive to help those who want no help. In fact, it only increases their ire and runs the risk of causing them to turn on us and do us damage. We are far better to move on to the next person. There comes a time when we must cut bait and try fishing in another spot.

This is a very serious decision to make and not one to be made lightly. In fact, it is a decision that is not offered much guidance in scripture. When must we, in fact, judge someone to be a swine or a dog and move elsewhere? I cannot fully say. I can say two things with certainty. First, we must not make that decision before we have tried. This is not a preconceived notion. We must attempt to remove the speck. If the person is unwilling to receive aid, we must move on. Second, this is not the same as a person who doesn't get the speck out on the first try. There is a difference between a person whose speck is deeply embedded needing a great deal of work to get it out and the person who violently rejects our aid.

As we make this judgment with multiple people, we will make mistakes at times. This, along with all matters of discernment and judgment, is a growth process. But, as we clear out our eyes and work with others on theirs, we will grow and God will use us to help people enter His kingdom.

Responding to the Sermon

What is your initial response to Jesus' teaching on judgment as presented in this chapter?

What logs have been in your own eye? What do you need to do to remove them?

Are there any specks in your brothers' or sisters' eyes that you know need to be removed? What can you do to help?

Meditating on the Sermon

By what standard of measure do you want God to judge you?

Why are you thankful for God's mercy? Meditate on these things today.

Praying the Sermon

Righteous Lord,

You are merciful. Your lovingkindness endures forever. I am amazed at Your grace, offered to me through Your Son. Through Him I am praying to You with awesome wonder. I deserve judgment in the severest way because I have turned from Your path of righteousness and have walked in the way of wickedness. Yet, You did not seek to judge me but to save me. Thank You for forgiving me and please continue to bless me with forgiveness.

Father, help me extend that same mercy to others. Do not allow me to seek vengeance. Do not allow me to think of myself as the standard. Do not allow me to want to see others judged. Rather, guide me in Your path of mercy and righteousness. Use me as a tool to draw others to Your forgiveness, even when they have sinned against me.

Please provide me with wisdom that I might know how to help those in spiritual need, knowing when to continue helping and knowing when to move on. Help me make that judgment with Your love, patience and instruction in mind. Help me do all things to Your glory.

I love You, Father, and I thank You for loving me.

Amen.

Our Loving Father:

Matthew 7.7-11

"Ask, and it will be given to you; seek, and you will find; knock, and it will be opened to you. For everyone who asks receives, and he who seeks finds, and to him who knocks it will be opened. Or what man is there among you who, when his son asks for a loaf, will give him a stone? Or if he asks for a fish, he will not give him a snake, will he? If you then, being evil, know how to give good gifts to your children, how much more will your Father who is in heaven give what is good to those who ask Him!"

No Blank Checks

"Ask, and it will be given to you: seek, and you will find; knock and it will be opened to you." This statement, or parts of it, have been so used and abused throughout our time they have become almost indelibly planted on our mind's eye separate from their context. Too many hear a blank check in this sentence. But Jesus did not intend that.

This is the second time Jesus has mentioned prayer in the Sermon. The first time we learned some very important points that provide context for this statement. We learned we are asking our Father who is in heaven. His heavenly residence, as taught by Ecclesiastes 5, means we are not merely to come into His presence with any old statement, request or otherwise, that pops into our mind. We must come thoughtfully and reverently. Further, we recognized His heavenly residence demonstrated He was beyond our power to manipulate, even via prayer. Prayer is not a magic lamp to be rubbed; God is not a genie under the control of whoever holds the lamp. He is God. He is in heaven. And He is not to be trifled with in prayer.

Further, Jesus' example of a request demonstrated there was no blank check. He said we should pray, "Forgive us our debts as we forgive our debtors." He then commented, "For if you forgive others for their transgressions, your heavenly Father will also forgive you. But if you do not forgive others, then your Father will not forgive your transgressions." There was no blank check with this request, there was a condition.

Finally, Jesus' introductory comments on prayer demonstrated God feels no obligation to respond to prayers of the self-righteous show-offs or the mindless rote repeaters. They have no blank check. Their prayers get no farther than the men in front of which they pray.

Beyond the context of the earlier teaching on prayer, there is a greater contextual issue within the Sermon itself. We notice the progression of asking, seeking and knocking. The careful student cannot help but notice he has already been brought through two steps of this progression. In Matthew 6.7 and the prayer that followed, we see asking. For what did Jesus teach us to ask? Daily bread. Forgiveness. Deliverance. We must not miss that we also ask for God's kingdom. In Matthew 6.33, we see seeking. For what do we seek? God's kingdom and righteousness. Of course, isn't that what the Sermon has been completely about? Getting into the kingdom.

The purpose of the Sermon was stated in Matthew 5.20: "For I say to you that unless your righteousness surpasses that of the scribes and Pharisees, you will not enter the kingdom of heaven." What is Jesus' audience most concerned with? Entering the kingdom. Of what do they need the most assurance? That they can, in fact, enter the kingdom.

Paul Earnhart said it well when he demonstrated a contrast between Matthew 7.1-5 and this section:

> If Matthew 7.1-5 is directed at those inclined to become kingdom Pharisees, this section is aimed at that far greater number who might despair before the demands of love. In their weakness and unworthiness, they see the lofty standards of the kingdom as unattainable. The Lord now makes clear that it is to just such hearts as long for righteousness out of a desperate necessity that the kingdom of heaven yields itself. It is not a kingdom for the deserving, but for the desiring—a kingdom for the asking.[17]

---

17. Earnhart, p. 124.

In the context of the Sermon, we see this prayer on three levels. First, we ask for the kingdom, not that we ask for the kingdom to be established in the earth, but in our hearts. This is asking that we be part of the kingdom and that God rule in our hearts with His righteousness. This is asking for His kingdom righteousness and all we have learned goes along with it throughout the Sermon.

Second, we ask for the strength to fulfill the teaching about the kingdom righteousness. As in the model prayer, we ask not to be led into temptation. The meaning of that statement is that we be led in the paths of righteousness. Whether that guidance takes us between cresting waves of the Red Sea or through the valley of the shadow of death, we will not fear, but will simply ask God to give us the strength to accomplish what He has required. We ask Him to help us in our poverty of spirit, our mourning, our gentleness and our hungering and thirsting for righteousness.

Third, we ask for protection. Again, we note the model prayer and the request to be delivered from evil. There is an enemy of Christ's kingdom and he will attack us. The devil is prowling about like a roaring lion, seeking whom he may devour (1 Peter 5.8). We learned early on that despite the great quality and character of the kingdom citizen, the world's response will often be persecution. Jesus' life, above all others, demonstrated this. There is only One who can deliver us and protect us, preserving us by His power for the reward He has promised. We must ask Him.

Jesus is not offering a blank check here. He is offering us a key to His kingdom. All we must do is ask, seek and knock. He will give us the kingdom and all the good that goes with it.

Ask...Seek...Knock

I cannot help but think there must be some significance to this progression, especially since Jesus had already started us down this path in the Sermon's context and here He stated it twice. I am further motivated to see this progression since we are now pushed to a new level of knocking.

Each of these words in vs. 7 is in the present imperative. That is, they are commands we are to follow right now. However, in a few moments, the commands will be as imperative as they are right now. Thus, this verse demonstrates a continual action. Jesus is not teaching us a one time action. "Ask once and you will receive the kingdom. Seek today and you will have the kingdom forever. Knock tonight and you will enter and never leave the kingdom." This is about a lifestyle of asking, seeking and knocking. Our lives are to be completely and totally governed by the hunt for God's righteousness.

The progression from ask to seek to knock is a progression on multiple levels. It is a progression of activity. It is a progression of intensity. It is a progression of desperation.

The asker hardly moves. He can remain in one place as he calls forth his request to the God of heaven. However, the seeker cannot remain in one place. He actively looks for the kingdom as the woman who lost her coin searched for it (Luke 15.8). The knocker has found something, but the door is closed. Instead of turning away to seek another opening, he pounds on the door seeking entrance. We see an increase in activity. For those who suggest all a person has to do is offer the Sinner's Prayer and be admitted to the kingdom, Jesus' words here are devastating. It takes more than words. It takes action.

The asker prays and, no doubt, prays fervently. But the asking is not enough. He knows God will give Him his request, but He must seek it out. He moves about asking and seeking. He runs to and fro searching with a deep hunger for the kingdom and righteousness of God. He sees the kingdom of God, like a city set on a hill, and climbing up to it he bangs on the gate pleading for entrance. We see an increase in intensity in the one who desires the kingdom.

The asker hopes his request will be granted. Yet, there is a sense in which it is not, else there would be no progression to seeking. One does not have to seek what he already has. He has asked and it is almost as if God has said, "Hmmm. Let's see. How desperately do you desire it? I will give it to you, but you must find it." The seeker rises from his knees and starts to search. Like the woman for her lost coin and the shepherd for his lost sheep, the seeker combs every corner, saying to himself over and over again, "I have to find it," crying out to God, "Let me find it." He finds it, but the door is closed. Will he leave it there believing his search has been in vain? No he grabs the door handle, shaking it, knocking, pounding on the door pleading, "Let me in, let me in. Please, let me in." We see an increase in desperation from the one who hungers and thirsts for God's kingdom and righteousness so much that he will stop at nothing to be satisfied.

We must not lose sight that this is still part of the surpassing righteousness. I cannot help but think of John 7.32-39. Read the entire section and see how it contrasts the scribes and Pharisees with what is taught here and throughout the Sermon:

> The Pharisees heard the crowd muttering these things about Him, and the chief priests and the Pharisees sent officers to seize Him. Therefore Jesus said, "For a little while longer I am with you, then I go to Him who sent me. You will seek Me, and will not find Me; and where I am, you cannot come." The Jews then

said to one another, "Where does this man intend to go that we will not find Him? He is not intending to go to the Dispersion among the Greeks, and teach the Greeks, is He? What is this statement that He said, 'You will seek Me, and will not find Me; and where I am, you cannot come'?"

Now on the last day, the great day of the feast, Jesus stood and cried out, saying, "If anyone is thirsty, let him come to Me and drink. He who believes in Me, as the Scripture said, 'From his innermost being will flow rivers of living water.'" But this He spoke of the Spirit, whom those who believe in Him were to receive; for the Spirit was not given, because Jesus was not yet glorified.

I don't want to get too sidetracked regarding the giving of the Spirit. The full discussion of all that meant is beyond the scope of this book. However, I think it bears noting that where Matthew said the Father will give good to those who ask Him, Luke wrote, "How much more will your heavenly Father give the Holy Spirit to those who ask Him?" (Luke 11.13).

Do you see the contrasts? The Pharisees are not thirsting, therefore they will seek but not find. But those who humbly come to Jesus, hungering and thirsting (asking, seeking and knocking) for His kingdom and righteousness will receive, will find and will be allowed to enter.

In Matthew 13, after Jesus taught the Parable of the Sower, the disciples asked why Jesus spoke in parables. He said it had been granted to the disciples to know the secrets but to the others it had not been granted. He said, "I speak to them in parables; because while seeing they do not see, and while hearing they do not hear" (Matthew 13.13). What was the difference between the ones who saw and heard and the ones who didn't? The former asked. They sought out Jesus. When the meaning seemed closed to them, they knocked.

If our righteousness will surpass that of the scribes and Pharisees, we have to ask, seek and knock because we are desperately, intensely hungering and thirsting for His kingdom and righteousness.

Of Fish and Serpents

Jesus once again supports His contention with an illustration. Who among us would give our children stones when they asked for bread? Who would give them snakes when they asked for fish? If we who are evil know how to give good gifts, how much more does our heavenly Father, in whom there is no variation or shifting shadow, know how to give good gifts to His children?

We must not read into this statement the Calvinism so many authors want to find. He called His audience "evil" but did not say how they came to be that way. He could call us all "evil" without stating how that happened. It is an assumption our Calvinist friends make to find any passage that calls people evil and assume it meant they were born that way. We know from passages such as Romans 3.12 that we have all become evil because we have turned aside. Romans 5.12 teaches death spread to all men because all sinned. This audience is not evil because they were born that way. They were evil because they had sinned. But that was already established when Jesus began His Sermon teaching we must be the mournful poor in spirit.

Here is Jesus' point. In contrast with the Pharisees, who are constantly looking for ways to judge and condemn, our Father wants to bless us with the good things of His kingdom and with the good things it takes to be part of His kingdom. However, He will not force these blessings upon us. We have to ask.

Please notice very carefully, Jesus did not say God gives good things to those who are worthy. He did not say God gives good things to those who need it. He did not say God gives good things to those who deserve it. He did say God gives good things to those who ask. How many of God's good gifts have gone unopened because His children did not ask.

As we read the Sermon, we may get discouraged thinking we just can't make it. We will never measure up. God is saying all we have to do is ask. This Sermon is not about those who measure up by their own strength and righteousness. It is about those who by faith in Jesus Christ ask, seek and knock for the kingdom and righteousness of God. 2 Peter 1.3 says God has given us everything pertaining to life and godliness through the knowledge of Jesus Christ. Romans 8.32 promises us, "He who did not spare His own Son, but delivered Him over for us all, how will He not also with Him freely give us all things?" The point is, just as God has promised to take care of us physically if we seek first His kingdom and righteousness, He has promised to take care of us spiritually if we ask, seek and knock. He has promised to do that and we can trust Him to follow through.

When we ask for loaves, He will not give us stones. When we ask for fish, He will not give us serpents. When we ask, seek and knock to be part of His kingdom and have His righteousness, He will not hand us over to the kingdom of the serpent of old. He will bring us into His kingdom.

Further, at times we may ask for stones and serpents and not realize it. We are not wise as God is. We cannot see all ends. Like children who ask to eat candy instead of vegetables, we sometimes ask for what is not good for us. In those moments when we ask for stones and serpents, God will give us loaves and bread anyway. Consider Paul's request in 2 Corinthians 12.7-10. Three times he asked for a serpent without knowing it when he asked for his thorn in the flesh to be removed. But God knew that thorn was actually protecting Paul, keeping him from arrogance and pride. Had God granted Paul's request, who knows what would have happened to his soul. However, God gave him the fish, leaving the thorn in place, forcing him to rely on God's grace. At times the fish may seem like a serpent, but we have to trust God. When we ask, seek and knock, He will give us the bread and fish.

What a great and loving Father we serve. Aren't we glad He is no Pharisee? Aren't we glad He cares and wants to care for us? Aren't we glad He will provide His kingdom when we ask?

Responding to the Sermon

What is your initial response to Jesus' teaching on the Father's love as presented in this chapter?

What issues have been hindering you in your quest for God's kingdom and righteousness? Ask God to help you with these.

What can you do to seek and knock for God's kingdom and righteousness regarding the issues you listed above?

Meditating on the Sermon

What are the blessings God has given us through the knowledge of Jesus Christ?

What will our lives look like when we are asking, seeking and knocking for God's kingdom and righteousness? Meditate on these things today.

Praying the Sermon

Loving Father,

Thank You. Thank You for loving me. Thank You for responding to my requests. Thank You for granting my requests. Thank You for denying my requests when they need to be denied. Thank You for bringing me into Your kingdom. Please, rule in my heart.

Father, I want to be in Your kingdom so badly. I want Your kingdom to be in my heart. Rule over my life. Take my cares and concerns. Take my wants and wishes. Take my desires and dreams. Mold them into Your desires. Make of me the servant You want. Use me in Your kingdom in whatever way You see fit.

Strengthen me in righteousness and lead me in Your paths. Guard me from the tempter and help me hold my shield of faith against His attacks. Lead me through the persecution and trials I will face and bring me into Your heavenly abode in the end.

I love You, Father, and I thank You for loving me.

Through Jesus I pray,

Amen.

The Golden Rule:

Matthew 7.12

"In everything, therefore, treat people the same way you want them to treat you, for this is the Law and the Prophets."

Summing Up

Admittedly, on the surface, this statement, though profound and deep, seems to be just thrown into the mix of the Sermon's conclusion. However, the use of "therefore" denotes some kind of connection with what has preceded it.

D. Martin Lloyd Jones suggests it connects back to Christ's teaching on judgment in Matthew 7.1-5. Thus saying, if we wish to judge others properly we can follow the practical rule of treating them as we want to be treated. Paul Earnhart suggests it is the logical follow through of Matthew 7.6-11. As God treats His children, we ought to treat others. He gives good gifts and we ought to give good gifts, treating others the way we want to be treated. Both make decent arguments. In fact, when reading both, we see the Golden Rule fits in both places.

I believe, however, instead of trying to simply make a direct connection back to the most recent statements in the Sermon, we should see this is a summary of the entire treatise. The reason the Golden Rule can so naturally flow from both sections in this final chapter is because it naturally flows from every part of the Sermon.

As stated in the last chapter, Earnhart has demonstrated a magnificent structure between Jesus' section on judgment and His section on the Father's love and gifts. The first section warned those kingdom citizens who would have tendency toward Pharisaic application of the kingdom principles. The second section flowed to those who might be paralyzed by fear that they cannot fulfill the kingdom principles. This Golden Rule summarizes those kingdom principles, providing a very practical rule of thumb for how to live up to the standards of the entire Sermon—treat others how you want to be treated.

The "therefore" of the Golden Rule links back to the Beatitudes. We sinned. We are destitute. We blow it all the time in our relationship with God and in our relationship with God's creation. Therefore, we are poor in spirit, mourning our condition, meekly submitting to God and before others, hungering and thirsting for righteousness. As we look around at those who have sinned against us, we do not see enemies. We see people in our same boat. We see people just like us. Therefore we treat them the way we want to be treated. We treat them with mercy striving to be peacemakers with them. That is how we want them to treat us.

The "therefore" of the Golden Rule links back to the principles of salt and light. Do we want people to hide the straight and narrow way from us? Do we want them to simply become just like us or hide the truth from us so we continue to wallow in our own sinful misery? Of course not. We want their salt and light. We want their help along the path of righteousness. Therefore, we strive to be the salt and light in our world to help others come to God's kingdom and righteousness.

The "therefore" of the Golden Rule links back to Jesus' "you have heard…but I say to you" statements. When we have messed up and angered people, do we want them to call us names, hating us and plotting evil against us even if it falls short of murder? Of course not. We want them to come to us, helping us overcome the tempter and forgiving us. Therefore, we do the same for them. When someone has sinned against us, do we want them to hang on to their sin, putting up a barrier between us? Of course not. We want them to apologize and make things right. Therefore, when we have sinned against others, we do not let the sun go down on the problem. Instead we go to them and reconcile quickly.

Do we want others coveting our wives or husbands, lusting after them? Of course not. Therefore we do not covet the husbands and wives of our neighbors. Do we want our spouse to lay a stumbling block before us, sending us out into the world even if it is with a certificate of divorce? Of course not. Therefore we do not do the same to our spouse, but strive to make our marriage work. Do we want others laying a stumbling block before us sending their spouse out into the world causing those who might marry the divorced spouse to commit adultery? Of course not. Therefore, we do not lay that stumbling block.

Do we want people to lie to us because they developed an elaborate system of verbal finger crossing? Of course not. We want them to tell us the truth and honor their commitments no matter how they were verbalized. Therefore, our yes means yes and our no means no.

Do we want people to take advantage of us or retaliate whenever we have messed up and done something wrong? Of course not. Therefore, we bend over backwards to endure the wrong ourselves instead of retaliating against others.

Do we want people to hate us because we are the enemy? …because we are a different nationality, skin color, socio-economic class or because we have messed up in the past against them? Of course not. We want them to love us, seeking our best interests even when we have not always sought theirs. Therefore, we treat them in the same way, loving them, doing good for them at all times.

As Jones demonstrates, the "therefore" of the Golden Rule links back to Jesus' teaching on judgment. Do we want people to judge us hypercritically and hypocritically? Do we want them to take every opportunity to castigate us into hell? Of course not. We want them to seek our eternal welfare, trying to be a help in removing the speck in our eye and not a hindrance because of the log in their own. We want them to extend mercy, helping us, not to extend judgment cutting us loose and letting us go into God's judgment. Therefore, we treat others with mercy, striving to help them overcome instead of merely judging them as awful sinners worthy of hell.

As Earnhart demonstrates, the "therefore" of the Golden Rule most definitely links back to Jesus' teaching on our Father's love. Do we want to receive stones and serpents from our Father or anyone for that matter? Of course not. We want the good gifts of loaves and fish. Therefore, we strive to give those good gifts to others as well.

When we fear that we cannot actually live up to the deep theological teaching of the Sermon and we wonder exactly how a particular principle applies to real life, we can follow this practical rule of thumb. However we want others to treat us. We should treat them.

Love

We most certainly recognize the link between Jesus' Golden Rule and the overarching principle of agape love. First and foremost, we recognize Jesus taught this same principle in different contexts. When Luke presented this statement (Luke 6.31), he did so in the context of teaching on love for our enemies. Secondly, Jesus' statement that this Golden Rule is "the Law and the Prophets" correlates with Matthew 22.34-40. There, Jesus explained the two laws of love. Love God with your all and love your neighbor as yourself together make the lynch pin on which all the Law and the Prophets hung. Jesus' teaching on love might be viewed as the more doctrinal approach. This Golden Rule is the practical approach. It is almost as if we have the following exchange.

"You are to love your neighbor as yourself and even love your enemies," teaches Jesus.

"That is deep. But how do we do it?" we reply.

"Treat them the way you want to be treated. That is the essence of loving others," Jesus responds.

No doubt, Jesus progressed from teaching to explaining in practical hands on terms to exemplifying that love. As I write this chapter, I am conducting a Gospel meeting in west Tennessee. The local preacher's son has graciously lent me his room and bed while he has been sleeping out on the couch in the den. Every time I walk into his room, I glance at the wall to the left of the door. There hangs a plaque I have seen in numerous places. It reads:

"Jesus," I asked, "how much do You love me?"

"This much," He said.

And He stretched out His arms and died.

Isn't that how we want people to treat us? Sacrificing themselves for us and our benefit, especially our eternal benefit? Of course it is. How then should we treat them?

On the surface, the Golden rule seems to be merely about our relationship with other people. However, in the Biblical context we learn it is very much about our relationship with God. The reality is, we cannot have real love for the people around us if we are not firmly anchored with real love for God. 1 John 5.1-3 says:

> Whoever believes that Jesus is the Christ is born of God, and whoever loves the Father loves the child born of Him. By this we know that we love the children of God, when we love God and observe his commandments. For this is the love of God, that we keep His commandments; and His commandments are not burdensome.

Consider the practical example of the Macedonians demonstrated in 2 Corinthians 8. Paul told the Corinthians that the Macedonians not only gave to help their brethren in Judea based on what they had, but even beyond their means. How were they able to do this? 1 Corinthians 8.5 says, "They first gave themselves to the Lord." Consider also the example of Lydia in Acts 16. Immediately after her conversion she offered the hospitality of her home to Paul and Barnabas. Why was she so generous? In Acts 16.15, she said, "If you have judged me to be faithful to the Lord, come into my house and stay." She was generous to Paul and Barnabas because she was first faithful to the Lord.

The anchor, therefore, to treating others the way we want to be treated is to love God. Of course, to have this love for God, we must realize how much He has loved us. 1 John 4.19 says, "We love, because He first loved us." When we learn and increase our faith in God's love for us, how can we not love Him in return? Further, how can we not love those around us no matter how they have dealt with us? When we realize God's love came to us while we were sinners, in rebellion, doing all we could to hurt God, how can we not be moved to show the same love to others even when they hurt us? How can we, with that realization, set ourselves up as somehow special people having the right to withhold our love from other people who have done exactly as we have done?

We will follow the Golden Rule to the extent that we increase our faith in God's love for us. How could we not?

Tarnishing the Golden Rule

Everyone admits this rule is Golden. It is praised by nearly all cultures. I am told nearly every moral teaching of history contains statements similar to Jesus' rule, though few actually reach its height and depth of love. Yet, we look around us and see nearly no one lives by this rule they applaud. Why?

The number one reason is selfishness. The opposite of loving our neighbor is not hating our neighbor. The opposite of love is selfishness. It is hard to love our neighbors as ourselves when we are too busy loving ourselves.

We subconsciously worry that if we spend all our time loving our neighbors as ourselves, who is going to love us? If we spend all our time treating others the way we want to be treated, who is going to treat us the way we want to be treated? We especially wonder if we love our enemies as ourselves and treat them the way we want to be treated, what incentive are we giving them to treat us any better than they have treated us?

With that mindset, we always have plans to love our neighbors and our enemies. But first, we have to take care of ourselves. We have to get our own first, preserve ourselves first, provide for us first. Once we have safely lavished upon ourselves all the love we need, then we can venture out into the world of vulnerability that is loving others.

But we have to ask this question. Is that how we want others to treat us? Do we want them to withhold their love for us until their love tank has been filled? Of course not. How then should we treat them?

Philippians 2.3-4 demonstrates the mindset we should have. We are to do nothing from selfishness. Instead of looking out for our own personal interests, we should look out for the interests of others. We should view them as more important than ourselves. That is, they are worthy of receiving our love before we bestow love on ourselves. In fact, they are worthy of receiving our love even before they have bestowed their love on us. As Paul goes on to explain in Philippians 2, that is exactly how Jesus treated us. Didn't He bestow His love on us while we were still focusing our love on ourselves? We must strive to be like Him.

However, there is still that part of us that wants to hold out. "What about me," we cry. "When do I get mine?" At this point, we see how the "therefore" of the Golden Rule links back to Jesus' teaching on secret service. When we act as God wants us to without regard to how other men will reward us, then the Father will reward us. His rewards are far greater than any reward men would grant us or any reward we might pour out on ourselves. Be patient. The Father will reward us and it will have been worth it.

Improving the Golden Rule

In modern business literature, the new catch phrase is "the Platinum Rule." We must keep in mind, of course, that Jesus did not name Matthew 7.12 the Golden Rule. Man has done that. It does seem appropriate because it is one of the most valuable rules in scripture. Yet men today believe they have figured out how to improve on Jesus' teaching and they have dubbed this improvement the Platinum Rule.

If the Golden Rule is to treat others the way we want to be treated, the Platinum rule is to treat others the way they want to be treated. On the surface, this sounds as though modern men have been wiser than Jesus. Yet, all this does is demonstrate modern man's arrogance and ignorance. Modern man is ignorant of how deep Jesus' statement really is.

After all, in the context of the Sermon, this rule is not a rule that says, "What would I want for my birthday? Well that is what I will get my wife for hers." My wife wants the car detailed for her birthday. If she did that for me, I would be highly disappointed. But that is not what Jesus is talking about.

What do I want people to most do for me? I want them to get into my shoes. I want them to understand where I have been and where I am. I want them to consider what my personal desires really are. Then I want them to treat me that way. How should I treat them? Not with some simplistic approach to the Golden Rule. I should strive to enter their shoes. I should strive to empathize with them. Where have they been? What are they enduring? What do they most need and want right now? Then I can treat them the way I want to be treated.

There is another principle we must keep in mind that demonstrates the Platinum Rule is no improvement on Jesus' Golden Rule. It is very similar to our final point regarding the Father's love for us. Remember that we learned we sometimes do not know what is best for us. At times, we think we are asking for loaves and fish when really we are asking for stones and serpents. In the moment, we have a hard time really knowing how we want to be treated. However, intellectually, we very much realize that when our deepest desire is actually a stone or a serpent, we really want people to give us the loaf or the fish. In the long run we will appreciate it.

How then should we treat others? At times, they want a stone or a serpent. Should we give it to them because that is what they want? Of course not. We know in the long run they will appreciate receiving the loaf or fish, even if they do not appreciate it now. We do not simply hand over what other people want just because that is how they want to be treated. We think in the big picture and do what is best for them, because that is exactly how we would want people to treat us.

How do we want people to treat us? Treat them in the same way and we will fulfill this Sermon.

Responding to the Sermon

What is your initial reaction to Jesus' Golden Rule as taught in this chapter?

What are some practical situations in which you can see the need to apply this rule? How will you apply it?

What obstacles make this rule hard to apply? How can you overcome them?

Meditating on the Sermon

How do you want others to treat you?

How has the Father treated you? Meditate on these things today.

Praying the Sermon

Gracious Father,

Thank You. You have treated me so well even while I was Your enemy. Though I was in sin and rebellion, walking according to the path of the enemy, You sent Jesus to die for my sins. Though I continued to rebel against Your Son's sacrifice, You patiently waited, giving me time to repent. Thank You. Please continue to offer Your forgiveness as I stumble along the path.

Father, help me treat others as You have treated me. Help me treat others the way I want them to treat me. Strengthen me to be a merciful peacemaker. Strengthen me to suffer wrong with graciousness wanting the wrongdoer to be forgiven. Help me grow through all I endure to be more and more like You.

Forgive me, I have been selfish. I have sought to provide my own reward. I have sought to love myself first, withholding my love for others until it would come more naturally because I felt my needs were met. Help me love even my enemies, treating them as I want them to treat me.

I love You, Father, and I thank You for loving me.

Through Your Son's love and grace I pray,

Amen.

Choices:

Matthew 7.13-23

"Enter through the narrow gate; for the gate is wide and the way is broad that leads to destruction, and there are many who enter through it. For the gate is small and the way is narrow that leads to life, and there are few who find it.

"Beware of the false prophets, who come to you in sheep's clothing, but inwardly are ravenous wolves. You will know them by their fruits. Grapes are not gathered from thorn bushes nor figs from thistles, are they? So every good tree bears good fruit, but the bad tree bears bad fruit. A good tree cannot produce bad fruit, nor can a bad tree produce good fruit. Every tree that does not bear good fruit is cut down and thrown into the fire. So then, you will know them by their fruits.

"Not everyone who says to me, 'Lord, Lord,' will enter the kingdom of heaven, but he who does the will of My Father who is in heaven will enter. Many will say to me on that day, 'Lord, Lord, did we not prophesy in Your name, and in Your name cast out demons, and in Your name perform many miracles?' And then I will declare to them, 'I never knew you; depart from Me, you who practice lawlessness.'"

The Take Away

We have heard a lot of teaching in this brief Sermon. Jesus has talked about everything from how to be saved to anger management to morality to proper relationships and on we could go. At this point, our heads are spinning.

Jesus now comes to the final wrap up. As all good public speakers know, one rarely speaks just to speak. With few exceptions public speaking is almost always persuasive speaking. Some few presentations are meant merely to entertain. Some are meant only to inform. But even in those cases, the speaker can rarely leave the platform without trying to persuade the audience to something. The speaker wants to affect some action in the audience. Either the speaker wants to change the audience's opinion, to get the audience to support something or get the audience to take some action. Jesus is no different.

He wraps up His Sermon explaining everything He has taught has been about the ultimate choice. Which path will His audience take? Whose lessons will His audience follow? Whose teaching will His audience trust? Upon what foundation will His audience build? This entire Sermon has been intended to persuade us to make the proper choice.

We have already learned in Chapter 2 about the two foundations. Hopefully, we have followed the directions we learned there throughout this entire period of study, using the Sermon as a foundation upon which to build our lives, digging out the dirt and muck, getting to the bedrock. It has taken work, but it will be worth it when the storms come.

These concluding paragraphs call to mind the choice Moses laid before the Israelites in Deuteronomy 30.15-20:

> See, I have set before you today life and prosperity, and death and adversity; in that I command you today to love the Lord your God, to walk in His ways and to keep His commandments and His statutes and His judgments, that you may live and multiply, and that the Lord your God may bless you in the land where you are entering to possess it. But if your heart turns away and you will not obey, but are drawn away and worship other gods and serve them, I declare to you today that you shall surely perish. You will not prolong your days in the land where you are crossing the Jordan to enter and possess it. I call heaven and earth to witness against you today, that I have set before you life and death, the blessing and the curse. So choose life in order that you may live, you and your descendants, by loving the lord your God, by obeying his voice and by holding fast to Him; for this is your life and the length of your days, that you may live in the land which the Lord swore to your fathers, to Abraham, Isaac, and Jacob, to give them.

The choice is ours. We can pursue life or we can pursue death. We can follow Jesus or we can follow the heralds of the broad way, the false prophets. We can trust God or we can trust ourselves. Will we let Jesus be our Lord or not? Will we obey His Sermon or not?

Gates and Ways

Just the other day, I saw a young lady wearing a shirt imprinted with the following statement: "There are three kinds of people in the world. Those who can count and those who can't." It took me a moment to process that. How many statements have we heard dividing the world into two kinds of people? I have even heard someone say, "There are two kinds of people in the world. Those who divide people into two kinds and those who don't."

Jesus is one of those who divide people into two kinds. You may remember He said, "He who is not with me is against me; and he who does not gather with Me scatters" (Matthew 12.30). Jesus certainly spoke in extremes. He saw no middle ground.

As He wrapped up this period of teaching He again spoke of stark contrasts. He explained there were only two gates, two ways, two crowds and two goals. No more and no less. No matter what we do we are walking through one of those two gates, on one of those two ways, with one of those two crowds, heading for one of those two goals.

The two gates are the narrow gate and the wide gate. We have asked for the gate to the kingdom. We have sought for it. We have knocked on it. Now that the gate is opened to us, we peer through and see it is not an easy passage. We cannot take anything with us but must leave everything that was gain to us behind. The second gate is wide. There is limitless space to carry along with us all that we want, our pride, arrogance, sin, selfishness, self-righteousness. We have no trouble entering through the wide gate. It is natural.

The narrow gate, no doubt, is the great Shepherd, Jesus. He is the door for the sheep; through Him we may enter and be saved (John 10.19). There is no other door to good pasture and salvation. Are we willing to shed all and enter through the blood of Jesus Christ? Once again, Jesus' picture sets modern religion on its head. Most today picture Jesus as the wide door, allowing any and all through Him. But Jesus Himself said His door was narrow. Only few find it and fewer still walk through it.

The two ways are the narrow or difficult way and the broad way. According to Vine's Expository Dictionary, the word translated "narrow" by the NASU in Matthew 7.14 refers to suffering and affliction. The way that leads on from the small gate is a way of trouble. It is not a rose garden path. Paul encouraged the churches he established saying, "Through many tribulations we must enter the kingdom of God" (Acts 14.22). The narrow road has only way. We can walk straight down that way, one foot after another. We cannot stall lest we get in the way of other travelers. We cannot linger. We push on ahead single file, shouting encouragement to one another, but not straying from the path lest we fall into the deadly ravines on either side. The other way is broad. It is spacious. There is room to wander how we want. There is room to stop and linger. We will not get in anyone's way and no one will get in ours. Picture in your mind a wide path and see people traveling upon it. They can walk down the right side. They can walk down the left. They can zigzag back and forth.

Sadly, today many people look at all the religious division and say, "We are all going to the same place, just walking different paths." You tell me. Jesus established the picture for the two possible roads. Which one is the way with people taking different paths but winding up in the same place?

The broad path is a way of tolerance and eclecticism. It is broad enough for all the ecumenical who believe sincerity is the most important trait of God's children. It is a way of situational ethics and self-government. The only thing for which the broad way has no room is offering righteous judgment. There is no room on the broad path for suggesting someone is going the wrong way. The narrow way, like the door, is Jesus Christ Himself. He is the way, the truth and the life (John 14.6). His way has been described in this Sermon. It is not a way of doing whatever we want. It is a way of self-control, seeking the will of God and what benefits others.

The two crowds are the many and the few. The strait and narrow way of Jesus Christ is a lonely road. We will not have a great deal of company along it. We will, no doubt, be able to see the broad way. We will see the easy time of the large crowds milling about on the wide path. No doubt, they will see us and will make our way even more difficult. They will invite us to join them. They will mock us for traveling such a difficult road. They will discuss how popular their choice has been. Though we look around us and see few other travelers on the narrow path, we must realize we are never alone. God is with us, having promised to never forsake us (Hebrews 13.5).

The two goals are life and destruction. What a contrast. The broad and easy way leads ultimately to the greatest of suffering. We must not follow the crowds like lemmings into the pit of despair. Rather, we must follow Jesus through pain and suffering to joy eternal. The narrow road is hard but the goal is worth it.

Here is the point. If our Christianity is rather easy, if the most difficult part about it is making sure to "get to church" regularly, we are probably not on Jesus' way, no matter what kind of congregation we work with. Granted, we must not assume because we have developed all manner of hoops through which to jump we are on Jesus' way. Some on the broad way have developed their own brand of ascetic religion filled with all kinds of self-denial. It looks good to man, but it is of no benefit for godliness and against the indulgence of the flesh (Colossians 2.20-23). However, if the service is easy and the grace is cheap, we are not on Christ's path.

Which gate will we enter? Which path will we walk? With which crowd will we run? Which goal will we attain? The choice is ours.

The Heralds of the Broad Way

Jesus and His Sermon shine as beacons of light, pointing to the narrow gate, lighting the broad way, leading the few on to the goal of life. However, there are other lights shining. There are other heralds. They speak of an easier way. They come alongside us, looking like one of us, whispering in our ear that what we are doing is too hard. Surely God would not expect this of us. Their father is the serpent of old who lured Eve away from the path of righteousness by merely adding one word to the word of God. "You surely will *not* die!" (Genesis 3.4).

Their path looks easy because it does not contain persecution. When we learned about persecution on Jesus' straight and narrow path, we noted the fathers persecuted the prophets of God. In Luke's rendition of the beatitudes he also said, "Woe to you when all men speak well of you, for their fathers used to treat the false prophets in the same way" (Luke 6.26).

According to 2 Peter 2, the way of the false prophets and false teachers appears good because it is sensual. That is, it appeals to our senses. It appeals to what comes naturally to us as we pursue the desires of our flesh. They are greedy and trained by covetousness. They appeal to the greed of others turning them from Christ's path. They promise freedom but are themselves enslaved by their own passions.

We must not follow the heraldry of the false prophets and teachers. If we do, we will be like the pigs wallowing in the mire after being cleaned and like the dogs who return to eat their own vomit. Sadly, we will not even realize how miserable we are.

How can we tell the false prophets (teachers) from the true? We can test them by their fruit. This can be seen twofold. We know the fruit that comes from walking on Jesus' narrow way. It is described in Galatians 5.22-23. "The fruit of the Spirit is love, joy, peace, patience, kindness, goodness, faithfulness, gentleness, self-control; against such things there is no law." Jesus revealed a second aspect of this root and fruit test when He applied the same metaphor in a different context in Matthew 12.33-37. He said, "Either make the tree good and its fruit good, or make the tree bad and its fruit bad; for the tree is known by its fruit. You brood of vipers, how can you, being evil, speak what is good?" The twofold test of the false prophet (teacher) is the fruit of his actions and the fruit of his words. Do his actions and the logical conclusion of his teaching bear the fruit of the Spirit? Do His words compare with those of Jesus? If he fails in either case you can know him as a wolf in sheep's clothing.

This is reminiscent of the twofold test God provided for Israel to find false prophets. In Deuteronomy 18.22, God provided one test. If a prophet spoke something, saying it was in the name of the Lord, and it did not come to pass, then the prophet spoke presumptuously. He was a false prophet and the people did not need to fear him or his warnings. However, in Deuteronomy 13.1-4, God provided another test. If a prophet spoke something that did come to pass and used that event to try to turn the people from what God had spoken, they were not to follow the prophet then either. He was false.

There will be many heralds trying to turn us from the message Jesus preached in His Sermon. However, their path only ends in destruction. They are ravenous wolves no matter how docile they seem. If we swallow their bad fruit, it will poison us form the inside.

Lord, Lord

We commented on Matthew 7.21-23 in Chapter 2. However, we cannot end this study without examining it again, if only briefly.

We have a choice. Will we make Jesus the Lord of our life or not. It is not enough to say Jesus is our Lord. It is not enough to say Jesus is our Lord and behave religiously. It is not enough to say Jesus is our Lord and believe we have done some amazing things.

Jesus is our Lord when we do what He says. Luke 6.46 says, "Why do you call Me, 'Lord, Lord,' and do not do what I say?" If we corrupt our salt or hide our light, Jesus is not our Lord. If we turn from His commandments and teach others to do the same, He is not our Lord. If we call our brothers "Fool," He is not our Lord. If we sin against our brother and do nothing about it, He is not our Lord. If we lust after our neighbor's spouse or send our own spouse away (except for the cause of unchastity), He is not our Lord. If we lie and do not follow through on our commitments, He is not our Lord. If we seek retaliation and revenge instead of suffering the hurt, He is not our Lord. If we love our neighbors but hate our enemies, He is not our Lord. If we seek the praises of men, He is not our Lord. If we judge hypocritically and hypercritically, He is not our Lord. If we despise others, looking out for our own selfish ends, He is not our Lord.

Jesus is our Lord when we do what He says. He is our Lord when we hunger and thirst for righteousness. He is our Lord when we are merciful. He is our Lord when we are pure in heart. He is our Lord when we are peacemakers. He is our Lord when we endure persecution with joy. He is our Lord when our righteousness surpasses that of the scribes and Pharisees. He is our Lord when we allow our light to shine as a city set on a hill. He is our Lord when we seek first His kingdom and righteousness. He is our Lord when we ask, seek and knock. He is our Lord when we follow the strait and narrow way.

We must not think we can pick and choose. We must not think we are alright because we have seemingly done some pretty impressive things religiously. We must seek to follow the Father's will. I am amazed at these people mentioned in Matthew 7.21-23. They were so convinced they were right with God, they were willing to argue with Jesus Himself. Yet, Jesus said He had never known them. Despite their religion, they had followed lawlessness. They were not kingdom citizens. They had not asked, sought or knocked. They had followed their own broad path and they had come up short. We must not let that be us.

The Sermon is ours. It sets before us life and destruction. Which will we choose?

Responding to the Sermon

What is your initial response to the choices Jesus offered as presented in this chapter?

What are the obstacles to walking on the narrow path? How can you overcome those?

On what path have you been walking? Do you need to make any course corrections? If so, what changes do you need to make?

Meditating on the Sermon

Describe in practical terms the broad way and the narrow way?

Describe in descriptive and practical terms the goal of the broad and narrow ways (don't just say hell and heaven). Meditate on these things today.

Praying the Sermon

Father in heaven,

Forgive me. I have sinned. I have entered the wide gate and followed the broad path too often. I have pursued the course of my own fleshly desires, producing rotten fruit. Cleanse me and make me whole. Purify me and make me sound.

Strengthen me to pursue the difficult way. Help me know You are with me when I feel lonely on Your path. Please, help me be a strength to others who are following Your path and help them be a strength to me.

God, grant me wisdom to discern between those heralds who are following in the footsteps of Your Son and those who are wolves in sheep's clothing. Help me discern the fruit of those who claim to show Your way. Help me know Your truth and Your fruit, that I might bear the fruit of Your Spirit and might proclaim words that echo Yours.

I love You, Father, and I thank You for loving me.

Through Jesus I pray,

Amen.

The Sermon in the Real World

Foundations

As we learned how to read the Sermon in Chapter 2, we examined Jesus' parable of the two builders and foundations. This Sermon is not an intellectual exercise but a foundation for how we live our lives.

The Sermon is not merely meant to be read; it is meant to be relied upon. It is not meant to be studied; it is meant to be lived. It is not meant to be discussed; it is meant to be demonstrated. It is not meant to be written about; it is meant to be followed.

It does us absolutely no good to merely read the Sermon, study the Sermon, sit around and talk about the Sermon. We must be the Sermon. We are supposed to be the salt of the earth and the light of the world. As such, we must allow the Sermon to shine through us.

Further, living the Sermon is not to be a weekend vacation; it is to be an all week vocation. How we live at home, how we work on the job, how we participate in school, how we act among friends, family, neighbors and brethren should all be founded on and governed by what we have learned in this Sermon. Therefore, before we finish our study of the Sermon we need to consider how our lives should be and can be impacted by it.

Hiding the Sermon in Our Hearts

"How can a young man keep his way pure?" How can any person keep their way pure? The psalmist said, "By keeping it according to Your word" (Psalm 119.9). If we want pure lives, they must be based on God's words. However, if we desire to have our lives based on God's words, we need to continue through the path this psalmist described through verse 16.

> With all my heart I have sought You;
> Do not let me wander from Your commandments.
> Your word I have treasured in my heart,
> That I may not sin against You.
> Blessed are You, O Lord;
> Teach me Your statutes.
> With my lips I have told of
> All the ordinances of Your mouth.
> I have rejoiced in the way of Your testimonies,
> As much as in all riches.
> I will meditate on your precepts
> And regard Your ways.
> I shall delight in your statutes;
> I shall not forget Your word.

If we want our daily lives to be governed by the Sermon, we have to heed these words. We need to seek after the Lord with all our hearts, learning His commandments. Then we must treasure what we have learned in our hearts. The New King James Version translates it saying we must hide God's word in our heart. What a powerful tool that is. If we really want our lives to be lived around this Sermon, we need to sink that word deep in our hearts. Memorization is not very fashionable among adult Christians today. Typically, we view it as a children's Bible class activity. However, it would do us well if we worked on memorizing, if not the whole Sermon, the major points.

Remember that in the one recorded direct attack on Jesus by Satan in Matthew 4.1-11, Jesus overcame and won the victory by saying, "It is written." He knew God's word. It was hidden and treasured in His heart. When temptation arose, He was able to rely upon God's word to know how to respond. If we want our lives founded upon the Sermon, we have to have it hidden in our hearts. We have to be able to say, "But Jesus said…"

The psalmist said he told God's ordinances to others. We need to talk about the Sermon. We need to let others know what we have learned. We should do this with our brethren, sharing with them how we have grown based on our learning in the Sermon. We ought to do this with others. When somebody asks us how our day is going or what we did this past weekend, let them know what you read or studied in the Sermon or how well you have been living in context of the Sermon. "I have had a great day. I read my Bible this morning and learned about being the salt of the earth and light of the world." Or "I am having a pretty good day, I have been struggling with what Jesus said about loving my enemies, but I am getting better at it."

Not only should we read it, study it, memorize it and teach it. We also need to meditate upon it. We need to think about what it says. We need to think about what our lives would be like if we were truly living it. We need to think about where it leads. We need to envision those things, implanting those mental images in our hearts. The more we see ourselves doing what we have learned in our minds' eyes, the more likely we are to do them when the actual opportunity arises.

When we have read, studied, memorized, taught and meditated on the Sermon, we will naturally delight in it. Then, when we have lived it and walked according to it, we will fully understand the wisdom and benefit of it. In that knowledge we will rejoice at God's grace for giving us the Sermon.

WDJT?

I am not much into religious fads. I have never put a fish on my car. I have never honked because I loved Jesus. I have never passed on an e-mail for fear that not doing so meant I didn't really love God. But there was one fad I really liked. Do you remember the "WWJD" fad? What would Jesus do? This fad said we needed to stop and think in every situation, with every choice, "What would Jesus Do?"

It has dawned on me. If I really want to know what Jesus would do, the more primary question I need to ask is "What did Jesus teach?" Perhaps that can be a new fad. Maybe we can get WDJT bracelets and bumper stickers. The reality is we know very little about what Jesus actually did. We mostly know what Jesus would do based on what Jesus taught.

The central point of Jesus' teaching is found in this Sermon. As we leave it (I hope you come back to it again and again), let us take this thought with us. In every choice, before we speak or act, let us consider what did Jesus teach? He taught us to love others in word and deed. He taught us to treat them the way we want to be treated. He taught us to want to save them more than we want to judge them. He taught us to control our anger, our eyes, our words and our reactions. He taught us to stand out with holiness and righteousness in a way that could not be hidden. How are we measuring up today?

What Did Jesus Teach?

From Today to Judgment Day

When we think about preparing for Judgment, we have a tendency to think about our big choices—who will we marry, what career will we follow, where will we live, what congregation will we be part of. These are the important decisions. We can very often miss that our lives are not really made up by these big decisions. Our lives are actually made up of all the little decisions we make every day.

Our lives are not really made up by what we can be. They are not made up by saying we are different on the inside. Our lives are made up by the thousand little choices we make every day. Our lives are made up by how we speak to our parents, our spouses, our children. Our lives are made up by how we spend the unmonitored moments on the job. Our lives are made up by where, when and how often we swipe that debit (or credit) card. Our lives are made up by the times we serve the Lord in prayer, study and service to others. Our lives are made up by how we respond to those in authority over us, even when they are not watching. Our lives are made up of the minor commitments we make and whether or not we keep them. Our lives are made up of the words we use, whether reckless or purposeful, whether edifying or destructive, whether true or false. The Sermon hits us in these every day, minor, moment-by-moment choices.

When Marita and I lived in Beaumont, TX, we had just bought our first house. We still had the hand-me-down furniture from our parents and wanted to furnish our home better. However, we just didn't have the finances to really do so. One Saturday Marita dropped by a yard sale. She found out the family was retiring, selling everything and moving into their motor home. Their plan was to spend several years just traveling all over the United States. They had to get rid of everything. She called me and I visited the house. They had bedroom furniture, an entertainment center, office furniture, living room furniture, pictures, lamps, the whole nine yards. What was better was they were willing to sell it cheap. We could afford it and would reasonably furnish our entire home. Their only request was that we not pick it all up for two weeks until the day before they actually moved. We were willing. We shook on it. We agreed to pay them on the day we picked up the furniture.

We were excited. We envisioned where we were going to put the new furniture. We told our friends about it. They were excited. Then about a week later, we received a phone call from the family who had agreed to sell us the furniture. They had a change in plans. They had contacted an estate sale company to try to sell the rest of their stuff. The company wouldn't take any of it if they couldn't have all of it. Despite our agreement, they were not going to let us have the furniture.

I still remember their words. "We don't normally do this sort of thing, but we just don't have any other choice." I remember thinking, and even saying, something along the lines of, "Don't deceive yourself. The fact that you are doing this now demonstrates you would do it again in the same circumstance." These were religious people. Did they think they were violating God's word? I don't know. Whatever the case, they were not making their choice based on Matthew 5.33-37. Their yes had not meant yes. Their no had not meant no. When the going got too rough, they were willing to back off of their word.

Of course, to be completely fair, for a day or two, I wasn't thinking about Matthew 5.21-22 or 5.38-48. I called them many names. Told several friends about how bad the people were and what victims we were. I tried to see if there might be some legal approach to get them to follow through. I never physically took vengeance, but I did verbally, calling them several times and trying to make them feel guilty. Gratefully, my friend and co-worker at the time, Max Dawson, finally had enough and rebuked me, pointing out it was only stuff. For all of my high-mindedness about how they weren't obeying Scripture, I wasn't following it too well myself.

How easy it is for us to read all of these passages, hear all of these teachings, but in the circumstances of life act as if they aren't really about us. If we even think about the passage at all, we can easily convince ourselves it is not about our particular situation. I am certain the people who agreed to sell us the furniture knew they were supposed to honor commitments. But in that situation the commitment was too big of a burden and caused too much hardship, surely Jesus didn't mean for them to endure that. I certainly knew that I was not to call people names, slander their reputation or try to get even. But in that situation the hurt and disappointment were too big. Surely Jesus didn't mean for me to endure that.

Sometimes it seems as though we believe what determines our outcome on Judgment Day is all the big decisions. Actually, what I am doing this very moment is building my Judgment Day. What I do this evening when I am driving will be building my Judgment Day. How I act when I get home and the children are too loud will build my Judgment Day. How I respond when my spouse jumps on me about something will build my Judgment Day. How I behave when my boss is not looking will build my Judgment Day. It is how we act in the combination of all these small moments that determines what we will hear when we face Jesus in judgment. If my righteousness in these moments does not surpass that of the scribes and Pharisees, I will not enter the kingdom of heaven.

Practice what Jesus Preached

Think about this scenario. You have come home from a hard day at work. You are tired and frustrated. You were supposed to be home an hour ago but at the last minute your boss dropped a bomb on you. It took you thirty minutes to finish it and then you got stuck in traffic because of a wreck. As you walk through the door, you are not greeted with hugs from your children or a kiss from your spouse. Instead, the children are fussing and your spouse looks at you and says, "You're late. You said you would be home an hour ago. You didn't call, you didn't e-mail. You didn't do anything. I just get so sick and tired of how thoughtless and careless you are." How do you respond?

The natural person is immediately geared up for a fight. "Thoughtless. Thoughtless?! I'll show you thoughtless. You want to talk about sick and tired. I get sick and tired of how selfish you are. Don't you even care about what happened at work today? You are so self-centered it is not even funny…" But what did Jesus teach?

Jesus taught that those of us who called each other names were guilty enough to go into the fires of hell. He taught that when people insulted us, we should turn the other cheek. Do we do that with our spouse?

What about this scenario? You are driving home, minding your own business when out of nowhere somebody just cuts you off in traffic or they pull out in front of you or worse they are not paying attention when the light turns green and they just sit there. How do you respond?

The natural person is rolling down her window, hollering, shouting, calling names, clinching her fist, honking her horn. The natural person tells everyone about "the idiot driver who almost got me killed today." But what did Jesus teach?

Jesus taught us about calling people names. But He also taught us not to judge and that we would be judged by the same standards we bestow on others. He taught us that we ought to bestow mercy instead of judgment. He also taught us to treat others the way we want to be treated. Have we ever pulled out in front of anyone, cut anybody off or been distracted when the light turned green? How did we want people to treat us when we made those mistakes?

What about this scenario? You have been working hard on the job. You know you are the most qualified for the upcoming promotion. You are certain it is going to be you. But one of your co-workers lies about you to your boss. You get passed over for the promotion and it goes to the liar. How do you respond?

The natural person seeks vengeance. They want to sabotage all that the co-worker does to prove to the boss he made a mistake. They want to start spreading lies about their co-worker to hurt them in the same way. But what did Jesus teach?

Jesus taught us to love our enemies. He taught us to pray for those who mistreat us. He taught us to let God be the one who takes vengeance. Our duty is to make peace.

We could go on and on with these kinds of scenarios. However, I think we get the point. We need to practice what Jesus preached. We need to do it every day, in every relationship, no matter how hard it is.

At times it may seem impossible. But remember, we are not alone. God has promised never to abandon us. If we ask, seek and knock, He will bestow His kingdom on us. If we enter by the small gate, walking the narrow way, leaving the teeming masses to follow their own path, Jesus will guide us. He will strengthen us. He will lift us up on wings of eagles. We will run and not grow weary. We will walk and not faint. By God's grace we can live the Gospel of the Kingdom.

We can enter the Kingdom of Heaven. Are you ready to take that journey?

Responding to the Sermon

What is your initial response to living the Sermon in the real world as presented in this chapter?

What obstacles keep you from living the Sermon in your daily life? How can you overcome those obstacles?

Are there any relationships you need to reconcile because you have not lived in them by the Sermon? If so, what must you do? When will you do it?

Meditating on the Sermon

How would your life look different if you were following the Sermon completely?

How did Jesus exemplify this Sermon? Meditate on these things today.

Praying the Sermon

Almighty Father in heaven,

Hallowed is Your name. Let Your kingdom and righteousness rule in my heart. Strengthen me to live Your word. Strengthen me to tell of Your word to others. Forgive me because I have often fallen short of Your holiness. I have not followed the message I have learned in Jesus' Sermon. I have taken revenge. I have called people names. I have lusted. I have hated my enemies. I have followed selfishness. I have hidden my light too many times. Forgive me.

Father, please abundantly supply Your kingdom and righteousness to me. Guide me to seek Your kingdom and righteousness first and foremost. Strengthen me to knock and enter Your narrow gate. Help me choose the wise and righteous path.

I thank You for blessing me. Thank You for granting me the time to study this Sermon and learn Your will. Help me not put it aside, but keep coming back to it. Thank You for reserving for me a home in heaven with You. Strengthen me through faith to press on to it.

I love You, Father, and I thank You for loving me.

Through Jesus I pray,

Amen.

Group Discussion

What are the most important lessons you have learned this week?

What questions do you have about what you have learned this week?

What practical improvement have you made in your life based on what you have learned this week?

What practical advice would you give others to accomplish what you have learned about this week?

With what issues do you need help or prayers based on what you have learned this week?

Why is it difficult to enter through the small gate and walk the narrow way? How can we help each other stay on God's strait and difficult path?

Summarize what you have learned throughout this entire month of study in the Gospel of the Kingdom. What were the most important lessons you learned this month?

*For more books by Edwin Crozier
and a full listing of DeWard Publishing
Company books, visit our website:*

www.deward.com

www.ingramcontent.com/pod-product-compliance
Lightning Source LLC
Chambersburg PA
CBHW022100090426
42743CB00008B/666